PURITANISM IN AMERICA

PURITANISM IN AMERICA

New Culture in a New World

Larzer Ziff

The Viking Press | New York

One of the years spent on this study was freed from all other duties by a grant from the National Endowment for the Humanities to whom I am very grateful. Several pages on Jonathan Edwards and Benjamin Franklin in Chapter Twelve are a revision of part of a brief essay that was published in my *The Literature of America: Colonial Period*, Copyright © 1970 by McGraw-Hill, Inc., and I thank the McGraw-Hill Book Company for permision to reprint.

L. Z.

For Joshua Ziff

and

for Oliver Ziff

Preface

This is a history of American Puritanism as a culture from its origin in the Reformation to its final, major colonial manifestation in the Great Awakening. It proceeds from the conviction that Puritanism is an important topic because it has had enormous consequences in America. Therefore, although I am concerned centrally with showing how Puritanism came into being as a result of crucial changes in the conditions of European life, and was brought to New England by men who used it as an outlook in terms of which they attempted to shape their lives in America, I also risk in more than one place conjectures about the presence of Puritan habits in nineteenth- and twentieth-century American life, and, especially, American letters.

The subject of this book has not been treated at length elsewhere, even though this book would not have been possible had American Puritanism not been studied in detail by so many scholars. New England historians of the nineteenth century, such as John Gorham Palfrey, preserved the records of the Puritans and told their story as an act of genealogical piety. Their labors are of the first importance. They were followed by other New Englanders, such as Charles Francis Adams and Brooks Adams, whose interpretations of Puritanism are acts of iconoclasm that they hoped would free Americans to learn from the past rather than to worship it. Then, in the twentieth century, most prominently in Perry Miller's large and immensely influential intellectual histories, scholars have prepared specialized studies of almost all aspects of American Puritanism. My reliance on their work is made clear on almost every page that follows.

Still, this is the first book that attempts to synthesize the special concerns of intellectual, social, and economic history into a single account of the American Puritans. In making the attempt, I have not granted ideas an independent existence, but have been concerned with the material conditions that brought them about and the individuals who held them. If I am concerned, as I am, with ideology, my concern is, more precisely, with ideological reflexes. If I am concerned, as I am, with theology, my concern is, more precisely, with the conditions of life that made a certain version of man's relationship to an omnipotent being more appropriate than others. The term that I have applied most frequently to Puritanism is, therefore, culture. I recognize Puritanism's significance as a political movement in a specific period of English history and I understand how it can be isolated and studied as a body of theological assumptions and ecclesiastical practices. But my view is that Puritanism emerged as a way of coping with the threatening conditions of masterlessness and landlessness in sixteenth-century England. In developing responses to these conditions that would enable men to make something of themselves, the Puritans developed a particular way of living the common life and developed a pattern of reaction to the problems they confronted in their daily reality. This is what I mean by culture, and in taking this meaning I am receiving more than a hint from the work, in a quite different area, of Raymond Williams.

I believe that men have ideas rather than the reverse. I recognize at the same time that the great majority of those who lived in the Puritan colonies, as indeed of all men who lived before the Industrial Revolution, are historically mute: they preached no sermons, kept no diaries, and read no popular press. If in attempting to explain the Puritan culture, therefore, I have had to rely in great part on the materials left by the dominant members of society rather than the masses, I have nevertheless attempted to improve documents that do provide insight into the common life. I found, moreover, that once one is alerted to look for the common people, then their condition is recognizable in familiar materials. For example, sermons, such as those of Thomas Shepard, that have served intellectual historians as sources for their studies of, say, the idea of the covenant of grace, also abound in the bases for safe inferences about the condition of servingmen.

Since Puritanism is my subject, I do not in the following pages speak of the other influences on American culture, such as the frontier, that are of the magnitude of Puritanism. I would not want as a result to be misunderstood as offering a modern version of the silly theory that the real history of America is the history of the spread on the continent of Anglo-Saxon habits and Anglo-Saxon ideals. The influence Puritanism exerts on modern life is great, but it is far from exclusive, and I here say so explicitly.

Contents

PURITANISM IN AMERICA

CHAPTER ONE

Man's Judgment of Himself

*The printed word—Two views of grace and nature—
Masterlessness and conscience—Puritanism as culture*

Folk patterns are fixed and transmitted by word of mouth and by imitation. A folk mythology cannot attain the force of a revolutionary doctrine because it is perforce the creature of tradition and grows in the confines of routine. Although it may speak of the abuses of power and the indignities of the common life it does so with a sly docility and outward acquiescence. Some may be encouraged to rebel, but the very process by which the lore was developed is one of acceptance. Legends transmitted by word of mouth are organically related to their sharers' condition, growing from it rather than breaking across it and calling for a new dispensation. Oral protest against the deeply established structure of life must await a specific instance of outrage for its effect and cannot spread beyond the local.

But the printed word can consolidate the images of protest against the conditions of the common life and circulate them beyond the local. The articulate few who have freed themselves from the conventions of their society can, in print, express themselves in terms that cut across that society, and if they touch the springs of outrage at conditions that oral myth has assimilated, they will restructure the way men perceive reality.

And so John Foxe saw the invention of printing as a miracle performed by the Lord for the express purpose of consummating the reformation of His church. "The Lord began to work for His

Church not with sword and target . . . but with printing, writing and reading," he said. "How many printing presses there be in the world, so many block-houses there be against the high castle of St. Angelo, so that either the pope must abolish knowledge and printing or printing at length will root him out." [1]

The claim is particularly English. In Germany from 1466 to 1522, twenty complete translations of the Bible were printed; in France from 1487 to 1521, Jean de Rely's translation was printed seven times. But the book-hungry English were not permitted a satisfaction of their appetite.

The Lollard movement of the fourteenth and fifteenth centuries attacked clerical celibacy, transubstantiation, indulgences, and pilgrimages by asserting that the Bible was the sole authority in religion and insisting that every man had a right to read the book for himself. As a consequence, the printed word and protest became one. [2]

The complete English Bible that arrived from the Continent in March 1526 included Martin Luther's prologue to Romans, the fundamental statement of his break from the Roman Church, and was equipped with references to parallel passages, more than half taken from Luther's translation. A symbol of reform because it was forbidden, the Tyndale Bible was also a textbook for reform.

The language that Tyndale used in his Bible was the language that other Continental exiles used to acquaint their fellow Englishmen with a new history of their religion. Although rarely seen in print, it was a familiar language, drawing its images from the pasture, the boat, the fireside, and the market. The claim that the people had a true history in opposition to official versions gained a validity from being urged in the people's language rather than in that of the pronouncements made to them by authorities in church and state. The Roman Catholic Church, they were told by John Bale and other propagandists, was not the true church to which Englishmen owed their allegiance. Rather, within that church was a true church that had since the days of the Fathers been in opposition to the official church, and that, now in the sixteenth century, was finally scheduled for triumph over it. The legend that print disseminated was that the Gospel had been brought to Britain by Joseph of

Arimathea, and that it had since been engaged in a vital struggle against malign forces such as the monks and friars of Rome. It had been suppressed, but because of the championing of Wycliffe, Gower, Chaucer, and Tyndale, it was never killed. In heeding Luther, England was not receiving a new truth from Germany but recognizing a native heir, Wycliffe's grandchild, sired by Wycliffe's heir, John Huss.

The legend received its definitive telling in John Foxe's *Book of Martyrs* (1563, and especially the enlarged version of 1570), because Foxe joined to the legend the anecdotes of contemporary history and in absorbing detail rendered the lives of the Marian exiles, those who suffered and those who fled. "Here," as William Haller says, "was what ordinary Protestant Englishmen for generations to come were going to believe had happened at that crucial point in their national history." [3] To belong to the community of Englishmen was to have a special relationship to the true church, one that was tempered in English martyrs' blood. Foxe fixed the equation of papacy and persecution and furnished the power for the fleet that met the Armada.

Puritanism, taking its rise in the days of the Armada, never relinquished its overwhelming insistence on the centrality of the word. So exhilarating did the Puritans find the liberating effect of a religion expressed in language, and so inseparable was it from the basic nature of the true church—the priesthood of all believers—that they could not halt at any halfway house of success, nor, when successful, could they consolidate their success. Once let loose, the word united men in revolt and divided them in victory.

Appearing in the Star Chamber on June 14, 1637, to press the Church of England's case against the Puritans Bastwick, Burton, and Prynne, Archbishop William Laud reminded the Lords of the Garter that they, in their great solemnities, reverenced almighty God "*Versus altare,* towards His altar, as to the greatest place of God's residence upon earth. (I say the greatest, yea greater than the pulpit. For there 'tis *Hoc est corpus meum,* this is my body. But in the pulpit 'tis at most but; *Hoc est verbum meum,* this is my word.)" [4] Laud was a Protestant churchman severely delimited by an English birth and an English career that the persistent slanders of the Puritan party were unable to transmute into a tendency toward Romanism.[5] He insisted that his assertion of divine right for the bishops in his church was as stoutly in opposition to the Church of Rome as it was to the Puritan humor. At the center of his faith was symbol, the rich mystery of the sacrifice of Jesus, and the focal point of his church was the altar that commemorated it. His imagination lingered on the architectural embodiment of Christianity in decorated churches as the necessary setting for the essential communion. All senses, not just the ear that received the word, were to be served by the church, for the progression from mortal limitation to becoming one with the godhead was, ultimately, not verbal. The mystery was ambiguous and all the richer for it.

To break with the traditional means of guiding man to his God by limiting that guidance to the words in the Bible and the words spoken from the pulpit was, for Laud, a perverse misshaping of the nature of man and his relationship to the divine. Words alone, unaided by symbol and ceremony, rent the fabric of society, he felt, and broke the delicate hierarchical structure through which, and only through which, man could realize God and the realities of his own existence. Ceremony was not dumb show but the provision of a pattern along which the questing soul could travel toward God and in which it could find peace in this life. Symbol went beyond word to inarticulate experience.

Laud perceived that in insisting upon the exclusive primacy of the word and thereby elevating the pulpit above the altar, the Puritans were doing more than reapportioning values. They were, rather, denying gradation and asserting a break between the human and the divine, with the word only as bridge. Sermons are not the only means to humble men, he repeatedly insisted in opposition to those who would bar the clergy from ritual reading of the Bible, ritual reading of homilies and devotional formulas, ritual reading of approved prayers—all the devices of religion through habituation. The printed word of the Bible, he recognized, was the common property of those who could read it. But unless controlled by the authority of the church as figured forth in its vestments and rituals, the word was chaos. Those who would control the chaos by elevating the sermon, a time-honored but minor guide to devotion and good behavior, to the status of being the definitive explication and release of the word into the consciousness of men were in reality compounding chaos rather than containing it. Some of the Puritan sermons, he knew, "are fitter . . . to stir up sedition" than to humble men to their condition as good Christians and good Englishmen.[6]

In asserting the importance of the altar over the pulpit, William Laud and his colleagues and heirs in the Church of England affirmed a world in which grace came to perfect nature rather than to combat it. In the tradition of the Christian Church they perceived a series of gradations that linked fallen man with the supernatural. Jesus had come not to separate the mortal world from the eternal but to link them by spreading grace among the fallen. He recognized the love and natural piety that existed among even sinners, children, and Samaritans, and the division He overcame was that between their restricted present and their boundless future.

Jesus had left behind Him the church as keeper of the treasury of grace. As an objective institution it was larger than the clergy who served it. Where it existed, there the God-Man existed and the connection between here and hereafter was complete. In Ernst Troeltsch's words: "The individual is born into it, and through infant baptism he comes under its miraculous influence. The priesthood and the hierarchy, which holds the keys to the tradition of the Church, to sacramental grace and ecclesiastical jurisdiction, represent the objective treasury of grace, even when the individual priest may happen to be unworthy; this Divine treasure only needs to be set always upon the lampstand and made effective through the sacraments, and it will inevitably do its work by virtue of the miraculous power which the Church contains. . . . It is the extension of the Incarnation, the objective organization of miraculous power from which, by means of the Divine providential government of the world, subjective results will appear quite naturally."[7]

This view of the mission of Jesus and the church built on it is rich in chronological continuity and temporal order. Given an absolute objective existence, which is its essence, the church can perfect itself through historical time in order to meet the demands of the world it serves as treasurer. For the sake of efficiency, the grace that flows through it is lodged more fully with some, so that the clergy is arranged in hierarchical orders of grace that forge the chain between the lowest in nature and the highest in heaven. Those whose lives lie in the world will, by supporting the church, join themselves with those whose lives lie outside the world and whose devotion acts to redeem them even as their works act to maintain the redeemers. On the folk level, a world in which grace streams down to all is one in which no natural object is separated from divinity, and even the creatures of the field retain some aura of the holiness they possessed when they were the agents of pagan gods.

In accordance with the absolute validity of order and the essential objective existence of the church, the reform in the Laudian manner of the Church of England's corruptions was conducted within a pattern that retained hierarchical order and recognized that the chronological connection with Jesus ran through Rome, even though Rome had become so compromised that its purer descendants must now disown it. But the Church of England did not have a separate history; rather, that church maintained, it was the rightful heir of a common history.

Paul, however, was read by others to serve a different view, one that saw the message of Jesus as a radical dividing line between those within the church and those within the world: the one the kingdom of God, the other of Satan. A stark abyss yawns between those who possess grace and those who remain in nature unredeemed by it.[8] There are no gradations of grace; its operation is total, and those who are gracious are equals in the city of God. Every believer is a priest, and the minister, therefore, although a superior in learning and an invaluable guide to the people of God, is not, in essence, holier than they. His special position with regard to salvation is as a guide rather than a dispenser. The saved are visibly in the world, just as are the damned, but their actions have been sanctified so that their doings in the world are free operations on an environment that, ultimately, is unresistant to them because of the power they have, whereas the same environment works to the damnation of those who have not been elevated above it by grace. The natural creation for those elected to salvation is not so much corrupt as neutral, their rightful inheritance to do with as they will to the glory of God. The church exists wherever true believers exist and does not have an objective character beyond this. Christ is not so much the eternally present God-Man residing in the sacraments of the church as He is the king of the church of the believers, opposed to Satan, the king of the damned.

The theology of Augustine gave fullest historical force to this view of the human condition as one of a divided mankind. Freedom means, he taught, to act according to one's nature without external compulsion, but one's nature determines the actions, and freedom is only relative to the lack of outside force. "There are two kinds of human beings and correspondingly two kinds of human natures," as Harry Wolfson characterizes Augustine's thought, "and each man belongs either to the one or to the other. For Augustine, the old definition of man as a rational animal would not do; for him, some men are concupiscent rational animals and some are grace-endowed rational animals." [9]

The Puritans held this view, and for them, therefore, history was, as it were, complete in a moment. The story of Christianity was not the story of the church, but, rather, the story of that band of true believers who had transmitted the saving word either within the institutionalized church, as was still possible in the days of the Fathers, or, more usually, outside or in opposition to it. The typical human career was, therefore, a stronger feature of their view of the past than the continuity of institutions. Foxe's *Book* gained its instant and persisting popularity because, appearing as it did in the days after the first arrival of the printed English Bible, it completed that book by providing an instant and less constraining past for those who would use the Bible to found a society unrestricted by the traditions that the established church regarded as of its essence. The martyrs in Foxe's *Book* live in conscious imitation of biblical models. Their careers reinforce a view of history as exemplary at any moment rather than as developing. Analogy takes precedence over chronology; the sense of tribal belonging over the details of historical change.

The denial of the importance of historical change and of the existence of hierarchies of grace was a denial in practice of structures of order, which many regarded as vital to the well-being of society. Although none who denied was a democrat—an anachronistic term at best—nevertheless the denial had a democratic force that was clearly perceived by those in authority in state as well as church. After the separation of the Church of England from Rome, loyal Anglican theorists had been forced to develop a counter-theory to that of papal supremacy, and in the sixteenth century they evolved a doctrine of the divine right of secular governments.[10] As did the Puritans, so they drew upon the exploding anti-Roman sentiment of the nation, but they worked to channel it into a force in favor of hereditary right. Since their doctrine drew ultimately on the model of the Holy Roman Empire, despite its origin in the need for a response to the supremacy of Rome, it presented the Puritans with a secular pattern of order opposed to Continental rulers, a pattern to which they as Englishmen could not help assenting, even though as church reformers they drew their theoretical strength from an outlook that was ultimately destructive of such order. Their condition in this respect is well summarized by George P. Gooch's remark that "Modern Democracy is the child of the Reformation, not of the Reformers." [11]

The Puritans were to achieve a notable, if in some respects temporary, social success over forces of order, tradition, and history. But the ground of that success does not lie in elaborations of their theology. This is vital, to be sure, but the Puritans prevailed because they met a felt if inarticulated need and shaped a new perception of the human condition for hundreds of thousands of Britons. This new perception, one that was essentially a new way of reacting to the problems of leading the common life, in short, a new culture, is at the center of what Puritanism meant in and to America, but the conditions that gave it its attraction were initially European.

In the course of the sixteenth century Spanish mines had increased by 400 per cent the amount of portable wealth that had been available in Europe in 1500. At the same time the expiring feudal system abandoned large numbers of people to the social chaos of masterlessness. Displaced from their position in the medieval social hierarchy, they were also displaced from the land as it was put to new uses, principally sheep-grazing, and they were desperately unable to attach themselves in socially useful ways to the vastly increased amount of wealth. Tudor law, forced to multiply the statutes directed at the burgeoning army of the landless and masterless, reflected the vastness of the problem by the distinctions it was compelled to make among the disinherited: there were separate regulations for the rogues, the vagabonds, and the beggars.

Even as it arrived at a church settlement halfway between Rome and the reformers, so Elizabeth's administration met the deteriorating social conditions with regulations that stood halfway between a conservative longing for continued practices and a radical discontent with loss of identity and worth. The Statute of Artificers, 1563, and the Poor Law, 1597, set themselves the task of overcoming the disastrous effects of vagrancy and the mobility of the poorer sections of the population. Justices of the peace were empowered to fix wages in their areas annually, persons in employment were forbidden to leave their work, and apprenticeships were rigorously enforced so as to be of seven years' duration and to require everyone, regardless of his trade, to work on the land at time of harvest. Medieval legislation that insisted that those who worked on the land until the age of twelve were not to be admitted to a handicraft was reiterated, but the medieval spirit was also modified and modernized in the national and well-planned character of the acts.[12]

A situation that threatened chaos was thus formally stabilized. But the deeper discontents of the masterless and the aggravations of lack of ready money persisted. What identity could be assigned these uprooted people? A man's bond used to be his line of fealty: the allegiance he owed his lord and the surety his lord provided in return. No device or institution seemed capable of providing a new basis for trust. The poor were whipped back to the parish of their origin as if identity were still to be earned on native soil even when native conditions no longer prevailed. All districts through which a fleeing thief passed became responsible for repayment of his theft because in the absence of any positive social bond liability could be assigned only on the negative principle of negligence. Splendid wars and splendid exploitation abroad; sharking, cadging, and dodging at home. "To England will I steal, and there I'll steal," says Shakespeare's veteran of the Continental campaigns.

Another Continental veteran, Captain John Smith, saw his England as a land in which many were consuming carelessly what some few got worthily. In urging colonization as a solution, he asked his countrymen why they should remain home if they were to maintain themselves only "by using that miserably, that maintained virtue honestly? Or, for being descended nobly, pine with the vain vaunt of great kindred, in penury? Or to (maintain a silly show of bravery) toil out thy heart, soul, and time, basely, by shifts, tricks, cards, and dice? Or by relating news of others' actions, shark here or there for dinner or supper; deceive thy friends, by fair promises and dissimulation, in borrowing where thou never intendest to pay; offend the laws, surfeit with excess, burden thy country, abuse thy self, despair in want, and then cozen thy kindred, yea even thine own brother, and wish thy parents death (I will not say damnation) to have their estates?" [13]

This was the England celebrated more than it was chastised, yet both celebrated and chastised in Ben Jonson's *Bartholomew Fair*. Gathered at the annual August Feast Day in Smithfield, pickpockets, panders, bawds, and bullies confront those who have money and go after it with a will and a lust. In and out of Jonson's scenes of quick-witted cant, deceit, and joy in the exhilaration of the chase for coin wanders a justice of the peace in disguise. Socially he represents the new custodian of equity, the J.P. charged with the local enforcement of the economic statutes. Dramatically he is the descendant of a long series of such play figures—the king or duke in disguise to observe how life is led in his absence, who eventually unveils, and in restoring himself, the object of fealty all hold in common, restores equity, order, and happiness.

But in the day of *Bartholomew Fair* society has gotten too far out of hand for such a restoration. The disguised justice, a good and a kind man, foolish only in that he clings to the belief that he can right all wrongs when he wishes, consistently misunderstands what is really happening. He mistakes a cutpurse for a young gentleman worthy of special protection, for example, and his persistent inability to penetrate to reality is climaxed when his wife is prostituted by the panders at the fair under his unseeing eyes. When he finally reveals himself, therefore, no great restoration of order such as he had originally anticipated takes place. Rather, through his mistakes he also has been compromised, and he prudently recognizes that the best measure is to invite everybody home for a feast rather than to court for a judgment. *Bartholomew Fair* is a celebration of a reckless and exciting social ride and an admission that no one is at the reins any longer.

Although not granting the justice the control that he believes he has, Jonson does introduce a Puritan into the play in recognition that a counter-force had come into existence. And, indeed, the attraction of Puritanism was that it was shaping a radical response to such a situation. Already on the Continent the Dutch were beginning to perform what was, for many Englishmen, to be the greatest wonder of the seventeenth century: with few natural resources the Netherlands was becoming one of the richest nations, while Spain in seeming helplessness was watching the gold and silver from its mines flow out of its control. Credit could compete successfully with cash, and Puritanism provided the best basis for credit.

Rather than accepting human nature and attempting to improve it, Puritanism disowned nature. The doctrine of the gulf between grace and nature and the overwhelming importance of standing on the spiritual side of that gulf responded to the collapse of economic and social hierarchies. Grace was all. Those who had it led their lives on a new principle: nature in them was all but destroyed. Piety, the possession of grace, freed men to treat the material world as wholly mediate, a malleable set of circumstances that would yield to their sanctified condition. Morality lost its centrality because morality conventionally addressed itself to the conduct of the natural man.

Piety replaced it with the argument that grace sanctifies action, but action uninformed by grace is theologically meaningless and socially useless.

Faced with the ineffectuality of authorities in everyday life, the Puritans dramatically and emphatically denied the chain of authority in the church and enthroned conscience in its place. Conscience, they asserted, was God's vicar. Its seat was the soul of man, and its edicts were meant to determine the quality of daily life. The radical solution to social deterioration was not the strengthening of external authority. It was, rather, the internalizing of authority itself. Conscience was put to the cause of civic duty.

The view of conscience that prevailed among the Puritans found its fullest expression in the writings of William Ames, who defined conscience as "a mans judgment of himself, according to the judgment of God of him." [14] That judgment of God was to be sought in the Bible, else the conscience was merely natural and unenlightened. In addition to the Scriptures, men must have available to them a constant flow of exegesis from the pulpit. Whereas Catholicism had seen exegesis as a partner of devotion and had proliferated spiritual meanings not implicit in the letter, the Puritans regarded it as crucial for clear, authoritative, daily instruction.[15] Their interest in the Bible was rational and practical rather than imaginative and devotional.

William Ames recognized the awesome dependence of the conscience on language and devoted a considerable part of his work on the conscience to an insistence on keeping language pure. Words were to replace religious symbols as instruments of precision for the Puritans just as, in a later time, mathematical symbols were to replace words in order to achieve greater precision in scientific matters. Ames therefore concerned himself with diction, and, for example, explained that obscene talk was to be distrusted not just because it dwelt on sin and exposed men to the hazard of sinning, but also because of its linguistic implications. "Obscene speeches," he notes, "out of a certain natural modesty, are not wont to be expressed in downright words, but insinuated obliquely by metaphorical phrases; whence it is, that upon occasion of the like words or

phrases, that godly discourse, meditations, and even prayers themselves are troubled, polluted, and hindered by such fancies intruding
themselves. And for this reason, the frequent use of obscene speeches
seemeth to be more hurtful to piety, than the simple act of
fornication." [16]

The simple act of fornication is a specific and redeemable sin. But
if language is poisoned, then the channel of redemptive guidance that
runs from man's judgment of himself through the word to God's
judgment of him is clogged.

If the conscience is maintained purely, then it comes into its own
as authority. The man who possesses an enlightened conscience has
found his identity. He is no longer masterless because he is his own
master. His own word is sufficient voucher.

In developing the doctrine of the conscience Ames, accordingly,
places extreme emphasis on the sacredness of the oath. Although an
oath is a promise given by one man to another, that oath, if it is
offered by the new man, will be offered to another only through the
oath-taker's binding himself to God to perform what he has
promised another. As Ames explains: "There is a double obligation
in every promissory oath; one to God, another to man." [17] This
means that even when a promise is extracted by force, the man who
makes the promise must make good on it, should the force be
subsequently removed. In traditional ethics force applied to extract a
commitment is immoral and therefore cancels the commitment when
it is removed. But Ames insists that "although the injury done, takes
away the wrong in respect of man doing the injury, because no right
is founded upon an injury; yet the obligation made to God
remaineth, which without irreverence and injury to God cannot be
both admitted, and then continued. This is the case of a man
constrained by thieves to swear to pay a price for his redemption.
Such a one either ought not to swear or swearing a lawful thing,
ought religiously to keep his oath." [18]

Time would soften this extreme view of personal accountability.
But the Puritan movement in its formative days drew power from
the idea that man was his own master and authority was to be sought
internally. He must, therefore, always be as good as his word,

regardless of the condition under which he gave his word, because he had only his word as his identity. Such a man could be trusted without the surety of a lord or a guild vouching for him. Such a man could be extended credit and, eventually, could claim political power.

The Marian exile who was elevated in Foxe's pages was given, among other characteristics, this new quality of self-mastery. "Physically exiled," as Michael Walzer has noted, "he had moved outside the world of political limitation into the new world of self-control." [19] William Ames formulated his principal works while living in Holland in the days of the first Stuarts and he too had the experience of exile as the crucible of his doctrines. His everyday world was that of the fantastic Dutch rise to commercial supremacy in the early decades of the seventeenth century, and his crystallization of Puritan thought partook of this ambience. The family, that indispensably basic unit of the social fabric, was for Ames based on oath, on the contract between man and wife, rather than on patriarchy. In Holland, before America and before Cromwell's England, the marriage contract was a matter of public record and secular regulation; the family was founded as a new business was founded, by an exchange of oaths. The parents were the proprietors of the establishment, and the children indentured to it. "The son cannot alienate or give any thing away of his fathers," Ames says, "without his fathers consent and consequently not himself, for he is his fathers." And the law, he went on, should not ratify a daughter's marriage unless her parents consent. "The punishment appointed for such marriage" in the primitive church, Ames insisted, "was, that, neither husband or wife, nor marriage, nor dowry should be acknowledged, and that the children which should be born, should be esteemed as bastards." [20] Even had Juliet risen from her drugged sleep in time to claim her Romeo, their relationship would have been illegal and unsanctified rather than the reverse that Shakespeare held. Views such as his or that of Francis Bacon were fast becoming outdated among a substantial part of the population. Bacon had maintained: "Unmarried men are best friends, best masters, best servants. . . . A single life doth well with churchmen for charity will hardly water the ground where it must first fill a pool." [21] On the contrary, said the Puritan voice, he who could be entrusted to enter the marriage enterprise was he on whom a new society could build with confidence.

Christopher Hill elaborates on this aspect of Puritanism by pointing out: "The social basis for this view of marriage was the small workshop or farm in which the wife was in fact a helpmeet to her husband; there was no such cooperation between the rentier landlord and his lady. In the Puritan conception fidelity in the wife and pre-marital chastity began to be insisted on with a new vehemence. Since love was ideally the basis of marriage, then the marriage must be inviolate. In practice in most marriages property was still the main consideration: and in the world of capitalist production expensive goods must not be shop-soiled or tarnished." [22]

Although striking, the Puritan view of marriage is but one example of the way in which Puritanism represented the merger of felt discontents at existing conditions with a new theory, initially theological, of man's social competence. William Bradford illustrates the commercial benefit of possessing an enlightened conscience when he describes the financial dealings of his exiled band in Holland. "Though many of them were poor," he says, "yet there was none so poor but if they were known to be of that congregation, the Dutch (either bakers or others) would trust them in any reasonable manner when they wanted money. Because they had found by experience how careful they were to keep their word, and saw them so painful, and diligent in their callings; yea, they would strive to get their custom, and to employ them above others, in their work, for their honesty and diligence." [23]

Diligence in his calling was the outward mark of the new conscientious man. Since grace did not come in greater quantity to some but came absolutely and divided the elect from the reprobate, no calling or vocation was intrinsically more gracious than another. Rather, all callings were equal so long as they were pursued by the gracious. John Carter, a Puritan minister, had a Suffolk parish from 1583 to his death in 1635. "There dwelled in that parish a tanner," says Carter's admiring Puritan biographer, "that was a very godly man, and one that had much familiar society with Mr. Carter. This man as he was very busy in tawing of a hide with all his might, not so much as turning his head aside any way: Mr. Carter coming by accidentally, came softly behind him, and merrily gave him a little clap on the back: the man started, and looking behind him suddenly, blushed, and said, Sir, I am ashamed that you should find me thus: To whom Mr. Carter replied, Let Christ when He comes find me so doing: What (said the man) doing this? Yes (said Mr. Carter to him) faithfully performing the duties of my calling." [24] Labor thus took on a direct dignity. Its holiness need no longer be validated by a chain of connections through which it supported more godly secular and ecclesiastical enterprises. The godly tanner and the godly minister were equal sharers in the kingdom of grace.

Diligence in one's calling also served to fence one from sin because to be busy about one's work was to put the mind into a channel that was not easily diverted. John Rogers of Essex explained to his parishioners, "An idle person must needs have a corrupt heart, swarming with ill thoughts, for if the mind be not occupied about good, it will be about evil; its like quicksilver, ever stirring: if we be riding, working alone, walking, waking in our beds, let our minds be on some good: and in duties we must keep our minds earnestly bent thereto, that being full already there may be no place of bythoughts; as when a vessel is full, no more can be poured in." [25] So firmly did this enabling doctrine take hold on the Puritans that, as Christopher Hill has pointed out, when they enshrined the Sabbath they did so, among other reasons, to stop their working themselves to death. [26]

In a society in which graciousness did not automatically find its public mark in titles, offices, or preferments but was, nevertheless, the crucial distinction between men, the Puritans wove a cultural pattern that would separate them explicitly from the reprobate. John Rogers put the necessity for the pattern thus: "If the young prince should come on foot in his working-day clothes through a town, and none knew who were his father, nor what he is born to, he might go through the street, and no man greatly regard him; but if in his best apparel, and known what he is, then every man would look after him, and reverence him: so the world sees us in our working days clothes, and therefore neglect us; if they did see us in our holy-day apparel, they would admire us: but being ignorant of the father that begat us, and that will give us this inheritance, how can they take notice of us?" [27] The answer was that Puritans would be noticed because even in the workaday world they separated themselves from its corruptions. The strictness of Sabbath-keeping was one of the more obvious means of separating oneself out, of wearing "holy-day apparel."

The authorities recognized the Puritan Sabbath for what it was, a mark of division where no division in their opinion should exist, a symbol of the denial of the wholesome integrity of society where they believed such integrity was essential. In 1585, when the Puritans were exhausting legal means to have their case heard, the authorities responded by encouraging plays and sports on the eve of Sunday and sometimes even in the afternoon of that day. Parliament passed a bill for the better and more reverent observation of the Sabbath, but the Queen rejected it on the ground that matters of religion were her prerogative, not Parliament's. The net force of this exchange was to establish Sabbath-keeping as a mark of Puritanism. In 1595 Nicholas Bownde's book on the Sabbath was published and had a wide readership for its attack on Sunday sports. It was called in by Archbishop Whitgift as disturbing the peace and tending toward schism, but after Whitgift's death the book was republished in 1606 with large additions, and, Daniel Neal reports, "such was its reputation, that scarce any comment, or catechism was published by the stricter divines for many years, in which the *Morality of the Sabbath* was not strongly recommended and urged." [28]

Speaking of the days during which Bownde's book was suppressed, Neal says, "It was the distinguishing mark of a Puritan in these times to see him going to church twice a day with his Bible under his arm; while others were at plays and interludes, or at revels, or walking in the fields, or at the diversions of bowling, fencing, &c. on the evening of the Sabbath, these with their families were employed in reading the Scriptures, singing psalms, catechizing the children, repeating sermons, and prayer." [29]

The battle over the Sabbath continued with vigor in Stuart days as the crown continued to insist upon an integrated society. On May 24, 1618, James decreed: "That for his good people's recreation, his majesty's pleasure was, that after the end of divine service, they should not be disturbed, letted, or discouraged from any lawful recreations; such as dancing, either men or women, archery for men, leaping, vaulting, or Morris-dances, or setting up May-poles, or other sports, therewith used, so as the same may be had in due and convenient time without impediment, or let of divine service; and that women should have leave to carry rushes to the church for decoring of it according to their old customs." [30]

Dancing, said Ames, is to be utterly condemned because it stirs up people and is an expression of the madness of the mind. In it there is a "defiling of that dignity, which ought to be kept by all Christians: and in that respect, they were used among the graver Ethnicks by hired prostitutes and musicians." [31] And plays also are utterly damnable, for "if lightness and scurrility be taken away from the scene; the common stage it self is likewise taken away: because it will be destitute of actors and spectators." [32] Here something more than the holiness of the Sabbath is afoot; the contention is that Christianity itself is a matter for everyday sobriety and gravity and that the common life of the gracious therefore deprives the playwright of his material. It is the description of a growing practice as well as the statement of an ideal.

The *Book of Sports* was promulgated in 1618, but its strictures were not enforced. In another climate, however, that of Laud's supremacy in 1633, it was revived and provided the ground for persecution of Puritans in the next seven years. In enforcing the book, Laud was only, in his own opinion, reducing the Church of England, which he had always endeavored faithfully to serve, to decency, beauty, and uniformity on the outward face of it. But in the 1630s and 1640s a growing number of Englishmen denied the objective existence of the church, denied the validity of an institution that was separate from its members and could therefore claim for itself a physical mien other than the way of life of the elect.

The controversy over the Sabbath is illustration of the growth in England of a new culture based on the pulpit as opposed to the altar, internalized authority as opposed to external, the superiority of the gracious as opposed to the primacy of the anointed. The Puritan outlook permeated large sections of the population who were unconscious of a connection between their shifted values and any political movement. So John Geree, looking back on Puritanism from the 1640s, with honest innocence disavowed any association with anti-monarchical or anti-episcopal plots, insisting that the Puritans willingly obeyed just laws and commands "not only for fear but for conscience also; but such as were unjust he refused to observe, choosing rather to obey God than man: yet his refusal was modest and with submission to penalties, unless he could procure indulgence from authority." [33] Geree's Puritan preferred sermons to superstitions, but his adhesion to the word rather than ritual did not blind him to the fact that the sermon must teach, not merely complain: "Yet could he distinguish between studied plainness and negligent rudeness." [34]

The Puritan culture contained a wide if ultimately limited scope for tractability within existing secular arrangements. But daily life patterns were preparing men for a new political dispensation. The world they lived in was not a world of their making. "What should I speak of the common sins of the times? The last assizes and every one shows what state we are in, what horrible incests, the daughter being with child by her own father, and the wife burning the child; another ravishing his own daughter, being thereof accused by his own child and wife; what cruel murders? besides the common mother sins, ignorance, extreme worldliness and that overspreading canker and leprosy of the land, the contempt of good persons." [35] So John Rogers spoke from his pulpit. There was no explicit conflict between this observation and his contention that "magistrates laws bind us by virtue not of them, but of God; we must obey them, and all their good laws bind our consciences; but why, and how? because they be mens laws? No; for no man hath power over the conscience, but by virtue of a commandment of the Lord who hath set them, and given them a power to make laws for His worship, and for civil things agreeable to His law, and bid us obey them." [36] No explicit conflict, but implicitly Rogers was teaching the elect that the world from which they separated was one that rightly should imitate them if not come under their direct control. He did not mean, nor did the vast majority of his colleagues mean, that political control should be seized. But it was as clear as daylight that if gracious and natural men behaved in contrasting fashions the regulation of daily behavior should be according to the standard of the gracious. None would be hurt if vice were suppressed, and many would be improved. The reverse, however, seemed to be taking place: "If any be more forward, careful, zealous than the common sort, he is hated, mocked, discouraged all that may be: Not the simplest fellow in town, though he cannot understand one petition of the Lord's Prayer, but will mock at those that be anything toward in religion, or forward to hear the word, refrain from disorder, and keep the Lords day, &c. this sin abounds most fearfully in this land." [37] Here through Rogers speaks the voice of Puritanism informed by village experience. Constables command no respect with the alehouse gang, and magistrates are too easygoing with petty idlers because they are reluctant to look like meddlers. As a result, sin increases and a sick society lingers on, although it contains those who could redeem it.

The Puritans in the village were those who condemned all immodest behavior in their wives, "rolling eyes, naked breasts, laying out the hair, painting the face, wanton talk, and delighting to be in the company of strangers at home or abroad, &c. so especially that foul and odious sin of adultery." [38] But they were also those who had learned to entrust their wives with a share of the joint enterprise: "It were a foul wrong for her to sit in a chimney-corner, or set about some base employment, a servant in the mean time carrying the keys, and having the whole disposal of the house." And once given a fit employment, the wife should be left to it and not followed by a husband "prying narrowly into everything and following her from room to room, and taking account of everything, and every penny made of it, as distrusting his wifes thrift, wisdom or faithfulness." [39] If the wife must patiently submit to the husband's judgments in all lawful matters, such as his decisions to buy or sell, even when she knows the matter better than he, nevertheless the husband must bear in mind that two pairs of eyes are better than one and should consult his wife in such dealings. Moreover, husbands should not delude themselves into believing that daily life's little cruelties are quickly covered by its pleasantries, "for they may speak such words in their fits, as can hardly long after be forgotten, they may pierce so deep, that the wounds made thereby are not soon healed, and when healed, not without scars." [40]

The village Puritanism that John Rogers so copiously documents is one that is most often reiterated in sermons in the imagery of trade and labor. To be sure this is a traditional expository technique: the familiar explains the less familiar, the common and physical explains the rare and spiritual. So Rogers says, in a strain that is close to what was to be Thoreau's: "We trade to the Indies and other dangerous places for gain, and that with great hazard; there's no hazard to heaven, send but out a well prepared prayer, it never returns empty." [41] But the ease with which the one is used to illustrate the other also argues a certain interchangeability in the Puritan's consciousness, a felt superiority in the way he leads his daily life. Thomas Shepard, at one time also an Essex minister, wrote to a former parishioner troubled by the fact that he found that religious thoughts came to him unseasonably. If he gave himself up to them, he would lose his custom; if he resisted them, he feared he would lose his sense of election through offending God. Shepard relieved him of doubt: "Entertain those thoughts as (it may be) you have done friends who came to you at that time you have business with strangers, (whom you love not so well as your friends;) you have desired them to stay a while, until you have done with the other, and then you have returned to your friends; and when the other hath been shut out of the doors, the other had the welcome, and hath lodged with you all night, and thus you have grieved neither, but pleased both. It is so in this case; worldly employments are our strangers, yet they must be spoke with. Religious thoughts and practices are our friends." Not only will the Lord Jesus not be offended at the sensible postponement of His entertainment, but, in fact, "you will grieve His spirit if you parley with the conceived suggestion of it at unseasonable times." The sum of Shepard's counsel is that his correspondent is working for Jesus in his worldly employments and that "you honor God as much, nay, more, by the meanest servile worldly act, than if you should have spent all that time in meditation, prayer, or any other spiritual employment, to which you had no call at that time." [42]

The sense among the gracious of the sanctity of their daily pursuits was a powerful enabler, reducing the resistance that resided in nature and converting it to an ally. "For success in our lawful business, when we have used the means, and commended the same to God by prayer, we should live by faith, and take no carking care for the event, for this is to overload ourselves needlessly and vainly." [43] Confidence in the means and trust in the Lord here achieve a coalescence in "live by faith."

The Puritans, clearly, were not ascetics in their removal from the world. An ascetic perceiving the sinfulness of his natural part might mortify his flesh in a test during which he took the viciousness of one solid part of himself so seriously that he underwent the experience of his limits of physical endurance for the sake of a higher principle. But for the Puritan nature was the damnation of the reprobate only, and the gracious believer had it available to him as instrument. It was no longer an obstacle with an intrinsic resisting force. The way to cope with sexual desires, for instance, was to marry; if widowed, to remarry; and if rewidowed, to marry yet again. In that way the sexual aspect of nature would be used and, in being used, reduced to its proper sphere and kept from leading one into irrelevancies. Natural affection was designed as the foundation of conjugal love and the continuity of the fellowship of believers. It was a means and was not to be taken seriously in itself.

The things of this world corrupt a sinner because he pauses over them, giving them weight, making an idol of them. But the believer uses them for godly purposes; they are sanctified to him through his gracious calling.

Those who remained outside such a culture were distrustful, at the least. Where piety dominated morality and the sanctity of the doer counted more than the deed, there was room for suspicion. Where most things were fit for the saint and few for the sinner, there was room for rage. And the term suspicion and rage most frequently prompted was "hypocrite." The Puritans recognized this but did not comprehend it. One of their number, John Ley, complained: "The most ordinary badge of Puritans is their more religious and conscionable conversation, than that which is seen in other mens: and why this should make them odious or suspected of hypocrisy amongst honest and charitable men I could never yet learn." [44]

The answer to his puzzlement resided in the manner rather than the matter, in a cultural style that was making so much of nature irrelevant. The offensiveness the style gave may be felt, for example, in the Puritan theory of the way to deal with a civil authority who offends against the true church. Do not summon him to you, says William Bradshaw with all due respect for his office, but go meekly to him and, once in his presence, "stand bare before him, to bow unto him; and if he be a king and supreme ruler, they are to kneel down before him, and in the humblest manner to censure his faults; so that he may see apparently that they are not carried with the least spice of malice against his person, but zeal of the health and salvation of his soul." [45]

Many a contemporary was well capable of pointing out to Bradshaw how drained of nature this ideal encounter would be. To endure the king's offenses but to stay out of his way as far as possible is the way of the prudent, whose human motives are to be appreciated. To defy that king by asserting one's principles to his face is the way of the heroic, through whom also the recognizable strain of humanity runs. But to kneel before him, speak humbly, and in that speech censure him for his offenses against your sense of right on the ground not that your main concern is for yourself but that he is thereby jeopardizing his own chance of salvation is a style which, though principled and temperate, has the flush of human blood drained from it. So much of nature is made irrelevant.

Laud persisted to the end in admitting nature into man's devotions through allowing grace to reside in it, saying again at his trial that the images of things visible are "not only for the beautifying and adorning the places of divine worship but for admonition and instruction";[46] but by the time of his trial those with new values based on the supreme word that divided were in triumph. Although

Richard Hooker had earlier joined issue in terms of the word, he warned the Puritans "not to exact at our hands for every action the knowledge of some place of Scripture out of which we stand bound to deduce it . . . but rather as the truth is, so to acknowledge, that it sufficeth if such actions be framed according to the Law of Reason." [47] He did not prevail among those who thought they knew that his law of reason was the rule of precedent, the collection of human compromises with natural weakness, whereas theirs was the rule of Scripture properly explained, so that nature was dominated.

The history of the steps by which Puritanism as a movement came to the fore in the government of Great Britain is a history of political measures, and the history of the Puritans as a whole must also be a history of their ideas. But the Puritanism that was brought to America was not centrally a political movement, English politics very quickly proving themselves remote from the most pressing daily problems of life on a new continent, nor was it centrally an intellectual experiment in applying theology in an unexplored territory.[48] Both political and theological ideologies were imported, and both political and theological ideologies were applied with frequent adaptations to the peculiar American condition. But the Puritanism that was brought to America was most crucially the culture of a people, a new perception of reality that located them in terms of their worldly chores and their God, taught them that they had brought all necessary for the church when they brought themselves and their Bible, and evaporated anxieties that other men felt when they sensed that by their physical removal they were also removing themselves from the sustenance of traditional institutions and a continuity with modern history. The Puritans knew in their bones that history in the sense of the chronology of human affairs had always been complete because there had always been such as they, who were of God, and others who were of the world. They were neither showing the way for the future nor fulfilling the past. They were out of history because they were all the history there was.

CHAPTER TWO

Home Is Nowhere

Calvinism—The congregation as revolutionary cell—
Communism at Plymouth—Rhetoric of colonization—
Family government—Colonial realities

The Puritan culture that grew in England in the latter half of the sixteenth century was based on a division of the elect and the damned that ran throughout mankind. The theology that most satisfactorily met the culture's sense of affairs was that of John Calvin. Systematic and weighty, Calvin's theology maintained that God, before time began, had elected some of mankind to enjoy everlasting bliss in heaven and others to live out eternity in the torments of hell. He had done so in His impenetrable wisdom for the sake of His own glory. When Adam sinned, all mankind sinned in him, and therefore in strict justice all men were damned. But God in His omnipotence had waived strict deserts and had singled out some for salvation. Initially those saved had been those to whom God revealed Himself directly, but in Abraham He had founded a tribe of the saved, the Jews. This was the old dispensation under which Abraham's seed were given the moral law—epitomized in the Ten Commandments—as their guide, although in their corruption they could not satisfy that law and received salvation from being of the chosen people.

Jesus had brought a new dispensation that extended beyond race. He was the son of God who took upon Himself a mortal condition and in His death destroyed the old dispensation. He had the perfect righteousness which sinful men cannot possess, and through belief in Him sinful men have His righteousness imputed to them and are saved by the imputation. They cannot live so as to deserve salvation because they are inherently corrupt and so on strict merits deserve only damnation. But some are elected to redemption through receipt of the gift of belief in Jesus. Once they have this true faith, although still clothed in their sinful bodies and still liable to human errors and human vice, they are purified and their lives are led piously. No deed is in its nature holy; the deeds of the pious are holy because of the righteousness of Jesus imputed to them, be those deeds the tawing of a hide, the tilling of a field, the vending of a bolt of cloth, or the preaching of the word.

One cannot know with absolute certainty that he is among the elect. But there are sufficient signs that can be built on. These signs are to be located primarily in the soul, in man's innermost disposition rather than his social behavior. Whereas it is true that he who is saved will behave graciously, it is not true that seemingly gracious behavior is a sound sign of salvation. Rather, the soul must be searched for such signs, and the search is ultimately verbal. Even though a man may have a feeling that he has been elected, that feeling must be subjected to an analysis that, human frailty being what it is, is conducted in words. The Bible provides an ample text for the difference between conviction and mere delusion and is, therefore, the indispensable companion of the saved.

But what of those who never had opportunity to see the Bible or hear the Gospel preached? Are they to be damned through accidents that are beyond their control? Yes, the Puritan preacher says, because they are men and as men in justice they deserve damnation; salvation is theirs only through divine mercy, and mercy has not been extended them. "They who never heard the Gospel, shall never answer for not believing in it as revealed or offered," the preacher admits, "because it was not so made known to them, but yet they shall answer for that habitual infidelity whereby they would have resisted it, and whereby they are opposite unto it." [1] The equity of the system is perfectly clear to those within it, just as a father's preference for members of his family is understandable.

In the parable he who begins work at the eleventh hour is rewarded equally with him who commenced at the first. This means that no man is too old or too young to experience the conviction of his salvation. The stages of the salvation experience he undergoes are, broadly: vocation, during which he is called to believe and suffers the severe pains of contrition at his inherent sinfulness so acutely that he is humbled and brought to an abject realization that he deserves no mercy from the Lord; justification, during which he perceives the inflowing of faith, a belief in Jesus that lifts him from the dust and attaches him to the community of saints; and sanctification, coincident with (or consequent upon—the debate will have serious consequences in New England) justification, so that now his actions are hallowed unto God, regardless of his walk of life.

The Bible, while it is the indispensable support of the saved, is not in itself the vehicle God employs for the salvation experience. If it were, then those who had hoarded the Bible and kept it from the people would have been in a fair position to secure their election. But the salvation experience must also have the initiating and sustaining force of the Holy Spirit. In the days of miracles the Holy Spirit came to man immediately from on high, calling him to repent and believe. But direct revelation is no longer available. Instead, the Spirit, although it still comes to man livingly rather than from a printed page, now comes ordinarily through the word spoken from the pulpit. Behind the uttered words of the preacher vitalizing the revealed word of the Bible, hovers the word itself, the Holy Spirit that will enter the soul of man and help him in his unbelief. No man can will to believe; he must be given that power by the Holy Spirit; he must be given faith in order to have faith. Those who restrict pulpit activity to the reading of set homilies and prayers are, therefore, chaining the word and denying the congregation full access to salvation.

Charged with conveying the word through his words, the minister has an awesome responsibility, one that he cannot meet if he is not learned, since only through learning can he interpret the Bible and minister to the range of psychological conditions presented by his parishioners. His sermons are acts, designed to initiate and support the salvation experience of his listeners, and are, therefore, to be judged by their consequences. They are not works of art, constructs that justify themselves in their formal balance and beauty of language. Imagery is for illustration, not for decoration, and need not, therefore, be elaborate or consistent; once the point is made, another, even a mixed, image may be most suitable for the next point. The only diction available to the preacher is that of the people because their salvation is his principal aim, and therefore, although he must be learned, his style must be plain. Learning is essential for the preacher because the church has no human existence except where the community of believers gathers, and its continuity is therefore jeopardized should the highest reaches of learning be denied its leaders, just as it is jeopardized by the illiteracy of parishioners who cannot read their Bibles.

Calvinist theology was not the exclusive possession of the Puritans. The bishops too adhered to it, although as its radical consequences became increasingly explicit in the culture that the Puritans were developing, they modified it and finally in Stuart days broke with it. Predestinarian belief did not, on the face of it, preclude government of the church by a hierarchical establishment, nor did it preclude ritualized worship. But the religion of predestination did insist upon the absolute difference between saints and sinners, and the difference, as it was lived out in everyday life, was destructive of the irreducible unit of the Church of England, the geographical parish to which all involuntarily belonged.

"God be merciful to the land of England," said John Rogers, "for it is a presumptuous nation, and a bold, and that without any warrant from God. They think most in England shall be saved. It is the voice of ministers and people. For do not many ministers everywhere admit all in their parishes to the Lords Supper, good and bad, believers and unbelievers, whether prepared or unprepared? now he that is a worthy communicant (as none else ought to come to the Lords table) shall be sure to be saved, as having right to Christ." The bishops could well point out in reply that it was consistent with the commonly held theology for all in the parish to join in communion and that election would work itself out in God's good time rather than by men insisting on making distinctions among themselves. But Puritan practice insisted that this seriously misled men and dishonored God: "And indeed if you should go into all parishes, even the rudest and most ignorant, and go from the chancel to the belfry, and ask them if they be not persuaded they shall be saved; is there any almost make any doubt but that all sorts ignorant persons, civil persons, profane worldlings, hypocrites, all shall be saved?" [2]

In 1595 the Church of England, in the Lambeth Articles, reaffirmed its adherence to predestinarian doctrine, but this was a turning point rather than a renewal. From that declaration on, the belief grew in official circles that Jesus died for all men, not just a group who were elect. The catholic parish could be better maintained on this principle in the face of those who were tearing it apart in favor of the saints separating to themselves the communion table and marking themselves off socially from their fellow townsmen. For the Puritans the unit that would provide the basis for replacing the parish with a voluntary congregation was the conjugal family. If the word was readily available, then the household could become the center of religious discussion and education, the focus of the sanctity of the Sabbath.

Although the family was the crucial building block of Puritan life, a model for the more formal organization of a purified ecclesiastical polity was also provided by John Calvin. In this area the bishops had never agreed with him even during the period when his theology was incorporated into the Church of England to fill the gap left when Scholasticism had been expelled together with Roman Catholicism. Calvin's polity was based on the individual congregation of the saved, who elected their ministers and elders and governed their church through them. It was a system admirably suited for revolutionary as well as reform purposes because it provided those who were forced into such a position by the opposition of authority with an organization that mixed clerical and lay participation, giving all a stake in its vitality, an organization that was local and therefore enjoyed the advantage of the cell, "extraordinarily difficult to root out," as G. R. Elton observes, "and sometimes even difficult to detect." [3]

Puritanism as a name had first emerged in the 1560s to designate those who wished to purify the practices within the Church of England beyond the degree of reform attained by the bishops, and the name was first attached to those who opposed the retention of ecclesiastical vestments, reminiscent of Rome, and insisted upon the suitability of the plain Geneva gown for the ministry. The term was, then, initially a quantitative one, and although the quantity of reform insisted upon by the Puritans came eventually to constitute a qualitative difference, it did so at no discrete point in time. Rather, well into the seventeenth century most Puritans would sincerely insist that they were reformers within the Church of England and not a separate group outside of it. "There was," as Patrick Collinson's study shows, "an extensive area of corporate religious experience within the establishment over which the official Church had little control." Once attention is paid "to the busy life of the puritan laity in sermons, catechizing and house meetings" [4] and the sense of this cultural pattern is felt, then the more public acts of ceremonial nonconformity come into proper perspective and the rationale by which these dissenters insisted that they were, nevertheless, within the church no longer appears to be mere casuistry.

In the 1570s the Puritan clergy managed to develop within the Church of England a system whereby the elect enjoyed the full force of the word. Gathered at local prophesying meetings, the people could hear three or four preachers in turn speak on the text of the day, each dealing with one of its formal divisions and the last concluding with the practical uses of the doctrine. After they had finished, learned auditors were invited to supplement or qualify what had been said. Collinson documents the heated public discussions that followed among "all of them, men and women, boys and girls, laborers, workmen and simpletons" when the formal group broke up and the ministers had departed to share among themselves their reactions to the day's proceedings. "This weekly (or monthly) session rehabilitated the unlearned clergy, promoted a unity of belief based on instruction rather than authority, and gained popular assent to the gospel and its adherents," [5] (as Collinson summarizes the matter).

Had the reformers been permitted to expand such exercises within the church, it is probable that they would have developed a network of communication from local gathering to local gathering that would, in time, have resembled what was to be the synodical structure of Presbyterianism. The pragmatic nature of their ecclesiastical organization would, in all likelihood, have yielded to a dogma. But the authorities in the 1590s annihilated these reformist events within the church and in so doing obviated the Puritans' need to develop a national program. At the same time, the annihilation drove English Puritans back upon the local cell and reinforced the pragmatic. Beginning in the 1590s a generation was trained to local independence, to the autonomy of the particular congregation of the saints. The fellowship of those who had the true faith was stimulated to affirm the cohesion of the folk, and the new man who was his own master had a full field for demonstration of his power. As Perry Miller notes, those who wanted a national church imposed upon the whole people did not believe "that the church could afford to rely upon the perseverance of the saints." [6] In so thinking, they gravely underestimated the strength of the Puritan culture.

Perhaps the most significant event in checking the early prophesying and classis phase of Puritanism was the Paul's Cross sermon delivered by Richard Bancroft in 1589, in which he convinced the authorities that the seemingly spontaneous outburst of petitions, acts, and tracts on behalf of the reformers' position was, in point of fact, the work of a definite party, small, well organized, and destructive in intent.[7] In this sermon also, Bancroft started among the Anglican clergy an interest in their church as catholic and positive rather than a compromise between Rome and reform. This view received its monumental embodiment in Richard Hooker's *Of the Lawes of Ecclesiastical Polity*, the first four books of which were published in 1594. But the *Ecclesiastical Polity* had to await the edition of 1632 before it attained a wide readership. The first edition of some twelve hundred copies was not sold out for eleven years, whereas the Geneva Bible went through thirty-four editions from 1593 to 1603. Explicit authoritarian restraint was being met by implicit popular self-sufficiency.

The check the Puritans received in the 1590s was made possible by the war with Spain. No Puritan doubted that the Armada that bore down on Britain in 1588 floated the minions of the Pope, whose principal aim was to reduce England to his rule once again, and the England that fought Spain was a united one. In the days of greatest nationalistic fervor the suppression of differences within the nation was relatively easy. But the accession of James I stirred up Puritan hopes again, only to frustrate them as the new King clearly indicated that he had learned that Puritanism was the way of those who claimed a self-mastery and did not wish merely to reform the church but aimed at reducing authority. Thus frustrated, the Puritans returning to the struggle amply revealed a sense that they must overcome the false security derived from victory in the Spanish war in order to muster their forces. "This land is wonderful bold, and confident against all enemies and dangers," taught John Rogers. "Tush (say the most) we have peace with all nations, and if we should have enemies, yet we need not to care for any, if we be true within ourselves. Also God hath defended this nation these sixty years, as in Eighty-eight, and at the kings coming in, and from the Powder-treason, and so he will do still, we have no fear." [8] Under this cover, the preacher said, abominations continue to abound in England as the Sabbath is profaned, the godly clergy are curtailed, and the saints are held in contempt.

A small minority of Puritans, under the chafing of the new Laudian Church of England, renounced the church itself and separated totally. In practice this amounted simply to proclaiming the local cell a church unto itself rather than a purified form of the national church, but such separation was, for most Puritans as well as the establishment, the heresy of schism and therefore punishable by death. Most separating congregations, threatened by fellow reformers as well as authorities, departed for the Continent, chiefly the Netherlands, to seek their security there. One such congregation, that which initially gathered at Scrooby, underwent twelve years of difficult living in Holland and finally emigrated to America, where its members founded Plymouth in 1620. They broke the path for their nonseparating brethren who were to follow within the decade, most often directly rather than by way of the Continent.

The war with Spain had marked the end of the first period of English colonizing efforts, one that was powered by dreams of wealth such as the Spaniards had achieved but that accomplished on the North American continent little more than the establishment of temporary fishing stations.[9] Theoretical interest in colonization, however, was high after 1586, although the war prevented application of the schemes. After the war such colonization was seen increasingly not as the means to develop a new route to the Indies and secure it strategically, nor as the basis for discovering and developing mines that would rival those of Spain. Rather, colonization was now entertained as a means of curing the social ills of a nation plagued with landless men desperately unable to attach themselves to the new, more liquid capital, and by England's acceleration toward technical development and industrialization. Medieval booms had been arrested by the refusal of overused land to yield further and by the consequent famines. But now colonization was seen as an easing of that pressure and a convenient area of disposal for the socially marginal.[10] As schemes began to be put into action under James, the Spanish Minister in England reported to his court that "their principal reason for colonizing these [American] parts is to give an outlet to so many idle, wretched people as they have in England, and thus prevent the dangers that might be feared of them." [11]

The outlet, however, was not to be provided by the state. Rather, the private entrepreneur now would test the liquidity of his capital and the strength of the credit system by risking some of his resources in founding a colony that he hoped would make him profitable returns. The Puritans were not precisely the "idle, wretched people" Minister Velasco had meant; indeed, their convictions were formed in reaction to such a condition. But they provided an ideal base for colonization in their fidelity to contract obligations; their conviction of the sanctity of hard work; their experience in the pragmatic organization of a self-governing community within the larger community; and their consciousness of their independence from human traditions in favor of their atemporal relationship to a true church and a true society that was timeless. These characteristics would gain them financial backing and would provide them with a psychological stability under the strain of isolation from the habitual conveniences of the English community.

But one further motive was needed before they could colonize; they had to be convinced of the lawfulness of their founding a colony rather than remaining and meeting the obligation to reform their homeland.

John Cotton, for instance, pondering his next move in hiding after having abandoned his Lincolnshire pulpit because of a summons to the High Court to answer for the purified congregation he promoted within his parish church, initially thought it a breaking of God's law to emigrate. He had to be convinced by the venerable John Dod of Northamptonshire that removal was not an act of betrayal: "I am old Peter," Dod told him, "and therefore must stand still, and bear the brunt; but you, being young Peter, may go whither you will, and ought being persecuted in one city, to flee unto another." [12] The model Dod offered seemed immediate and appropriate to both, more relevant than any chapter of modern history. And John Rogers, preaching in the region that supplied the migration with such leaders as Thomas Hooker, Hugh Peters, and Thomas Shepard, all acquaintances of his, insisted that it was "lawful for a minister or any other tied by calling, either when persecution is only or chiefly intended against him . . . to go aside, seeing it be best for the rest: Its lawful for any, either when God makes a way for them that seems to call them thereto (whereunto if they should not yield, we are to think they have some extraordinary motion of the spirit of God to the contrary, as its written of some of the martyrs) or find themselves as yet not strong enough to endure their rage; those, I say, may fly to be reserved as a seed to propagate the church afterward." [13] The example of the martyrs comes to the fore naturally and is used not to assert the need for a divinely inspired sense that one must flee but for the propriety of flight if no divinely inspired sense to the contrary is received. The new phenomenon of colonization is to be seen as God making a way.

Persecution after Laud's assumption of control provided the final motive and in so doing also held the Puritans in their settlements to a belief in their unity with those who remained at home. Even Cotton Mather, who some sixty years after the great migration was developing a version of the Puritan colonies that would make them peculiarly American, recognized that the initial transplantation was more fitly seen as "a banishment rather than a removal." [14]

When negotiations with the Virginia Company and with the crown came to naught, the group who were to settle Plymouth accepted the offer of Thomas Weston, a London merchant, who formed a company to sponsor them. The terms of the incorporation were limited to seven years, thereby providing a chafing point typical of a number of colonies, since profits were not usually forthcoming from such a radically new enterprise in so short a time. The settlers were to contribute labor and the merchant adventurers, capital. Shares were rated at £10 each, and went to any who contributed that amount in money or supplies, with each settler receiving in addition a share for himself and a share for every member of his household over sixteen years of age, servants included. Children under that age were rated at a half-share. In exchange, the settlers contributed their labor. All profits from "trade, traffic, trucking, working, fishing, or any means" were to go into the common fund from which the settlers were supplied and from which all shareholders anticipated eventually taking their profit.[15] Such serves as a fair example of the financial basis of Puritan colonization.

The leaders in the Plymouth colony, however, had had long experience in Holland, living the separated life of sainthood, and were thus encouraged in their American isolation to embark upon a form of communism that no other colony was sufficiently idealistic to attempt and that they themselves were forced to abandon as a manifest failure after a two-year trial. The patristic view of private property with which they were well acquainted was that it was a necessary institution in a fallen world because it made possible the production of the wealth each individual needed to support his status in society, strengthened and structured the human need to labor, and encouraged charity.[16] But their severe isolation in an unfurnished wilderness, together with the high idealism of their belief in the potential of the special community of the saints, led them to attempt to make total a pattern that was in Europe imperfect because of its countless contacts with other communities. God's ideal for the sons of Adam before the fall was communism, and those sons, encountering again a primeval world, might overcome their corruption and attain that ideal. They decided to act on "that conceit of Platos and other ancients applauded by some of later time; that the taking away of property, and bringing in community into a commonwealth would make them happy and flourishing." [17]

In so doing, William Bradford reluctantly concluded, they had acted "as if they were wiser than God." The fallen state of man worked against the success of communal property. "God in His wisdom saw another course fitter for them"—private property.[18] Single men resented the fact that they worked for other men's families; hard workers resented the fact that they received only as much as did weaker workers; older men resented the loss of dignity they suffered by receiving no more than did younger men; and wives who deemed it little better than slavery to do domestic chores for those not in their family—dressing the meat and washing the clothes of other men—were supported by husbands who could not brook it.

At the core of the failure of communism, then, was the powerful sense of family on which Puritanism had been built, one that was insupportable without private property. Although alarmist opponents of other communistic experiments in Europe later in the century were hysterically inaccurate in their contentions that such experiments included also the community of women so that communism meant free love, they were operating from within a widespread perception of reality. The family founded on new self-mastery was vitally connected to private property as the essence of its physical existence. Those who disregarded the sanctity of such property could, therefore, with probability be maligned as destroyers of conjugality and promoters of free love. The vanishing patriarchal view of the family had sat more loosely with regard to its essential relationship to private property and would prove a better model for socialist experimenters in later centuries. In their brief and painful flirtation with the ideal, the Plymouth settlers were doing more than flying in the face of the theory of human corruption; they were attempting to cut across the social pattern that defined them.

The failure of communism at Plymouth was also indicative of uncertainty about the nature of authority in the secular lives of the saints. Living in states where such authority already existed in the form of royalty, aristocracy, and magistracy, they had accepted it and come to certain compromises with it in order to fulfill their need to assume more authority in leading their daily lives. Their pragmatic instincts had been addressed principally to the organization of the church, the special governing of the society of the saints within the larger government. Now that they were to supply that larger government also, they were uncertain about its nature. Practically they saw that the very structure of their financial incorporation provided the explicit structure of government: stockholders in the company voted for that company's officers, and, located as they were, this, in effect, constituted a government. All that was needed was a brief compact wherein they recognized that they were a civil as well as an economic corporation.

But they had received their emotional outlook in a civilization in which titles and respect were due certain men, and as much as their social condition and the ideology based on it may have brought them into conflict with authority, their structure of feeling was one that was built upon a perception that God had made distinctions among men. They did not consciously aim at the overthrow of civil hierarchies; these they found compatible with the absence of ecclesiastical hierarchy. They hoped only that civil authority would support the true church. So far were they from a perception that rank and its dignities were ultimately unessential for their society that their imaginations still attuned themselves to distinctions and yearned to recognize them where they no longer existed. Three thousand miles of ocean might dilute the rule of bishops to the vanishing point, but they did not dilute the sense that the equality of men came far short of annihilating distinctions between the wiser and the simpler, the graver and the more flighty, the advantaged and the disadvantaged. Not merely were these distinctions to be allowed to emerge in practice but, since they were made by God, they were also to be recognized formally: some were worthy of a special respect and address beyond others, and society should, as it were, institutionalize this. The function of such distinctions was emotional rather than rational. The ambience of order in the wilds as well as the fact of it was sought as a necessary comfort.

The communist experiment foundered on this also. Men who shared property equally were tempted to think that they were equal in other respects, and the community's deeper sense of "mutual respects that should be preserved amongst them" [19] was so greatly offended that the experiment was further weakened.

Plymouth and the Puritan colonies to follow were vitally dependent on a line of supply from those in England who were jointly ventured with them. The readiest form of supply, the merchants in the homeland recognized, was not fluid capital but that which could be supplied by the small holdings and the labor of potential colonists. In promoting their colonies, therefore, they promoted emigration, and the rhetoric in which they promoted emigration, if it did not achieve the status of Puritan colonial policy, did at least cohere into a definite theory of colonization. Since their promotional literature had to be published where bishops as well as laymen could read, they were guarded in appealing to the desire for freedom from ecclesiastical restrictions. But, in point of fact, it is highly questionable whether that motive would have been worked upon more fully even if the authorities had been better disposed. Private letters from early settlers do not make much of this motive either. Such as would be persuaded to undertake so momentous a chain of events as selling out their holdings, giving what was most probably a final farewell to their friends and their native air, and cramming themselves into a vulnerable bark for a voyage that might end in death by drowning or captivity by pirates[20] were not going to respond in appreciable numbers to an appeal that was addressed centrally to their spiritual condition, for the very good reason that improvement of that condition, even when actively sought, was utterly dependent upon the presence of certain material conditions. Insofar as the godly needed ideological assurances, they did so in terms of the legality of their move in God's eyes and according to the laws of nations. The Puritan businessman who addressed this audience offered it a definition of itself as well as a description of America.

The most typical Puritan colonial appeal spoke centrally of the probability of the settler's improving himself materially, and surrounded this attractive proposition with a justification of the legality of migration. The justification went first to the Bible. Just as the new dispensation had been extended to gentile as well as Jew and the chosen people were no longer a particular race, so there was no longer a chosen land for the elect. God had promised Canaan to the Jews, but the attachment of place to promise was abrogated by Jesus. America was a lawful place for settlement not because it was a promised land, but, on the contrary, because there no longer was such a particular locale—neither England nor America nor Canaan —and therefore all places were suitable for the elect, provided the law of nations was not violated in their taking them up. Under the new dispensation, "our dwelling is but a wandering; and our abiding, but as a fleeting; and, in a word, our home is nowhere but in the heavens; in that house not made with hands, whose make and builder is God; and to which all ascend, that love the coming of our Lord Jesus." [21] If America was not a promised land, however, its discovery and development at just that point in history did argue that it was providentially provided. So Cotton Mather was later to reflect, "If this New World were not found out first by the English" (he acknowledged only with reluctance that Columbus was its discoverer), "yet in those regards that are all of the greatest, it seems to be found out more for them than any other." [22] The term "New English Canaan" would receive its first prominent use not from the Puritans but from Thomas Morton, an Anglican opposed to them, and it would be applied ironically. [23]

John Hull, the Puritan merchant who rose to wealth in Massachusetts, spoke not of Canaan but reflected that settlers such as himself had come "to make this wilderness as Babylon was once to Israel." The choice of the model is striking because Babylon was most commonly held to be the epitome of the corruptions of human society, the city of Satan. Hull did not intend this meaning, nor did he intend irony. Rather, he explained, just as the persecuted Jews found material supply in Babylon, so New England was like Babylon in being "a wine-cellar for Christ to refresh His spouse in." He quickly added that God "made this Babylon like a Jerusalem." [24] But the priority of terms is indicative; even if the saints were to achieve a new Jerusalem in the wilderness, they were to do so because the wilderness provided ample physical nourishment, not because it was in itself a promised land.

Settlement in America, as it was spiritually lawful, was also lawful according to the doctrines of nations because of English discoveries on the New England coast and because the first settlers had come to terms with the native inhabitants, who through their chiefs, considered by the Puritans to be autonomous and imperial, had acknowledged their submission to King James. This acknowledgment was gained, the Puritans felt, through friendly usage not the sword, and if any still had cause to wonder that a native people would yield so reasonably to English claims, they need only reflect upon the great amount of space the Indians knew they could spare and the benefit the settlers would confer through bringing them to Christianity. Indeed, even if they did not wish to colonize, they had a Christian duty to use all means to bring the Gospel to the savages, "and the means cannot be used, unless we go to them, or they come to us. To us, they cannot come: our land is full. To them, we may go; their land is empty." [25]

With theoretical questions thus answered, the Puritan businessman was able to get to the center of his appeal for new settlers, and in it he pictured an England so packed that "each man is fain to pluck his means, as it were, out of his neighbor's throat. There is such pressing and oppressing, in town and country, about farms, trades, traffic, &c.; so as a man can hardly anywhere set up a trade, but he shall pull down two of his neighbors." [26] Even those who have learned the lessons of self-mastery—temperance, husbandry, and discretion—are driven to the wall by the straitness of England, and for them especially New England lies ready.

The appeal is not primarily to the class of propertyless laborers but to those with some little means who are unable to improve them through no fault of their own. If they remain in England, they are warned, they might soon be forced into poverty. It is foolish to linger at home in the belief that you cannot live adequately without the range of comforts available in England, said Robert Cushman to potential colonists, because that range is not for you anyway but for the few: "The rent-taker lives on sweet morsels; but the rent-payer eats a dry crust often with watery eyes." What does it mean, then, to argue from the presence in England of things that only "some one of a hundred hath"? [27]

Although the appeal was made to the small farmer and tradesman, it was actually answered in high proportion by those to whom only dry crusts were available. The New England colonies in their early years seemed capable of absorbing a limitless number of those who needed initially to contribute only labor, and indentures were easily arranged. Under the terms of the indenture, not only did these laborers have their short-range economic future spelled out for them in terms of a servitude that was one stage short of enforced, but also, in binding themselves to their employers, they surrendered political and domestic control of their lives. They became for civil purposes part of the families they served and were bound to the rule of the head of the family in all things, even as were the children in that family. The commandment to honor father and mother was commonly accepted as a commandment that applied also to the magistrates who stood to the members of the community as parents stand toward children, and the proposition was, in Puritan culture, reversible: parental authority in the home was magisterial.

William Ames had taught that "there is some difference between servants and free people, for matter of striking, which comes hence; in that servants and slaves, are by their condition obnoxious to blows and stripes, and are compelled to answer their faults by the pain of their bodies." [28] For the servants to be governed in a family was to be governed in such a way. Conscious of a possible duplicity in ruling one part of the family, the servants, in a fashion different from another part, the children, the Puritans sought to obviate the confusion that mere natural affection might introduce. They followed in high degree the practice of putting out their children to be governed in other families, even when, apparently, no apprenticeship or financial consideration was involved. Edmund Morgan suggests that "Puritan parents did not trust themselves with their own children, that they were afraid of spoiling them by too great affection." Such a practice, as he shows, already existed in sixteenth-century England, where it was justified on the ground that a child learned better manners outside of his home, and he concludes that "the Puritans in continuing the practice probably had the same end in view." [29] To this should be added the observation that such a practice fitted well with the Puritan view of nature as mediate and therefore to be avoided when it became an object in itself; the affections should be weaned. And to this also must be added the fact that in a community faced with having to control a high proportion of workers who did not have an entrepreneurial stake in that community's future it was efficacious to govern them with a consistent authority. Since the seat of that authority was the family, uniformity of government was better assured if children were ruled by others rather than by their own parents.

Richard Mather, for example, detecting the gratifying brilliance of his son Increase, deemed it wise that Increase be removed from the dangers of parental indulgence and placed him in another town under the guidance of John Norton. Roger Williams wrote of his sixteen-year-old daughter that she was too young for marriage and "desires to spend some time in service." [30]

There is good evidence that natural affection consistently proved too strong for enlightened convictions and that the tribal sense that fueled the migration also undercut one aspect of its rationale. The Indians, as was frequently noted by the settlers, indulged their children, especially the boys, and Cotton Mather's is but one of many voices that mean, when they lament the "Indianizing" of the country, that the poor family government of the Indians is being shamelessly imitated. Indeed, for Mather this figured as an important cause of the Indian wars of his day: "Now the judgments of God have employed Indian hatchets to wound us no doubt for these our Indian vices." [31]

Other evidence of the resisting force of natural affection was provided, as will be seen, by the Half-Way Covenant movement and the witchcraft furor that, in one sense, might be called the revolt of the children abetted by the servants. But the system also had its successes, and to it may be attributed the fact that seventeenth-century New England culture bears most prominently the stamp of the few who were served rather than the many who served them. In a number of significant ways the latter were knit to the pattern rather than establishing patterns of their own, so that the merchant adventurers' appeals to the independent, although answered in high numbers by the dependent, still stand as typical of the culture.

There was, however, early cause for worry that the nature of the Puritan colony might be misapprehended through confusion with the promises held out by other promoters. Captain John Smith, whose 1614 exploration of New England provided the maps and descriptions of natural resources on which the first Puritan colonists based their plans, who was himself willing to accompany them but rejected on the prudential ground that his book was cheaper, had publicized a New England in which nature and liberty afforded freely that which in England was just about impossible to come by. In Smith's New England it was difficult to avoid becoming affluent. Why, even if, after a day of profitable work in contriving your own fields, gardens, orchards, buildings, and ships, you set out to recreate yourself with a little fishing, you found that there too you were unavoidably profiting. Any man, woman, or child could take fish of excellent quality at his pleasure: "And is it not pretty sport, to pull up two pence, six pence, and twelve pence, as fast as you can hale and veer a line?" [32]

The reality was far from this, and although the Puritans did not believe that many took the captain's bountiful fantasy seriously, they experienced dissension from those who expected to meet with a greater prosperity than they actually encountered. Edward Winslow, on a business trip back to London on behalf of the Plymouth colony in 1624, took care to prepare those whom he hoped to recruit for a severe reality, while at the same time maintaining the advisability of emigration. He managed this feat by pointing out that "he that walketh London streets, though he be in the midst of plenty; yet if he want means, is not the better but hath his sorrow increased by the sight of what he wanteth, and cannot enjoy." [33] In coming to America you will come into the midst of another kind of plenty, he said, "of abundance of fowl, store of venison, and variety of fish." But you must provide yourself with the means to take advantage of these, and if the means are not the money needed to avail oneself of London's supply, they are at least the materials required to set yourself up as farmer, hunter, and fisher.

On the London stage in 1605 John Marston had satirized the view of America that was to receive only a more qualified tone from Captain Smith. Marston's Captain Seagull had called his English tavern companions to share Virginia's maidenhead: "I tell thee, golde is more plentiful there then copper is with us . . . Why, man, all their dripping pans and their chamber pottes are pure gold . . . and for rubies and diamonds, they goe forth on holydayes and gather 'hem by the sea-shore." [34] Remote as is this extravagance from any man's sense of reality, Winslow, nevertheless, felt the need more soberly to warn: "And can any be so simple, as to conceive that the fountains should stream forth wine or beer; or the woods and rivers be like butchers shops, and fishmongers stalls, where they might have things taken to their hands?" [35] The fantasy of an earthly paradise undergoes an informative change in the Puritan consciousness. Natural resources that have immediate value without the intermediary of work are supplanted by those that argue some form of production: gold and rubies and diamonds are replaced by free butcher shops, fishmonger stalls, and fountains of beer and wine. Even when it runs loose and free, the Puritan imagination fantasizes in terms of the abundance of the products of labor.

Winslow's advice is that if you cannot live without luxuries or if you haven't the means to procure necessities you should stay here in England: "For as a proud heart, a dainty tooth, a beggar's purse, and an idle hand be here intolerable; so that person that hath these qualities there is much more abominable." [36] The year before he said this, William Bradford at Plymouth had welcomed a new group of settlers and through their dismayed eyes received a sudden insight into what his daily life really was. The people of Plymouth, he suddenly saw, were ragged in apparel and the only dish they had for the new arrivals "was a lobster or a piece of fish without bread or anything else but a cup of fair spring water." [37]

The New England reality that finally emerged in the first decade was neither so grim as Bradford's 1623 experience nor so bright as that of even the qualified promotions. It was one of a land in which hard labor combined with some resources could provide necessities. "Little children here by setting of corn may earn much more than their own maintenance," [38] Francis Higginson reported from Salem in 1629. In that sentence he fixed the essentials: a land which demanded that children labor but that yielded some profit beyond subsistence. And as for the Indians, a few years' experience had taught the settlers not to fear them or to trust them. If they were not bloodthirsty savages, neither were they a society of helpful neighbors. With tallow wanting, Higginson had to prepare his sermons in the light of burning pitch drawn from the pine, but its smokiness was compensated for by its plentifulness. If the winters were severer than those in England, they were also drier, and he found that he no longer had to wear his cap in the house, although before coming across the ocean he had "not gone without a cap for many years together." [39]

Only at the end of detailing the modest advantages of his new home did Higginson mention that the greatest comfort it afforded was "plenty of preaching and diligent catechizing," and he asked, "If God be with us, who can be against us?" [40] Some disadvantages had to be accepted: mosquitoes in summer, sharp frosts in winter, and rattlesnakes whenever they were least expected. But one disadvantage could be remedied—the sparsity of Christians. Higginson, however, made it clear that he and his fellows wanted more than the spiritual comforts additional Christians would bring. He asked for "a good company of honest Christians to bring with them horses, kine, and sheep to make use of this fruitful land." [41] America was that rare place where, in Edward Winslow's words, "religion and profit jump together." [42]

CHAPTER THREE

The Smith's Dog

Identity and the Antinomian controversy—
Education limits conscience—Magisterial supremacy—
Economic basis of heterodoxy

The Puritans ruled in the New England colonies. Situated in control, they had to work out a church and a civil polity far more fully than they had in England, where the practice of their ideas received sufficient check to confine them to organizing within the society rather than for it. Although they proceeded from principle, their church and their state were arrived at pragmatically.

One striking illustration of this is the relationship of Massachusetts Bay to Plymouth. The latter, founded in 1620, was avowedly separatist and was, therefore, the subject of reproach from the noncomforming but nonseparating Puritans in England who, in 1628, founded the Massachusetts Bay colony at Salem under the leadership of John Endicott and followed this within the next five years by the settlements of Dorchester, Watertown, Charlestown, Roxbury, Saugus, and the chief village, Boston. The flow of immigrants was steady throughout the 1630s under the pressure of the increasingly severe antipuritanic measures of the church ruled by William Laud. Nonconforming clergy were the establishment's primary target in its attempt to restore the church to order, and this learned body was represented in the immigration in disproportionate numbers, even as the need for a labor force encouraged the acceptance of many who could contribute nothing but their hands.

By 1643, it was estimated, Massachusetts contained the extraordinary ratio of one university-trained man for every two hundred residents, or one for every forty families.[1] At the center of the colony stood the self-employed man of small property who related his control of his destiny to the word held forth by the clergy and who relied upon the work of those who came without other forms of capital to invest.

All the leaders professed abhorrence at the schism of separation from the Church of England and were sincere in their belief that in Massachusetts they were merely setting up a purified form of worship within that church. Yet when Endicott brooded about the practical details of just how such a reformed body could be gathered—what the forms of the contract that would bind them, the source of the ordination of its minister, the manner of selection of its officers—he consulted the avowed separatists at Plymouth and copied their procedure in every essential.[2] The Salem settlers established a church that was local and that refused communion with members of other churches who were not so reformed (although it communed with Plymouth). The church admitted to membership only persons who evidenced signs of being elect, was united by a covenant signed by its members, and chose its own officers, who were designated as pastor, teacher, and ruling elder, the first two constituting the clergy and the last representing the lay members in all matters of church administration. This model, although it differed in extreme degree from what the nonconformists proclaimed and practiced as well as possible in England, was not modified in the new churches that followed, even though the influx that led to the founding of new churches included many a learned minister. The Salem settlers had found in the New World that they were not really so different from the separatists as Old World politics indicated and that their distance from England permitted them extremes scarcely talked of when they resided there. They acted accordingly. Regardless of what they had theorized in England, the ministers who arrived after them fell in with this practical fact.

That the crossing of the ocean was the key to the new polity was dramatized by John Cotton, who, after his arrival in Boston in 1633, was to become the Puritan colonies' prime intellectual. Cotton had talked with Samuel Skelton, minister of the Salem church, when Skelton had paused in Lincolnshire preparatory to departing for New England, and had found him to be, as he himself was, unwilling to conform with certain of the practices of the Church of England but still a member of it.[3] When word reached Cotton in England, therefore, of the nature of the Salem church that Skelton had assisted in founding, he wrote Skelton to admonish him for going over to the ways of separation. Cotton was typical of Puritan ministerial leadership in believing that New England congregations should reform distasteful ordinances but not refuse communion to members of the Church of England: he condemned separatism; he urged nonconforming congregations in Holland to receive members of the Church of England into their fellowship; and in preaching the farewell sermon to John Winthrop's group in 1630 he reminded them they were seeking liberty of ordinances but he did not confuse this with separation and told them that England was the Jerusalem at home. "Forget not the womb that bare you and the breast that gave you suck." [4] Yet John Cotton, too, when he arrived in 1633, quickly fell in with a congregational form that was separatist in all but name.

Three years later, in a sermon delivered at Salem, John Cotton provided the Massachusetts Bay churches with the roots of the theory they would use to justify their practice.[5] But the theory came after the fact, and in the sermon Cotton admitted that American experience had altered his judgment. Indeed, throughout the 1630s practice outsped theory. In response to the frequent inquiries during that decade from the brethren at home questioning the surprisingly extreme form their churches took, Massachusetts ministers replied with descriptions of their practice and with assertions that it worked rather than with theoretical constructs that sought to establish it as the very church that Jesus ruled and that true believers had kept alive through the ages. The latter documents—treatises of ecclesiastical polity—came only in the 1640s, after the New England fact and during the Puritan ascendancy in England, when there existed some faint possibility that New England congregational forms might be widely adopted in England also.[6]

On May 8, 1631, the infant colony of Massachusetts Bay ordered that "no man shall be admitted as a freeman, to the freedom of this body politic, but such as are members of some of the churches within the limits of the same." [7] The circuit was thus completed. None could be admitted to the church who did not possess signs of saving grace, and none could have a say in matters of government who was not a member of the church. At the same time, it was recognized that the Holy Roman Empire, that unforgettable model of tyranny, was founded on a satanic mixture of civil and ecclesiastical authority, and therefore that the institutions of church and state, while they supported one another, the church certifying fit citizens and the state enforcing the procedures of the true church and prohibiting others, would not overlap. Magistrates were not to rule in the churches and ministers were not to take civil office. The cooperation was to be assured through consultation.

The ordinance that was most abused in England and most sought after in New England was preaching. Since the continuity of the church was nothing other than the continuity of believers, and since the continuity of believers was ensured only by the word being made available from the pulpit to a congregation versed in its Bible, sermons were of the first importance. No single feature of Puritan life had been more longed for in England than constant preaching, and appetites so long fed on starvation rations rushed to glut themselves. Sermons went beyond necessity to luxury; they were the colony's chief refreshment as well as chief mental sustenance. Notes were taken during sermons so that the event could be enjoyed again in family discussion; the purpose was edification, but the effect was also recreation. On Sundays there were sermons in both morning and afternoon, and in most towns the minister delivered a further lecture on a set weekday. In some town on any given day there was a lecture available to the man who had the time and the horse. So obstructive to the more mundane needs of the colony did the abundance of preaching threaten to be that in October 1634 an agreement was reached whereby the ministers consented to reduce the lectures to only two weekdays: "viz., Mr. Cotton at Boston one

Thursday . . . and Mr. Hooker at Newton the next . . . and Mr. Warham at Dorchester one 4th day . . . and Mr. Welde at Roxbury the next." [8] The culture that so deeply indulged itself was putting a strain on the sermon that would shortly prove intolerable, asking it not only to satisfy the need to be edified by the learned but also to permit the laity to test their own intellectual competence through questions and comments, which followed either in the congregation itself or in more private discussions elsewhere. The occasion of the sermon was the only regular weekly occasion on which the settlers would meet together under one roof and therefore was a moment of solidarity, a crucial means of psychological reassurance of the sanity of an arduous daily life in a wilderness. But the sermon also offered display to a number of men who differed in intellect, delivery, and opinions, and those differences were susceptible to invidious distinctions. Other forms of intellectual recreation and social assembly would have to be developed, but they did not emerge significantly before the invidious distinctions grew into a crisis—the Antinomian controversy.

Disparaging comparisons were the manner of that controversy, and had the abundance of preaching not been so indulged, they might have been contained on a private level. But the matter of that controversy rested deep within the Puritan psyche, and its eventual outbreak on a public level was inevitable in a community that was no longer contained by a larger, traditional society with whose laws compromise must be made. In a land where the godly ruled in church and state, the moral law, given under the old dispensation to guide corrupt man and preached in the new dispensation as a means of calling those who were elected to come out from under its penalties, now had to be redefined. The political longing for liberty of ordinances was matched among many by a psychological longing for the spiritual liberty of the new man, to whom the rule of law was no longer applicable. A crucial conflict developed in Massachusetts about the nature of human nature, its liberty and its responsibilities, and about the relation of the flux of power that flowed through the new man to the forms of the society in which he was located.

Released by a culture whose frame of thought was theology, it was fought, in great part, in theological terminology, but it touched every aspect of the culture's sense of identity.

The theologians of the Reformation had offered varied if not opposed views on the question of the role corrupt man unaided by divine assistance could play in the process of his righteousness. Augustine had emphasized sudden grace as the indispensable starting point of the salvation experience, and Peter Martyr and John Calvin had re-emphasized the idea that before it received grace the heart "cannot produce anything but what is corrupt." But another reform view, exemplified by Johann Bullinger of Zurich, who had corresponded with Henry VIII and Edward VI and also offered hospitality to the Marian exiles, held that corrupt man was capable of confessing his fallen state to God and that such confession was "necessary for the obtaining of pardon for sins," otherwise "we shall never by true faith lay hold on Christ." [9] In sinful England, where the Puritan minister addressed a parish made up of all who resided in the locality, the Bullinger interpretation of preparation for salvation best suited conditions. Faced week after week with sinners, the preacher could more relevantly address them by urging them to prepare themselves for righteousness than by emphasizing the exclusivity of sudden grace. The latter course was better suited to a congregation that already had signs of its salvation.

"Faith," preached John Rogers, "is the mighty work of the Holy Ghost, whereby a sinner is humbled by the laws, and quite driven out of himself, by or upon the gracious and sweet voice of the Gospel, and the free and unpartial offer of mercy from God in Christ, come in time to cast himself upon Christ, and trust to Him as the all-sufficient and only means of his salvation, and withal is willing to be subject to Him all his days." [10] There is some margin here for the action of man's will in affecting his own salvation, and the Old Testament—the laws—is made to function as an organic part of the Christian experience by being the means that humble him and prepare him to will his salvation. Rogers considered himself to be a firm predestinarian, as did the many others who believed his doctrine of faith, and he therefore anticipated the objection that since man cannot please God without faith it is meaningless for him to pray for faith unless he already possesses it, because unless his prayers proceed from faith the prayers will not only be ineffectual but also so presumptuous as to be abominable in the sight of God. "True," Rogers replied, "I grant, one without faith cannot do a thing in the right manner pleasing to God, yet it is a thing that God requires to attend His word, and to pray that His Spirit may make it effectual; which if we do not we sin double, both by abiding in unbelief, and disobeying Gods commandment too." [11] He insisted, "None can prove or show precedent, that faith was wrought in an instant at first, without any preparation going before." [12]

The moral law, then, was an instrumental part of preparation. If the minister preached only on the inability of corrupt man to fulfill the law's requirements and consequently on corrupt man's certain damnation, he would "terrify, torture, and drive to despair." But if, on the other hand, he preached only the Gospel, he would "make folks licentious Christians, and to look for salvation by Christ ere ever they know what need they have of Him." [13] Both must be preached, and if in England the Puritans seemed to place heavier emphasis on the law it was because they faced a hardened people who "be like the smiths dog, who can lie under the hammers noise, & the sparks flying, and yet fast asleep." [14]

English reality shaped predestinarian doctrine, therefore, in the direction of preparation rather than sudden grace, and established a consequent reliance on preaching, in good part, the moral law. This was not quite the hell-fire preaching of the eighteenth-century evangelists, but it shared a common motive. When the community addressed is one in which the preacher can assume that corruption is widespread and that most saints are yet to be called forth, the terrors of the law are emphasized to give the call its proper urgency. Thomas Shepard replied to claims that his preaching was too legalistic for one under the Gospel by saying, "Where there are no law sermons, there will be few Gospel lives; and were there more law preaching by men of gifts, there would be more Gospel walking both by themselves and the people." [15] And, gifted stylist that he was, Shepard recognized that the preaching that would move men to prepare themselves for their salvation was one that had to be directed at their emotions (which he called affections) rather than at their reason. "In natures school we conceive first, then believe;" as Rogers put it, "but in Gods, we believe first, and then conceive." [16] Shepard built on this central Puritan notion. "Being among a people whose hearts are hard enough," he said in England, he would work upon their feelings rather than their understanding "for the understanding, although it may literally, yet it never savingly entertains any truth, until the affections be herewith smitten and wrought upon." [17] Shepard, as a consequence of his ability to fit his outlook with an affective style, was the seventeenth-century preacher to whom those of the school of Jonathan Edwards were to turn most frequently for inspiration in their eighteenth-century evangelical efforts.

The dominant attitude toward vocation among English Puritan thinkers, then, was one that distinguished between contrition and repentance in that first stage of salvation. True repentance, to be sure, could only come with the gift of grace, but it must follow contrition, and that preparative act was within man's power. The minister's assumption of a corrupt congregation also gave a crucial shape to the way he handled the concept of sanctification, the condition of the justified man whereby his acts were deemed gracious. In the midst of corruptions, the justified man should strive to show his saved condition in all aspects of his everyday behavior. A century later, Benjamin Franklin, dramatizing the advent of the new commercial man, was to point out that he should not only be truly industrious but also give the world the appearance of industriousness: Franklin took care to be seen in the streets in his shirtsleeves, bustling away at his work.[18] John Rogers at the outset of the tradition had also seen the importance of the appearance as well as the reality: "We should not only labor to have sound testimonies to ourselves of our election and salvation, but so live, as we may get a good and full testimony thereof in the conscience and mind of the church and brethren with whom we live." [19]

Sanctification was what publicly marked off the believer and most readily identified him to the other members of his community. Consequently, as has been seen, the new men dramatized their solidarity in Sabbath observance, sober dress, oath-keeping, sexual propriety, and so on into an entire range of behavior. Sanctification, the badge of their justification, was a crucial social fact, and although theoretically none who were not justified could be sanctified, the political need of Puritans to add to their strength in order to affect the world in which they lived led them to seize upon sanctified behavior as a sign of justification. Their way was a way of life as well as of belief, and, with opposition to it manifestly evident in so many features of their environment, they welcomed those who had the courage to act as they did. In a world in which the common sort "are shamed of no evil (as of covetousness, swearing, Sabbath-breaking, &c.) but do even strive who should exceed others therein . . . and would not be seen with a Bible in their hands, or in good company, or to speak a good word, lest their companions and betters should upbraid them," in such a world he who dared to act differently could well be accounted among the elect. In a world in which those who have some goodness in them "are yet ashamed of being seen to be too forward, who would hear [preaching] oftener, but for fear they should be counted Puritans," [20] in such a world those who were forward in goodness were, to all intents and purposes, among the elect.

A perception of reality shaped along such social lines was brought to New England by the Puritans, but New England reality no longer contained institutions dominated by sinners. All church members were now of the elect (even though sinners attended compulsorily) and the magistrate encouraged rather than opposed such an arrangement. The man who was not forward in his goodness was the man who would be flying in the face of convention, and there were laws to punish his flights. Yet the perceptions of English Puritanism were built upon to shape the new institutions, most strikingly so in the extensive use of the covenant concept.

Only one prominent man in the first decade of settlement is on record as believing that democracy should be so embraced as to make the surrender of liberties consequent upon a social compact unnecessary. At the founding of New Haven in 1637, the Reverend Samuel Eaton dissented from the proposal that magistrates be chosen from the free burgesses who were church members. He granted that the magistrates should be men fearing God and that the church was the company where such were ordinarily to be found, but he questioned whether free men ought to yield magisterial power to a few. When he was told that the magistrates' power originated in the will of the people and therefore the magistrates acted for the people through delegation, he replied "that all the free planters ought to resume this power into their own hands if things were not orderly carried." [21] Since the constitution made no provision for such a contingency, he regarded it as defective. But his view did not prevail; indeed, it was overwhelmed. Civil government was based firmly on the sacredness of the oath explicit and implied in the social covenant into which men entered and by which they voted and their magistrates took office. Their votes bound them to obedience to the magistrate; his acceptance of office bound him to serving them to the best of his ability. They had covenanted with one another.

So the church too was a covenant whereby men bound themselves to worship together and whereby officers were elected and served along lines parallel to those of the state. One chief difference was that the clerical officers were elected for life rather than annually, as was the case in the commonwealth, but there was a feeling that such might also be a good idea for the state, even though the feeling never prevailed.

The covenant concept was one that applied also to man's relation to God. The old dispensation had been a covenant between them wherein man was promised salvation should he meet the standard of the moral law that God had announced. Since man in his fallen state was incapable of such obedience, God in His mercy had covenanted with Abraham to save all of his seed. This was the old covenant, the covenant of works, whereby a man was to save himself by his works. The new covenant brought by Jesus was the covenant of faith, whereby a man is saved by the grace given him by God that enables him to believe in Jesus and have Jesus's righteousness imputed to him.

A covenant is a hypothetical proposition. There is an "if" that must be performed to assure the "then" that will follow: thus the old covenant of works and thus the covenant entered into by freemen in the state and saints in the church. But how is God's free offer of grace in the new dispensation to be called a covenant except if the term is used loosely to satisfy the desire for rhetorical balance: as one balances old with new dispensation, so covenant of works with covenant of faith? Is God in His omnipotence bindable to a contract?

The English view of vocation and sanctification provided the answer. Man-made contrition preceded God-made faith and was an instrument in securing it; and sanctification, good behavior, was a mark of justification, the state of righteousness. There were, then, two areas of behavior in the salvation experience that came under human control. Even though, it was admitted, sanctification, which was the outward mark, came only after God had given grace, the causal order was reversed in the human perception of the matter. Thus God could be seen as binding Himself to certain conditions, certain "ifs" which when performed brought about the "then" of His grace. The convenant of grace could also literally be accounted a covenant.

Peter Bulkeley of Concord preached accordingly: "After . . . you have broken your covenant with your sins, judged yourselves for them, submitted yourselves to the will of God, and come in the name of a Mediator, then by faith look at the gracious invitation of God, and consider His readiness and willingness to enter into covenant with you." [22] With that view of preparation he combined this of sanctification: "God hath so linked together the blessing of the covenant (which is His to give) with the duty and way of it, (which is ours to walk in) that we cannot with comfort expect the one; but it will work in us a careful endeavor of the other." [23] Such was the view of almost every minister in Massachusetts Bay in the 1630s, understandably so in the light of a lifetime of experience in England.

But if New England truly was the community of the saints, then a headier prospect could also be taken, one in which the old covenant was truly dead and the saved were governed by grace not by laws. Those who were saved were possessed by the Holy Spirit, and their relations with one another were therefore transcendental, it could be argued, conducted through the gracious motions they commonly received rather than in fear of punishment by the laws. The dicta of the moral laws were dead to them. Under the reign of grace they were liberated into a new world whose spiritual scope matched the physical scope of the new continent. To be sure, such an enabling power could be dangerous if pretenders claimed it. But since there was no acting against the true grace that possessed one—election was irreversible—the danger was to be contained by a rigorous search into the qualifications of those who claimed to be elect. Sanctification, seemly behavior, therefore, should not be regarded as a sign of justification. Rather, the premium must be placed on internals, on the actual possession of grace. Psychology took precedence over ethics as the science of the salvation experience. If one objected that a tree is known by its fruits, the obvious answer was that the tree does not know itself by its fruits but by its roots. Not the outer form but the inner flux marked the saint. His every energy should be bent to insuring access to that flux and opposing the imposition of forms and formulas that arrested it.

Such a view was hopelessly hampered and hedged in a corrupt society. But now in America it was for a significant number an irresistible outcome of their liberated situation. In order to become attractive the view needed an eloquent spokesman, and it received this in Anne Hutchinson. In order to become a movement, it needed some base in the values shared by the entire community, and it received this by fastening on the teachings of the highly respected John Cotton.

Cotton himself, though he finally chose flight to Massachusetts rather than answer a 1633 summons from Laud's Court of High Commission, had enjoyed a success in England unmatched by that of any New England minister of his generation. In Boston, Lincolnshire, his reforming practices had for more than twenty years been adroitly maintained, in the face of episcopal visitations and royal inquiries, by a congregation devoted to his person, a wide number of influential people, including bishops and noblemen, impressed by the humility with which he held his vast learning, and a group of aldermen—the living he held was controlled by the city as a corporation—cunning in the ways of dealing with outside authority and compliant when confronted with the need to bribe. So extraordinary was the relative tranquillity of the course Cotton was enabled to pursue that Samuel Ward, the Puritan incumbent at Ipswich, remarked, "Of all men in the world I envy Mr. Cotton, of Boston, most; for he doth nothing in way of conformity, and yet hath his liberty, and I do everything that way, and cannot enjoy mine."[24]

Thus shielded from the chafings of the world by his grateful and infinitely more practical supporters, John Cotton was enabled to turn his great learning to the development of a doctrine of the covenant of faith that partook more fully of Calvin's emphases, arrived at in secure Geneva, than of those of the majority of his colleagues who had followed Bullinger. Man could do nothing without the saving Spirit, he taught, not even bewail his unbelief. No condition is first to be fulfilled, but grace comes directly to those who are elect. The corollary of man's utter passivity in the first act of his redemption is that no man can put his trust in sanctified behavior: "Though his mind be enlightened, sometimes to fear, sometimes to joy, to humiliation, to enlargement, to zealous reformation, yet rest in none of these, for these you may have and yet want Christ, and life in Him; common graces may and will deceive you."[25]

Other Puritan preachers went to their authorities to shore up a reliance on common graces and made distinctions between actual grace and habitual grace,[26] but Cotton did not recognize the need for such distinctions. Rather, what he felt compelled to insist upon in free New England was that the people be not deluded by their ability to attend godly services into believing that they could rely upon their association with the church for their salvation. Of course, the true ordinances as practiced in New England should be cherished, but "while you enjoy them, trust not in them, nor think not to stand upon this, that you are blessed in regard of them." Such trust was a reliance on the letter, and the letter was "loss, and dross, and dung."[27]

Cotton in America was thus able to break through to a new perception—although as the event proved he was not able to own up to its social consequences—and faced the idea that even the word of the Bible is a dead letter if the Spirit does not cooperate. The believer needed no other matter than the word of the Bible for his salvation, but there was need of greater means than it provided, "for it is not all the promises in Scripture, that have at any time wrought any gracious changes in any soul, or are able to beget the faith of Gods elect: true it is indeed, whether the Father, Son, or Spirit reveal any thing, it is in and according to the word; but without the work of the Spirit, there is no faith begotten by any promise." [28]

Adherence to such a doctrine brought the accepted idea of the covenant into serious question and made that term when applied to grace merely metaphorical without any legal parallels. The separation of the covenant from conditions that man must perform and the centering of it in the soul exclusively was a further, even a final, step in the internalization of authority begun when Puritan doctrines first called the men of post-feudal England to seek a new master within themselves. Since both church and Bible were of the Spirit, the believer would, of course, proceed in conformity with them, not because he followed their teachings explicitly, however, but because what motivated him also motivated them. The Holy Spirit would not contradict itself. The moral law had application to the combined community of saints and sinners, indeed should, ideally, provide the basis for its statutes, but it no longer held any punitive power over the saint. Should he through lingering human weakness go aside from the path of righteousness "the Lord will school him thoroughly, and make him sadly to apprehend how he hath made bold with the treasures of the grace of God," [29] but he no longer needed the school of the law. His enlightened conscience was sufficient to a totality.

No preacher of the 1630s matched Cotton's popularity in New England, and the residents of the new Boston recognized that the rise of their village to the status of the principal market town and the capital of the commonwealth was strongly assisted by the desire of so many to live under his ministry. As unworldly there as he had been in old Boston, Cotton did not concern himself with the social complications of his immensely successful preaching—successful, among other features, in the higher rate of conversion in his church—if, indeed, they ever penetrated his consciousness. He was an intellectual guide to be enjoyed by his parishioners. His radical doctrine could possibly have remained in the realm of ideas, with its only practical consequences being felt in the stirrings to salvation experienced by his listeners. But the probability was high that eventually he would reach the ears of more pragmatic saints who would not rest with doctrine alone, and, in point of fact, his preaching soon found such ears.

Anne Hutchinson, when she proceeded to act upon the teachings of John Cotton, however, was not so doing as the result of having been suddenly converted by him. She was, rather, familiar with his doctrines from the many occasions she had taken to hear him preach in Lincolnshire, although she was not of his parish, and she had thought deeply and long about such matters on her own. Indeed, the presumption, so obvious to most of her fellows and so strongly to be urged against her, that she, a mere woman, dared to elevate her thoughts into an area of expression beyond her family, had, in her own eyes, come about as power, not presumption, precisely because the doctrine of the full force of the Holy Spirit had so freed her that she was enabled now to respond to it rather than to the mere externals of the law that bound a woman to silence in a public assembly. As Cotton's doctrine gave Anne Hutchinson a purchase on her perceptions, so the habit she shared with most saints of listening to a number of sermons outside of their own congregation provided her with the basis for the distinctions she was to make in advancing her insights.

Anne Hutchinson was a woman of considerable personal attraction, with a fund of practical knowledge of the problems of women, especially childbirth. These brought her into more homes in Boston more frequently than was common of others, men as well as women. In addition, her strong intelligence attracted to her home a widening circle of people who found that the benefits to be derived from the domestic discussions of religion—most frequently centered on recent sermons heard—were increased when they were conducted under tutelage rather than confined within family discussion. By 1635 she was the center of two large weekly gatherings at her home, gatherings that were popular, it may be assumed, because of the social occasion they afforded as well as the religious edification they provided.

At the meetings in Anne Hutchinson's house, notice was taken of the difference between John Cotton's doctrine of grace and that of the other ministers in the colony. Indeed, to most gathered there it became increasingly clear as they pursued the topic from week to week that really John Cotton alone preached the true covenant of grace. In the conditions to salvation that they taught men to meet before faith would come, the other ministers were holding forth nothing better than the old dead covenant of works. They were binding men to the form of the letter rather than opening them to the free flow of grace.

The pattern of Massachusetts community life allowed for an outlet to the ideas of Anne Hutchinson's group. Most sermons were followed by discussions, and the Hutchinsonians could, therefore, attempt publicly to point out to others the errors of their ways; to show them, for example, that if they built their hope of salvation on signs of sanctification rather than on soul-searching for justification they were going on in a covenant of works and courting their damnation. Precaution had to be taken, of course, against giving offense. Although the members of the group were influential in Boston, the most powerful man in their town, John Winthrop, was not of their number, and most in other towns were suspicious of them. But after October 1635 they could afford to be less guarded, for in that month the colony received its most eminent new resident, Sir Henry Vane, son and heir to the comptroller of the King's house, who had come, he said, to "enjoy the ordinances of Christ in their purity," [30] and who joined the Hutchinson group. Especially after May 1636 could they be outspoken, because then Vane was elected to the colony's highest office, the governorship.

As the Boston opinions were broadcast openly, dissension set in. They did not take with a large number of people outside of Boston and they were greeted with almost unanimous abhorrence by the magistrates. Unworldly John Cotton, when forced to contemplate the division of opinion now erupting into public controversy, saw little reason to become heated by it. Although he clearly believed his doctrine to be correct, he felt that the differences were ultimately in emphasis and not central to what all saints must believe. Neither side was heretical.

But Cotton was almost alone in his calmness. During 1636 tempers ran higher and higher, and the oral clashes that followed sermons were becoming slanderous. In view of the undeniable Christianity of the Hutchinson group, the heat generated and the sense of danger acutely felt by those who opposed them indicated that the doctrinal battle was touching the deepest assumptions of the culture. Since, however, the growing outrage sprang from the unarticulated structure of the society's sense of reality rather than from a mere disagreement on theological interpretations, it was intensified by the majority's frustration in being unable to find a correlative in the disputed opinions for their intense feeling of being threatened. It was difficult to procure witnesses who had heard any of the Hutchinson group say things that could be called downright heretical, and although John Cotton was perfectly willing to go more than halfway in conciliation, there was really no ground for asking him not to preach what he preached so well.

Yet something had to be done about the dissension that was fracturing the fellowship, and something was done and with a vengeance. In 1637 Vane was voted out of the governorship in favor of Winthrop, and during the course of that year John Wheelwright, a newly arrived minister, a relative of Anne Hutchinson's, and the only clergyman other than Cotton to preach the unconditional covenant, received a civil censure that served as the basis for his expulsion. In the autumn of that year the magistrates summoned a synod of the churches to pronounce on a long list of opinions that were hastily compiled with the insinuation that they were all current, but without their being assigned to any particular holders; then, in the early winter, Anne Hutchinson, under cover of the synod's pronouncements on the heresy and blasphemy of most of the listed opinions, was tried. After an ineffectual though forceful attempt to fix a number of these opinions on her, she was triumphantly expelled from the colony for a belief that was not at issue when the trial started. In the course of her examination before the magistrates she had attempted to show the centrality of inner experience, and, referring to her own case, spoke of how she had been guided to distinguish "between the voice of John Baptist and the voice of Antichrist." When asked how she knew that the Spirit was her guide in this matter, she replied "by an immediate revelation." "How!" exclaimed Deputy Governor Dudley; "An immediate revelation," [31]—and this remark served as the basis of her banishment. Following her civil trial, the movement collapsed and the authorities found there was remarkably little mopping-up to do.

But the question remains. What was there in the Puritan community that was so deeply offended by Anne Hutchinson's group that her opponents moved swiftly and massively to suppress them, even though the suppression could not find a meaningful correlative in the doctrine of that group and took place in the name of whatever could be made to apply: sedition, or dishonor to magistrates, or an injudicious expression?

When John Winthrop wrote the history of the controversy as a sterling display of the ability of the churches in Massachusetts Bay to regulate their affairs according to the best principle of reformed Christianity, he commented upon Anne Hutchinson's claim to an immediate revelation. "For here she hath manifested," he wrote, "that her opinion and practice have been the cause of all our disturbances, & that she walked by such a rule as cannot stand with peace of any state; for such bottomless revelations, as either came without any word, or without the sense of the word (which was framed to humane capacity) if they be allowed in one thing, must be admitted a rule in all things; for they being above reason and Scripture, they are not subject to control." [32]

The members of any civil society, of course, must be subject to a control external to them. The question raised by Anne Hutchinson was whether such control extended to the enlightened conscience in all the areas of daily life that were not the explicit concern of the civil law. Did a society ruled by saints need to continue to insist for its well-being on conformity to a code of behavior that was based on commonly accepted restrictions, or could it, confident of the sanctity of the individual conscience lit by grace, permit a wider range of individual expression in word and deed? The victorious party called its opponents' position Antinomianism: the view that Christians are by grace set free from the need of observing any moral law. Such a view was not in itself heresy—indeed could with some justice be derived from such teachings of Paul as Romans 3—but it had come to be heretical in meaning because some early Christian groups that held the view had fallen into licentiousness as a result. The need existed among the majority in Massachusetts to see their Antinomians as those who would run amuck in their enthusiasm if not forcibly restrained, although the facts of their behavior did not pose such a threat. But Anne Hutchinson had crossed a border of her culture and menaced it with a concept of the individual as finally being more important than the state. She held forth the view that social norms were rooted, ultimately, in human needs, and that, as human experience led to new insights, those norms should fall in favor of the new enlightenment rather than become fixed and worshiped, as it were, as idols. They were a dead letter when opposed to individual insight rather than made responsive to it. Like transcendental thinkers who were to follow in her New England, she saw no conflict between the freedom of the enlightened individual and the well-being of the community, but, like them also, she insisted on the priority of conscience.

Most men who had elevated conscience into an instrument of self-mastery against the collapse of external authority wished nevertheless to bring that conscience under control, once freedom from misguided authority had been secured. The prospect of following it further was too anarchic. Conscience had to be bound to the service of society. They recognized that although specific examples of excessive behavior based on claims of conscience could be dealt with punitively, a more positive bonding of the conscience to communal principles was desirable. How could they retain their insistence on freedom of conscience and at the same time limit that freedom to socially acceptable behavior? They answered the question by charging the institution of education with the task of inculcating in developing minds the limits within which the free conscience might range.

Nowhere in the English-speaking world was schooling so widely available to children as in Massachusetts. Education was a sincere response to the observation that in the absence of other insurances of cultural continuity—an objective church, an aristocracy, communities that had existed for centuries—schooling must serve that function. Literacy was the key to the survival of the culture because it assured the learned ministry and the reading congregation that was the culture's essence. Winthrop had pointed out that reason and Scripture were to furnish the standard, and since the standard could be ambiguous, schooling was made to serve as the inculcator of a common interpretation of the teachings in these sources. In domestic gatherings and in the church, as well as in schools themselves, reason was to be exercised within an acceptable range and the Bible was to be given an acceptable interpretation. Thomas Shepard noted that "the Lord having delivered the country from war with the Indians and Familists [the Anne Hutchinson group] (who arose and fell together,) He was pleased to direct the hearts of the magistrates, (then keeping Court ordinarily in our town [Cambridge], because of these stirs at Boston,) to think of erecting a school or college, and that speedily, to be a nursery of knowledge in these deserts, and a supply for posterity." [33] Consideration of such a matter had, to be sure, been postponed by the turmoil, but the speedy establishment of Harvard after the settlement of the controversy emphasizes the role education was meant to play as the agency of implicit conformity to the limits of the conscience. In the absence of other traditional restraints, the New England Puritans pioneered in the field of education as the means of shaping the individual to a psychological acquiescence in the norms of his community, to educating him, as it were, for citizenship.

The institutionalization of education as the prime agency of limitation of the conscience was accompanied by other institutional shifts during and immediately after the Antinomian controversy. That event had forced the community to arrive at a sharper sense of itself. Through attempting to articulate and control what was deviant it reapportioned responsibilities within the system and asserted what the culture was by showing what it was not to be. Of extreme importance in this reassignment of duties was the initiative the state took over the church.

Although the trouble was at first doctrinal, the numerous conferences and correspondences among ministers were ineffective in coping with it. The Congregational system insisted on the autonomy of each gathered church: there was to be no superinten-dency over them as was characteristic of the Roman Catholic and Anglican churches. Churches were churches only insofar as they originated in the freedom of the saints and were controlled locally by them. But this view, founded on the bedrock of suffering under an episcopacy, was inadequate to meet the problem of the straying of any particular congregation. Ideally, through voluntary consultation with neighboring churches, the errant congregation could be reset on the proper course—in modern terminology, nonbinding arbitra-tion would suffice. In practice this seemed to work until the Antinomian controversy.

When consultation failed, compulsion followed. But since com-pulsion of recognized believers by other believers had too distinct a flavor of the familiar European oppression that had been fled, the godly magistrates stepped in. Doctrinal differences were read as sedition rather than heresy and as such were liable to civil action. It was the magistrates who acted first when they claimed Wheelwright had preached a seditious sermon, and it was the magistrates who continued to act as they convoked a synod for guidance. The members of the synod need not fear they were establishing a precedent for the ecclesiastical coercion of the particular church, and, indeed, they did not. They gathered for consultation only. But the magistrates were free to use their deliberations, as they did, as the basis for popular support of their continuing actions, chief of which was the civil trial and banishment of Anne Hutchinson.

Until the controversy the developing relation of church and state was sufficiently fluid for the settlers to regard it as that of two cooperating forces pulling abreast. The churches, with magisterial cooperation, regulated matters of the relation of man to God, matters such as those dealt with in the first table of the Ten Commandments. The state, with ecclesiastical cooperation, regulated matters of the relation of man to man, matters such as those dealt with in the second table. The Hutchinson group called into question the separation of the two areas by asserting that if one stood in a wholesome position with regard to the first table, matters of the second table were irrelevant, not because the commandments were not wholesome but because they would be met by the believer as the result of his grace and that grace would define them. In its reaction the community could not, indeed, maintain the separation and therefore moved to an implicit acceptance of the fact that the magistrates and the ministry were concerned with both tables. In order to keep its deep-seated sense of the importance of the moral law it needed to continue to envisage a world of which the principal feature was the constant presence of the sinner under threat of punishment and therefore under need of external regulation. Since this world was not that of the church—as the opinionists vividly insisted in their exposition of the free condition of the saint—it had to be that of the state. And since their psychological needs, shaped by life in England, were for explicitly regulated order, they permitted the state rather than the church to become the institution that most fully represented their view of the world.

At the May 1637 meeting of the General Court, during which John Winthrop had been elected governor to replace Sir Henry Vane, an order was passed "that no town or person shall receive any stranger, resorting hither with intent to reside in this jurisdiction, nor shall allow any lot or habitation to any, or entertain any such above three weeks, except such person shall have allowance under the hands of some of the council, or of two other of the magistrates." [34] Suitably stiff penalties were affixed: offending towns to pay £100; offending individuals, £40 initially and £20 for each month's continuance of the offense. The arrangement had been that a man must be admitted to a church before he could apply to be a freeman, and local communities, therefore, had a significant voice in determining citizenship. But with the Antinomian troubles upon them and the rate of immigration continuing high, the magistrates had moved to control the nature of such as could be received as residents, and thus came in before the churches in determining qualifications.

The intent was clear to members of the Hutchinson group. Massachusetts was to be not the home of the saints, but the home of saints who held acceptable opinions; even though a would-be settler were an acknowledged Christian and acceptable as a member of a church, he could be turned away by the civil authorities. Vane promptly protested the court order, noting that a fundamental shift in the nature of the society would take place, and Winthrop admitted this but maintained firmly on behalf of the concept that prevailed: "A man that is a true Christian, may be denied residence among us, in some cases, without denying Christ." [35] Vane could only note ineffectually that the law was really aimed at those who were, in his opinion, "truly and particularly religious." [36]

The area of intersection between church and state, and therefore the area into which the state first entered in assuming total control, was that of individual responsibility for behavior. It was the area created by the doctrinal recognition that man's receipt of grace was conditional upon his actions, and broadened by the acceptance of sanctified deportment as a sign of justification. The state needs good citizens and the state, therefore, is anxious to improve upon beliefs that maintain that civic behavior and piety are just about identical.

Most men felt the magistrates had saved their commonwealth through prompt action, and following the controversy the pulpit supported the civil officers in their newly extended authority. The practice of questions, answers, and comments after the sermon was dropped as "an occasion of much contention, vexation, and folly." [37] Shepard preached absolute obedience to the magistrates. Derision of laws or appeal from them, he said, was a sure way to break down the commonwealth. Assertion of individual liberty was the mother of discord. Tyranny came, he pointed out, not when the magistrates were respected in their power but when they were disregarded and authority was turned to a mere vanity. This would be accomplished if the people "open the door to all comers that may cut our throat in time; and, if being come, they do offend, threaten them and fine them, but use no sword against them." [38] If his severity were opposed by any misguided enough to believe that doctrinal differences among Christians came well short of deserving such punitive measures, he replied that the way to make oneself vulnerable to oppressors is to keep saying "they will not assault us first by craft and subtlety, but openly and violently." [39] The retrenchment in favor of greater civil power that he advocated was to receive its greatest challenge when immigration died suddenly after Puritan prospects took an upward turn in England in 1640. In the short run, it prevailed sufficiently to establish as an article of almost permanent belief the notion that New England's strength resided centrally in its civil charter and the magistracy therein provided.

When, in talking of the foundation of Harvard, Shepard had pointed out that it was undertaken speedily after the trouble with the Indians and Familists, he had used the term Familist advisedly to describe the opinionists in order to underline the licentious consequences of their outlook. "Familists" meant members of the Family of Love, a sect that believed free love was a permitted result of the gracious life freed from the law. Historically, sects that hold this view, indeed most pietistic sects, are drawn from the disinherited of the earth, who thus attempt to comfort themselves with a counterculture in which they may at least take full enjoyment in the little they do possess. But scrupulous analysis of the church membership, civil offices, property, and English background of the supporters of Anne Hutchinson points undeniably at the fact that they came from the richest and most prominent members of her society.[40] Repression of the opinionists, therefore, was repression of a very significant and influential element of the community.

In confronting this fact, one is led to confront again the material motive so dwelt upon in the propaganda of the merchant adventurers. Mercantile theory emerging in England during this period insisted that the welfare of society or the welfare of the state be substituted in place of the amelioration of the individual. In addition, that welfare "was conceived emphatically as materialistic or economic." [41] New Englanders, of course, resisted some of the implications of this outlook that had provided the necessary condition for their migration. They distrusted interest, still regarding it in a biblical and pre-mercantile manner as usury, although they would in the next decades change their minds; they did not approve of luxury, linking it with the vicious manners of their oppressors in England, although it provided new markets, including that for the beaver fur they dealt in; and they would not tolerate freedom of religious expression, although such freedom, as practiced in Holland, assured that trade would flow unblocked by arbitrary obstacles. But their lives were led in response to the general economic structure of mercantilism, and their society was increasingly vulnerable in those areas in which it attempted to qualify or arrest parts of that economic outlook.

The relative isolation of the community, however, did leave such qualifications of the mercantilist outlook relatively unchallenged, especially in the first ten years, when a high rate of immigration postponed the need to consider a colonial source of capital by providing a constant influx of consumers with funds brought from outside. The settlers thought of an economy based on a pre-established distribution of business opportunities among certain numbers of people in given trades. If they distrusted monopoly except in cases of demonstrable public benefit such as the encouragement to develop local ironworks, they were also far from accepting free competition. Their patristic models combined with their lives in post-medieval England to inculcate in them the need to protect the buyer through fixing prices, even as they sought to achieve social stability through an oligopoly in crafts and trades and a strict regulation of laborers' wages. This economic ideal was drawn from a static view of society, one that would inevitably come under pressure as events in the wider economic world destroyed isolation. Put more bluntly, such a point of view had to be based on a self-evident wage level, else the structure would collapse, and when immigration halted, the wage level was bound to turn upward.

Even prior to 1640 the attractions of freer trade than that permitted by the state were making themselves felt, and, indeed, the first major war with the Indians, the Pequot War, was the result of traders' machinations among the tribes. In order to insure a supply of furs from any given tribe, traders were encouraged to enter into alliances with that tribe against its rivals, and therefore traders acting independently made difficult a consistent Indian policy for the entire commonwealth. The Narragansetts and the tribes who paid them tribute were the crucial allies to be retained at all costs in the first decade, both because they would be a powerful military enemy and because they had developed a specialty in currency: for goods received, the Narragansetts would supply wampum, a portable currency handier for use than goods in dealing with remoter Indians.[42] The Narragansetts, moreover, were jealous of the trade with inland tribes and preferred to serve as middlemen in such transactions, themselves trading English goods for Indian furs.

Through 1635 the fur trade was more important than the fisheries in providing the resources from Europe necessary to sustain internal trade and agriculture. Since it profited from a labor force outside the English community, it was unhesitating in responding to whatever demands would ensure supply without a corresponding regard for the well-being of the Indian community. The fur trade corrupted the Indians by introducing artificial demands into their culture. It also led to the unhesitating need to kill Indians to assure the security of the trader. After the Pequots had killed John Oldham, an English trader, in July 1636, punitive action was compulsory.

But Vane was Governor at the time, and Vane dragged his feet. Lieutenant Gardner, out in a fort on the Pequot frontier, claimed that adequate support was denied him on the ground that Indian arrows were of little force, and he took care, when one of his men was killed by an arrow that entered his rib cage on the right and penetrated through to stick in a rib on the opposite side, to extract the rib and arrow and send them with a letter to Governor Vane in order to chastise his reluctance.[43] But an effective punitive force had to await the replacement of Vane by Winthrop, and even then, Winthrop claimed that although Boston had met earlier emergencies by sending more and better men than other towns, in the Pequot draft "they sent not a member but one or two whom they cared not to be rid of, and but a few others, and those of the most refuse sort, and that in such a careless manner as gave great discouragement to the service." He felt he well knew the reasons for this conduct: "Mr. Wheelwright had taught them that the former governor [Vane] and some of the magistrates then were friends of Christ and free-grace, but the present were enemies, &c. Antichrists, persecutors." [44]

Boston reluctance was attached to Boston Antinomianism. This does not argue that the opinionists had any specific brief on behalf of the Pequots; it indicates the negative fact that they were unwilling to join in a communal enterprise with those with whom they had so profound a disagreement in other matters and who had so rudely turned their representatives out of elective office. But it is clear also that the Pequot War did not present a national emergency so overriding as to qualify their reluctance. The relatively wealthy and well-positioned group behind Anne Hutchinson was attracted to her doctrine because free grace above the legalistic restrictions of the moral law meant freer enterprise beyond the specific regulations of the state. The protection of the fur trade clearly did not enlist their sympathies; their worldly interests lay elsewhere.

More than a hint of where they resided is provided in a letter to John Winthrop from John White, a Puritan minister in Dorchester, England, who had had an interest in the Christian benefits of colonization that predated the migration. White held to a patristic vision of a static society centered on the producer and believed that this ideal must be pursued if Massachusetts were to realize its Christian promise. "I hear shopkeeping begins to grow into request among you," he wrote on November 16, 1636. "In former ages all kind of retailing wares (which I confess is necessary for mens more convenient supply) was but an appendix to some handicraft, and to that I should reduce it, if I were to advise in the government. Superfluity of shopkeepers, innholders, &c. are great burdens to any place. We in this town where I live (though we are somewhat reformed that way) are of my knowledge at charge of £1000 per annum in maintaining several families in that condition which we might well spare for better employments, wherein their labors might produce something for the common good, which is not furthered by

such as draw only one from another & consequently live by the
sweat of other mens brows, producing nothing themselves by their
own endeavors." [45]

White's attitude was one with which Winthrop might have had
sympathies, but which he was too practical to act upon. It is
representative of a widespread view in Massachusetts, evidenced,
among other things, in the maintenance of the doctrine of the fair
price and the civil prosecution of Anne Hibbins when she opposed
oligopoly in the joiners' trade. The attitude that White represented
was one which chafed a number of merchants and would-be
merchants, and these were to be found in significant quantity in the
Anne Hutchinson group. Free grace struck a responsive if inarticulate chord among those who felt the attractions of freer trade.

When the Transcendental Movement developed in New England
two hundred years later, it did so in a climate of *laissez-faire*
capitalism. Even as they sincerely and severely attacked the
materialism of their countrymen, Emerson and Thoreau preached a
self-reliance as the essential starting point of reform in their society.
In so doing they responded to the same current of thought that
empowered their fellow citizens to engage in open commercial
competition. The differences between their movement and Anne
Hutchinson's are many, but not so many as to veil the crucial
similarity: belief in the absolute sanctity of the enlightened individual
finds favorable soil among those who wish to cross the older
boundaries of restricted commerce. Emerson and Thoreau spoke at a
time when the boundaries had been crossed, and their transcendental
philosophy was expressed in reaction to the extravagances of the
materialism of their culture. It was based, however, on a recognizably similar view of the freedom of the individual. Anne Hutchinson
spoke theoretically, with no conscious reference to material conditions, when the vocabulary of free trade was as yet unthought of. But
the group who supported her show in their makeup the early
stirrings of resistance to impediments to such freedom. The
Antinomian controversy, in addition to giving education as an
institution a crucial bent and redefining the relationship of state and
church, had also given preliminary expression to a class of people

who opposed the regulation of commerce in the interest of the consumer and farmer—though their criticism of such regulation was to remain latent until the sealed community of Massachusetts was opened to the wider economy of the Atlantic and their stirrings achieved a publicly acceptable vocabulary.

Dominant Puritan culture had in the 1630s defined itself through defining deviancy from it. It was one that needed its quota of sinners, hence the priority of the state over the church, and that sought communal solidarity through the psychological inculcation of the limits of reason and scriptural interpretation. Those who had come out of the world now shaped the world, and self-mastery rather than opposing a decaying order drew a perimeter and ruled within it.

CHAPTER FOUR

A Good Fence

American Puritanism versus the sect ideal—
New England and the Civil War in England—
Laboring class and other economic pressures—
Indian policy—Control of dissent

In the sixteenth century Puritanism was a sect and manifested the characteristics of a movement governed by the sect ideal. Members were not born into the group but entered it consciously, and the spirit of fellowship was promoted by the gracious behavior of the members who thus set themselves apart from the larger community. At the same time, individualism had considerable play, for it was through self-expression that the believer achieved the identity that qualified him for membership and marked him as different from those who remained in the world. The sect assimilates within its framework all secular matters crucial to its members; what cannot be assimilated is rejected and avoided. Should such rejected matters, in the long view, be of relevance, they can be met with varying degrees of compromise as the necessary consequence of a mortal existence. But the sect insists on exclusivity and is not concerned with humanity in the mass. Universalism is postponed to the Day of Judgment, and the sect ideal is, therefore, eschatological. Since a strictly defined purer life is led by believers in the interim, the sect ideal is also, therefore, ascetic, not because, as in medieval asceticism, this ensures salvation, but because asceticism is the outward mark of difference from the world.

Although the Puritanism of the New England settlers originated in such an ideal, and although certain characteristics of the pursuit of that ideal, such as a strict code of manners, were to continue to be insisted upon by the leaders of the community, nevertheless the Antinomian controversy with its redefinition of the roles of church and state put an end to the essential similarity between American Puritanism and sectarianism. Henceforth Puritanism was to be the way of the New England world rather than of a group within it. The main forces of the culture strove to sustain this concept.

In the emphasis they placed upon commonwealth, the New Englanders committed themselves to the proposition that the glorification of God, their ruler, in His omnipotence outweighed considerations of a fellowship of those who communed with God and in that communion overcame all conflict and all law. The radical ethic of love, prominently held forth in the Sermon on the Mount, sustains the sect ideal, but it was diminished to the vanishing point in a society that made its Christianity coextensive with the claims of social and political life. After the Antinomian controversy New England thus came into a closer correspondence with the ethic that governed Calvin's Geneva rather than with that of the reformed German communities inspired by Luther. Ernst Troeltsch's characterization of Calvin's social ethic is a just description of what the leaders of Massachusetts came to think. "With piercing insight," he wrote, "Calvin singles out of the Christian morality of love the religious element of activity for the glory of God, and of sanctification for God and for His purpose, which has always distinguished Calvinism from any mere sentimentality and humanitarianism. Without hesitation he regards everything as commanded and permitted which can serve the glory of God—and by that he means that the Church is to be set up, maintained, and kept pure as a community of saints closely connected with the State and with Society. When it is claimed that the Christian ought to renounce authority and law, wealth and possessions, rewards and worldly honours, Calvin takes care to explain that his renunciation only applies with certain limits—that is, that a renunciation of this kind must be solely designed to serve the spirit of holiness and brotherly love, but that it must not be permitted in any way to endanger the glory of God Himself. Where this is concerned, all those methods are not merely permitted, they are commanded." [1]

The sword of the magistrate is thus placed squarely at the service of the church, and religious persecution becomes a duty when divergent opinions threaten the unity of the commonwealth. The Old Testament character of Puritanism in New England, frequently noted and commented upon, stems from its emergence out of the sect ideal into one of the holy commonwealth. Apologists who lived through the shift were to rely on a rhetoric of analogy between their migration and that of Abraham. What had been described in propaganda addressed to would-be settlers as a removal for the sake of liberty of ordinances, economic improvement, and national welfare, came in such apologetics to be described as the calling forth of a chosen people. [2]

In 1640, however, as Puritan fortunes in England began to rise, the sect ideal rose with them. The broad popular support attracted by the brewing revolution against Charles included many good statesmen and a multitude of good soldiers and suppliers who felt the hour had now arrived for the expression of their particular beliefs, and the revolution was conducted, as a necessity, through permitting the widest variety of sectarian expressions. Toleration was the beacon that attracted men to the Parliamentary cause and secured its victory. [3] Polemics, not persecution, ruled the day. During a period when Massachusetts was consolidating itself and putting stricter limits on freedom of religious expression as a consequence, England rushed into its period of greatest permissiveness. Indeed, before the 1640s ended, all other compromises having failed, the successful revolutionaries had embarked upon republicanism as a matter not of principle but of expedience. And foremost among those who proclaimed liberty of conscience were the New Englanders' closest ecclesiastical allies, the Congregationalists, who perceived that in England they would never achieve a majority and that therefore their only welfare resided in such liberty. [4] In 1646 John Winthrop received a letter from England reporting on the activities of Hugh Peter, former minister of Salem but now a member of Cromwell's staff, who had returned to England as an agent of the Massachusetts colony. "I could wish," complained Giles Firmin, "he did not too much countenance the opinionists, which we did so cast out in New England." [5] American isolation, which had provided the context for a galloping reform of episcopacy, would have to provide stabilization against such trends now that the saints were so recklessly on the move in the homeland. Moreover, such stability would have to be achieved in terms of a radically changed economic situation.

During the 1630s Massachusetts had been able to import heavily without producing capital to meet the bills because the steady increase in immigrants who brought their holdings provided the colony with funds. But with the first promise of Puritan success in England in 1640 immigration stopped, and while imports continued to call upon the colony's money, new sources of capital had to be developed.[6] The mission that first brought Hugh Peter back to England was one of appeal for continued support. The "seasonable supplies" he craved from fellow Puritans on behalf of the colony were means to carry further their infant trade, continued shipments of ammunition and powder, and contributions for the maintenance of their schools, especially the college. He also hoped to overcome the labor shortage in Massachusetts "by stirring up some well-minded to clothe and transport over poor children, boys and girls, which may be a great mercy to their bodies and souls, and a help to us, they being super-abundant here [in England] and we wanting hands." [7] The response was sympathetic but not adequate. Some £875 was raised in furtherance of the scheme to send impoverished children, although few children were actually sent, and on March 10, 1643, the House of Commons exempted New England exports from the duty of 5 per cent that was levied on the rest of the plantation trade.

The combination of Parliamentary sympathy with short supply that England extended New England provided the opportunity for the New England merchants, who had been held in check in the earlier period by an economic policy designed to protect the farmer. Although a widespread distrust of merchants as unnecessary middlemen still existed among the predominantly agricultural population, and although this distrust continued for decades to keep the merchants from almost all elective offices, the enterprise of these men now found its outlet. This release of their energies permitted them to assert themselves in the commonwealth without resorting to political factionalism. It also permitted those who distrusted their activities to continue in control of the government while allowing the merchants a fuller range of freedom.

The Civil War in England had interrupted the sequence of fishing voyages from English ports, and the bases of such operations were shifted in great part to New England ports.[8] New England agricultural produce thus increasingly found its way to those active in the Newfoundland fisheries, and the fish and train oil received in exchange by the merchants was sent in New England ships to southern European markets. Credit obtained there served as the source for importations from England to the New England market, so that the colonists, in spite of their predilection for direct barter without the profit-takers in the middle, found themselves, as Bernard Bailyn points out, "utterly dependent on them [the merchants] for the most essential goods and equipment."[9] In the twenty-year period from 1640 to 1660, the form of commerce developed by New England merchants in response to the opportunities and hardships brought about by the Civil War "had become the dynamic economic force in New England. Such it remained for a century and a half."[10] Boston traders had occasionally brought in Negroes from the West Indies prior to the Civil War, but in 1644 they actively entered the slave trade through direct voyages to Africa. In fear of possible reprisals from Dutch and English competitors, they soon pioneered in opening the more distant East African coast to such commerce.[11]

The end of Stuart supremacy, while it provided Massachusetts with certain favors from Parliament, also brought about certain threatening changes in English attitudes toward the colonies. Now that the godly ruled England, it was argued there, the men of Massachusetts need no longer cling to their location for political reasons; theirs was not the only English area of liberty of ordinances. The entire extent of British possessions was now open to the saints, and, in view of the severity of the Massachusetts climate, they should consider removal to the more fruitful West Indies. When Cromwell came to power he was to consider the economic value of New England trifling when compared with that of the islands, and his view was foreshadowed by the powerful Puritan nobleman Lord Saye and Sele, who once was a strong supporter of New England but who in 1640 was diverting men and money to the West Indies. When Winthrop protested that his primary support should still go to Massachusetts since it was a godly plantation, that nobleman would not take seriously Winthrop's contention that Massachusetts was a special place, providentially provided for His people by God.

"Thus may I argue with as much probability as you," Lord Saye and Sele wrote Winthrop on July 9, 1640, "for it is as likely that you have in providence been cast upon that place, to remove from thence upon due occasion, as to stay there, and much more likely, when in some other you may do service, and receive more means by much of comfortable subsistence." He went on to remark the coldness of the air and the barrenness of the land in New England, and asked, "Is there any impiety in me to move men to live in a warmer climate and in a more fruitful soil, when it is free for them to make their choice?" Moreover, word had reached him of the tendency toward popular government in Massachusetts, a tendency strengthened by the labor shortage and the consequent increase in importance of the lower classes, and he said, "No wise man should be so foolish as to live where every man is a master, and masters must not correct their servants." [12] Even as the Massachusetts government strove to contain the democratic threat presented by the colony's altered economic condition, Saye and Sele chided Winthrop for his opposition to large land grants to an established or newly created aristocracy.

The defense Winthrop bravely offered was that such grants would mean the enthralling of some "to advance other mens posterity." And, indeed, one significant aspect of the sympathy in Massachusetts for Mosaic law was that under such law the eldest son did not inherit all but only a double portion, the remainder being distributed among the other children. [13] This contributed importantly to the maximum utilization of resources in a new land. But in the straitened economic circumstances of the 1640s, land itself became a drug on the market. Those who had established themselves in agriculture in the previous decade protested to their government in dismay at the ease with which large tracts could now be acquired and at the consequent cheapening of their own holdings. "Our neighbor towns are much grieved to see the lavish liberality of the Court in giving away the country," Nathaniel Ward of Ipswich said.[14] In blissful ignorance of economic laws, he protested that in England sixty-eight towns existed side by side within the bounds of what was regarded as room for but one town in New England. And five years later, in 1645, the General Court was petitioned by the residents of Concord, who claimed they could no longer get a subsistence from the land allotted them. Unless some aid was forthcoming they would move, and let no man tell them they would meet the same difficulties elsewhere: "Such as hardly subsisted with us and were none of the ablest amongst us, either for labor or ordering their occasions, have much thriven in other places they have removed unto." [15] At the least, they insisted, some reduction had to be made in their assessments.

Boundary disputes became a frequent feature of life in the 1640s. "Would you have rapines, thefts, injustices abound?" asked Thomas Shepard: "Let not man know his own by removing the landmarks and destroying property." [16] In the same atmosphere of land jealousy, Ezekiel Rogers of Rowley feared the results of too rigorous a maintenance of one's land, and raised a theme that was to retain vitality in New England from his day through Timothy Dwight's to that of Robert Frost: "A good fence helpeth to keep peace between neighbors; but let us take heed that we make not a high stone wall, to keep us from meeting." [17] The land that was plunging in value was the principal resource the town and colony governments had to offer in their pursuit of immediate funds, and as a result most new grants in the 1640s went to those who had some ready means of payment rather than to those who would have to labor on that land for a season before beginning to make a slow return. In Boston, for example, as Darret Rutman has shown, by 1649 that town's "gentry—some thirty families—had received almost one-half of the land granted by the town. Some had additionally obtained land from the commonwealth government, which regularly granted land outside the towns in return for investments in the old company or for public services." [18]

While the shortage of labor permitted those who were without property to exert pressure on the wage level, therefore, the overall situation was not one in which they could readily rise into the ranks of property-owners. "Class conflict" is too strong a term for the situation that emerged, but certainly the difference in class interests became sharper. Under the original enthusiasm of settlement, when the church stood at the center of each town's social vision, servants were bound to the community's ideals by the Christian concept that they too could attain equality in the area that most counted, the city of God, and they were included in family religious services and instructions as well as required to attend church. As the civil replaced the ecclesiastical as the dominant concept of social organization, such guidance in families became more a matter of governance than of fellowship.

In 1641 Thomas Shepard believed it necessary to take extended note of the deteriorating relations between masters and servants. Although he believed in the equality of spiritual opportunity extended by Jesus, and had said "out of men fallen, He picks out usually the poorest and vilest," his example of the lowliest was far from that conventionally offered by priests who recognized the centrality of the Sermon on the Mount. Rather, as illustration he cited that the Holy Spirit frequently chooses "the younger brother less loved out of a family, leaves elder," [19] thereby revealing that his thoughts ran principally along the lines of the relatively established elements in his society. In a similar manner he linked subjection to Christ with subjection to masters and took seriously communications such as that of Lord Saye and Sele to John Winthrop: "Reports are abroad that no men of worth are respected, and hence the country is neglected," he warned.[20]

To counter such reports Shepard preached respect, and in so doing he had words for the haves as well as the have-nots. He reminded them that "good fellowship hath been the bane of the flourishing state of England," and warned them away from taverns and such places where dicing, feasting, excessive drinking, merry tales, and whoring would soon ensnare the most hopeful young men. "Next to communion with wanton women," he said, "I have ever looked on unnecessary fellowship with graceless men" [21] as the greatest source of spiritual poison.

But his principal strictures were reserved for the restive serving classes so anxious to move out from under that, even if they could not procure their own property, they elected, at least, to trade in their labor as free men rather than be bound to one family; men, as he put it, whose "reins are on their necks." Such were under no family or church government and neither prepared nor desired to be so. "I confess," Shepard preached, "if under heathen masters, then desire liberty rather; but when men will live as they list, without any over them, and unfit to rule themselves, I much doubt whether this be according to God." [22]

He went on to catalogue the errors into which the unattached servant fell, and the emphasis of every one of them was social, pointed toward the damage done the community rather than that done the individual so freed. His list stands as a revealing summary of the culture's attitude toward the pressure that class was now enabled to assert. Servants without masters do not behave according to the word of God because:

"1. Hence they come to live idly, and work when they list." Work is not a matter of choice; it is a public duty.

"2. Hence men of public use can have little use but when they please of them." Labor is a commodity that is rightly in the control of those charged with the public interest.

"3. When they be with them, they have no power to correct or examine, or call them to account, in regard of spiritual matters." Although all saints are equal in the city of God, the social distinctions in the city of man serve as instruments to shape men for the city of God.

"4. Hence they lie in wait to oppress men that must have help from them, and so will do what they list." The town's food supply is central to the success of the commonwealth and it must be assured at a price the town wants to pay rather that at one dictated by the workers in the fields.

"5. Hence they break out to drunkenness, whoring, and loose company." The more people were paid the less they worked, mercantilist writers said in advancing the doctrine of the utility of poverty.[23]

"6. Hence they make other servants unruly, and to desire liberty." [24] The independent servant not only suffers from an economic disease, he is its carrier and unless cured will cause an epidemic.

Reflecting back on the first decades of settlement, Edward Johnson of Woburn used military imagery, since he visualized his topic as one of the movement of the army of Christ—a very militant Church Militant—and said, "Here must laboring men a little be minded, how ill they recompensed those persons, whose estates help them to food before they could reap any from the earth, that forgetting these courtesies they soon by excessive prices took for their work, made many file-leaders fall back to the next rank, advancing themselves in the mean time." [25]

The pulpit came four-square to the service of the commonwealth in this area, but it did so at the expense of closing down a considerable part of its attraction for the serving classes. Church membership was still, of course, an important step to social advancement, but it also brought a servant under surveillance of his economic behavior by yet another authority. He would enjoy his spiritual equality with his master by religiously observing his economic inequality. Darret Rutman's study reveals that approximately 14 per cent of those admitted to the Boston church in the 1630s were servants, and this dropped to approximately 8.5 per cent of those admitted in the 1640s. Although the church drew its members from all walks of life, he concluded that only the upper class was inclusively represented: "Those outside the church were most often of low status . . . holders of minimal or no property and

designated 'laborer,' 'wheelwright,' 'housecarpenter.' " [26] He esti-
mates that fewer than one-half of the town's total adult male
population were church members at the close of 1649.

A contemporary and critical observer of Massachusetts church
procedures felt that the insistence on exegetical sermonizing and
especially the Massachusetts prejudice against set forms of prayer, as
practiced in the Church of England, in favor of spontaneous prayer
served to keep the lower classes from developing their qualifications
for church membership. Church practices that proceeded from an
abounding faith in the literacy and articulateness of the saint,
Thomas Lechford said, may "dull, amaze, confound, discourage the
weak and ignorant (which are the most of men) when they are in
ordinary performed too tediously, or with the neglect of the word
read, and other premeditated forms inculcated, and may tend to
more ignorance and inconvenience, than many good men are aware
of." [27] The very service developed in reaction to ecclesiastical
authorities who would have men sit dumbly and adore, which
asserted the freedom of the common man in opposition to such
authority, now released its potential to immure another kind of
believer in his fearful silence.

Economic realities in this period led also to the development of
intermediate degrees of political responsibility and power between
the absolutes of freemanship and lack of it, as was the original case.
In Ipswich, as in all probability in most towns, ownership of a house
and land within the town bounds carried with it a right to pasturage
that could be bought or sold. Men with such rights, even if they
were not church members or freemen, were commoners and voted
on all questions relating to common lands. In addition to commoners
and freemen there was a third body called residents: men who,
having resided within the town for six months, were required to take
the residents' oath and to bear the burden of taxation, compulsory
military service, and other public duties. Residents had no voice in
the direction of affairs initially, but by 1647 they could be chosen for
juries by the freemen and could vote for the town's selectmen
although not for the deputies and magistrates of the commonwealth.[28] The Concord petition had come from the residents, and

Rutman summarizes a similar situation in Boston by saying there was "a tripartite division of the town, some men being inhabitants, freemen, and church members; others being inhabitants and church members; still others being mere inhabitants." [29] Relief was thus obtained from the pressure that the disenfranchised middling classes put on the system, and they were thus carefully distinguished from the serving classes and disinclined to unite with them in their grievances.

The culture that had defined itself in the Antinomian controversy was severely tried by the economic reversals of the 1640s, but it was not found wanting. If merchants finally achieved an outlet for their aspirations, this outlet was in the service of the godly commonwealth and did not, in the short run, bring with it political power. If the disenfranchised classes now had opportunity to exert pressure on a community in need of their labor and their civic services, they could be divided so that some local power was accorded the more substantial of these, who accordingly identified their lives with the welfare of the state rather than the grievances of the less substantial. The pulpit powerfully supported the magistracy against the antisocial activities of all classes, but especially the laboring class. Now loosened from the sect ideal, the ministry emphasized Christ the King rather than Christ the Carpenter, bringer of love. Subjection to Him was subjection to the principles of a godly magistracy. If brethren in England now saw in New England only another band of believers, and that band located in a singularly harsh, unpaying climate, New Englanders could add to their belief in their providential situation a fund of experience that proved it—Massachusetts endured. England was in a flux of confusion, they noted, tolerating all manner of nonsense and heresy, and this led them to see themselves as superior. Whereas initially the New Englanders felt they were the one group among all true believers who sought to better themselves in New England, they now, in the face of English permissiveness, rationalized the fact that they had purified the English church without opening the gates so wide as to render it a Babel, and they saw themselves as constructors of a model way of life.

The many signs of dissension in the Massachusetts of the 1640s combined ultimately to underline the great strength of the culture that could adjust to them without a significant shift in its particular perception of reality. Until 1643 Massachusetts, being the most populous Puritan colony—some 14,000 of a total of 18,000 people[30] —had been tempted to pursue a policy of dominance over its neighbors, but in that year it signaled its desire to consolidate shared interests in the face of outside threats and accepted Articles of Confederation with the other colonies for common defense, even though this meant equal representation rather than representation proportionate to its far greater numbers. Threats from within could be managed by compromise, persuasion, and coercion only if the threats from without that demanded more drastic measures could be met by a united front.

Indian policy, for example, was in need of consolidation. With the fur trade waning in significance as the beaver population neared extermination and as the Atlantic commerce, especially the fisheries, came to the fore, the Indians were no longer regarded as essential to the economy. Rather, considerations of expansion of agricultural lands into Indian areas became more pressing, and a concerted civil policy toward the tribes took precedence over the particular activities of traders with the Indians.

The Pequot War had called forth in its most vigorous form the Puritan culture's sense of itself as an armed band of the Lord. This sense had been made bloody by the frustrations of academic dispute with the opinionists in Boston, and the field of battle provided the militia with an unambiguous outlet for the sense of righteousness that had been baffled in Boston. Driven to all-out war by English insistence that such was the way to punish the killing of John Oldham, the Pequots' policy was to retaliate against the most vulnerable English settlements. For the Puritans the war came very rapidly to be a matter not of capturing and executing the Pequots who had committed criminal acts, but of exterminating the tribe altogether. Less capable of exterminating the entire race of their foes and without such a precedent in their culture, the Pequots fought defensively and planned skirmishes against the weaker elements of the English advance. They were after supplies primarily, as Lieutenant Gardner realized when he sought in a parley to dissuade them from a raid on Connecticut by pointing out that all they would capture would be horses and cows that would spoil Indian cornfields, hogs that would spoil Indian clambanks, and women "who would do them no good, but hurt, for English women are lazy and can't do their work." [31] Gardner hoped thus to divert them to an attack on his well-positioned fort, finally indicating to them that within it were the supplies that the Pequots most wanted.

The Puritan colonists, however, wanted the very lives of the entire tribe. Captain Underhill, one of the two military leaders of the expedition that achieved this extermination, came to admire the bravery with which the Pequots fought, and, professional that he was, he began to respect them for their skill in an art he valued most highly, and to see, therefore, a humanity in them that hysteria in the less professional would not permit. Creeping into a swamp before dawn, the combined force of Puritan soldiers and Indian allies from tribes hostile to the Pequots, principally the Mohegans, surrounded the fenced village of the Pequots. Then at break of day, when the village was still asleep, they loosed their first volley. The Pequots, according to Underhill, "brake forth into a most doleful cry; so as if God had not fitted the hearts of men for the service, it would have bred in them a commiseration towards them." [32] But God did steel the Puritans' hearts, and, forcing their way into the village, they put it to the torch and, from their encirclement, proceeded to pick off those who sought to escape. More than four hundred men, women, and children were killed. An entire tribe was obliterated.

The slaughter that took place on that day in May 1637 taught the Puritans that a united policy—troops were drawn from Massachusetts and Connecticut, and the New Haven colony would later aid—would succeed not only because of the superior force it could bring to a war but also because it prevented the various settlements from working at cross purposes in allying with certain tribes in order to discipline others. With their economic value sinking into insignificance, the Indians were now to be considered primarily in terms of their military value, and the Puritans must keep them divided in order to procure their aid, on one hand, and to defeat them, on the other.

The Indian allies also learned their lessons in the swamp. The Puritan commanders of the expedition believed that the skill of the English troops resided principally in classical military maneuvers such as besieging or defending a fort, or head-on engagements in an open field. They felt the Indians had greater skill in dodging, skirmishing, and chasing, and in individual combat in the woods. When some of the Pequot warriors broke out of the encirclement, therefore, the Puritans ordered the Mohegans to engage them. The results filled the Puritans with disgust. The Mohegans and Pequots exchanged arrows "after such a manner," reported Underhill, "as I dare boldly affirm, they might fight seven years and not kill seven men. They came not near one another, but shot remote, and not point-blank, as we often do with our bullets, but at rovers, and they gaze up in the sky to see where the arrow falls, and not until it is fallen do they shoot again. This fight is more for pastime, than to conquer and subdue enemies." [33]

"Conquer and subdue" was the Puritan goal, and consequently the English entered into the skirmish with such a will that their Indian allies cried out to them, "Mach it, mach it; that is, It is naught, it is naught, because it is too furious and slays too many men." [34] Victory and annihilation were not the same thing in their outlook. But English war, the Mohegans learned that day, was not symbolic and exemplary of the superior art of the victor; it was massive and aimed at annihilation. The English imagination pictured the Indian as bloodthirsty because he fought by stealth and cut down the weaker at the perimeter while attempting to avoid direct confrontation with the full military power of his enemy. The Indians now came to see the English as incredibly furious, bent on the kill at the expense of all else.

The great Narragansett sachem Miantanimo was an ally of the English at the time of the swamp fight. This led him to a dire conviction of the consequence of English policy for all Indians. Even as he continued his nominal alliance with the English, he attempted to bring the insight he had gained home to the neighboring tribes, but without effect. "So are all Indians, as the English are [all of the same race], and say brother to one another," he told them. "So must we be one as they are, otherwise we shall all be gone shortly, for you know our fathers had plenty of deer and skins, our plains were full of deer, as also our woods, and of turkies, and our coves full of fish and fowl. But these English having gotten our land, they with scythes cut down the grass, and their hogs spoil our clam banks, and we shall all be starved." [35] He first sounds clearly the unavailing call for Indian union in the face of European ferocity that descends through American history more as a litany than as a war cry. Miantanimo himself was soon to fall victim to the Puritan policy of dividing the tribes, and was in 1643 delivered by the commissioners of the united colonies, whom he had previously aided, into the hands of Uncas, his foe. Uncas's brother "clave his head with an hatchet, some English being present." [36]

The downfall of Miantanimo and the destruction of the power of the Narragansetts were the consequence of the Massachusetts determination to keep from its frontiers English dissidents who would prove an attractive nuisance to the discontented within the colony's borders. The Indians were pawns in the doctrinal as well as the military wars. One result of confederation with Connecticut, Plymouth, and New Haven, it was hoped, would also be the elimination of free territory where those who were in opposition to the Puritan way could establish themselves and offer a haven to runaway servants while conducting an opinion mill that undermined the doctrines on which the security of the commonwealth was based.

After her banishment, Anne Hutchinson and some of her supporters had moved to the island of Aquidneck, where they purchased land from Miantanimo and other Narragansett sachems. Moves to bring this group under Massachusetts control were ineffective; a number of them were recognized Christians and, in keeping with the policy Winthrop had insisted upon against Vane, such were invulnerable to control once they had departed, although they could be refused residence in Massachusetts. Their numbers, moreover, included several men of substance, such as the merchant William Coddington, a former magistrate, and these men had good friends in England.[37] But the raggle-taggle dissenters who began springing up in New England as a consequence of the liberty being accorded sectaries in England during and after the Civil War were another matter. These were heretics who posed a clear danger, not only should they be tolerated within the commonwealth, as they most certainly were not, but also should they be allowed breeding space on its fringe.

Typical of such a group were Samuel Gorton and his followers. He was received as an inhabitant of Aquidneck in 1638, but, failing to achieve harmony with the original settlers there, he led his party to Pawtuxet in 1642, where he purchased land from the Indians. Massachusetts moved against him through accepting the allegiance of its Indian traders in Gorton's neighborhood as a ground for its civil jurisdiction over that area. Gorton's group, as a result, packed up again and moved six miles farther south to Shawomet in January 1643. But Massachusetts continued to insist through the subjection of the Indian traders, who were by that time selling powder to friendly Indians but not to Gorton's group, that Gorton came under the Bay government, and the small group finally dug in.[38]

Samuel Gorton well realized that the territorial claims of Massachusetts were secondary to its refusal to tolerate his dissenting opinion. Proceeding with full pietistic fervor beyond the point at which Massachusetts had consolidated the gains of the Puritan revolt against hierarchy, Gorton's group now held forth that the priesthood of all believers was so literal a fact that a community built on a formal church with an ordained clergy was the Antichrist. The word of God was free to all and it was possessed in abundance at Shawomet, while it had become distorted and used as the basis for a monopoly of the few in Massachusetts.

The threat that Gorton's patently weak little band posed was a threat to the way Massachusetts had structured reality, not to its physical power. Although held by men who would be ineffective in any overt political or military move, Gorton's doctrines were too dangerously close to what was being tolerated in England for his settlement to be suffered by the commonwealth's citizens. Such dangerous laboratories of dissent would undermine the system seriously if they were to link up with sympathizers in England who could affect governmental policy toward New England. This possibility might, in the main, be checked by astute diplomacy. But the cultural threat sensed was one that went beneath theology to the very organization of daily life.

Any sensible man of Massachusetts, it was presumed, was able to refute the garbled theology that Gorton proclaimed. But some might be very sympathetic to the perceptions from which it proceeded. "They were not learned men," the colonies' commissioner to London explained in justification of official policy, "the ablest of them could not write true English, no not in common words, yet they would take upon them to interpret the most difficult places of Scripture, and wrest them any way to serve their own turn." [39] While this might be a weakness in the dissenters that could be used against them in some circles, at the same time it constituted one of the principal attractions the group exerted on those chafing under a ministry committed to the maintenance of the status quo. If all men were priests, then the learned clergy were superfluous; the doctrine could, in undermining the church, undermine the state.

Gorton saw the allegiance between the Puritan reliance on learning and Puritan social control. He loudly raised the voice of anti-intellectualism in defense of the disinherited because of intellectualism's alliance with suppression. "You know not, neither can you, with all your libraries give the interpretation [of the light of God] . . . but have lost it in the wilderness," [40] he told the authorities in Boston. For himself, he scorned such reliances: "I was not bred up in the schools of human learning; and I bless God that I never was, lest I had been drowned in pride and ignorance through Aristotles principles and other heathen philosophers, as millions are and have been who ground the preachings of the Gospel upon humane principles to the falsifying of the word of God." [41]

There was a distinct class basis in Gorton's arguments, although he himself did not separate out the distinction, but tangled it with his theological views. Still, it bristles throughout his diatribes. When he assaults learning he does so in terms of its association with worldly wealth: "All those who triumph in a calf, though the most costly and beautiful that the jewels and earrings of learning (either in language or art) can possibly bring forth." [42] When he assaults the ordinances of Massachusetts that he claims are invalid in the days after the Revelation, he does so in terms of their being built on economic exploitation: "The passions of sin, which are by the law, having force in your members, you going about with great labor and industry to satisfy them by your submission unto the word of God, in your fasting and feasting, in contributing, and treasuring in retiredness for study, and bowing the backs of the poor, going forth in labor to maintain it, and in the spirit of the hireling [the minister who accepted a salary] raising up your whole structure and edifice." [43] And when he defends the right of his group to remain at Shawomet he does so in terms of their free labor: "We have wronged no man, unless with hard labor, to provide for our families, and suffer of gross, idle, and idol drones [Indian traders who do not produce what they market, and the colony's soldiers] to take our labors out of the mouths, and from off the backs of our little ones, to lordane it over us." [44]

A military expedition, which included Edward Johnson, the historian of New England as an army of saints, was sent to reduce Shawomet. En route its leaders replied to Gorton's inquiry as to their intent by saying that they were sent to correct his errors through persuasion but "if there be no way of turning them, we shall then look upon them as men prepared for slaughter, and accordingly shall address our selves." [45] That expedition arrested Gorton and some of his associates, seized their property to cover expenses, and brought them back to the Bay, where they were tried in civil court for heresy, even though heresy was, technically, not a civil offense, and were convicted for blasphemy. After their sentences had been served, they were received so kindly into some homes in Boston that the Governor, without any consultation with other magistrates, issued a warrant commanding them to leave the jurisdiction within two hours.

Gorton finally received the protection he sought in London and settled in Rhode Island under the aegis of the Earl of Warwick, after whom his settlement was called Warwick. He eventually won his personal battle and could triumph in his success over the superior power of Massachusetts. But the authorities in the Bay had won their larger struggle to affirm the superiority of their way. By the time Gorton settled peaceably in Rhode Island, the Narragansetts had been so subdued as to afford Rhode Islanders little military leverage, and Rhode Island was compelled to assist, informally at least, in the united effort. The tolerating policy of Rhode Island, moreover, enabled so many differing doctrines to exist side by side that the very variety of opinions diffused the danger that vigorous dissent would pose, although in the long run, of course, Massachusetts had constantly to confront specific problems presented by a tolerating community in its vicinity. Of special importance in Massachusetts was that the short-range appeal of Gorton's class-consciousness and anti-intellectualism had been effectively squelched. In spite of the sympathizers he found in Boston, Gorton's opinions could not gain wide acceptance in a society in which schooling was broadly established and laborers separated into a minority position.

The need to subdue the Indians was thus related to the need to maintain authority over dissenters. Until the Indians recognized that their dealings with any English must first gain the approval of the united colonies and that this prohibited them from selling land or providing room to those whom the colonies did not authorize, Indian wars would continue. Gorton had claimed that the Narragansett sachems who had sold to him were thereby recognizing their submission to the government in England, since he was an Englishman, and that this took precedence over submission to the colonies. But official policy in New England had to be that the established colonial governments were the agents of England in such matters and submission must be made through them. In pursuit of this policy they divided the tribes and punished those sachems and their followers who claimed an allegiance to the English through London rather than through Boston.

The right of appeal to England from their civil judgments was not recognized by the New England authorities, such appeal patently tending, as they saw it, to the overthrow of any effective control they might have over their constituents. Encouraged by the existence of a Presbyterian Parliament, in 1646 seven prominent inhabitants of Massachusetts felt the time was ripe to petition that Parliament for the establishment of English laws in New England.[46] Such laws, rather than the code that the commonwealth government had adopted, best suited English tempers, they maintained. They asked that civil liberty be granted to "all truly English" in the colony, equal to that liberty now granted only church members and freemen, and asked that the sacraments of the church be made available to all who were not scandalous in their behavior rather than just to those who had been admitted to church membership through convincing the elders of their possessing saving grace. At the root of their request was a desire to align New England conditions with old England and with history by introducing into New England what they took to be the immense value of tradition in guiding men, rather than continuing in the ahistorical framework of submission to the judgments of men who behaved as if they had the world to make over without regard to precedent. "Neither can we tell," said the petitioners, "whether the Lord hath blest many in these parts with such eminent political gifts, so as to contrive better laws and customs, than the wisest of our nation have with great consideration composed, and by many hundred years experience have found most equal and just." [47]

The lowly Gorton had argued against Massachusetts law by asserting the priesthood of all men: magistracy among Christians was to be submitted to as an ordinance of God, but only as a natural one like the submission of the subject to his hereditary prince, not as the delivery of rights to delegated authorities. Now from the other end of the economic and political spectrum the superiority of tradition rather than of divine light was being used as an argument against the Massachusetts way. All the petitioners were men of substance engaged in entrepreneurial activities in trade and industry. Unlike the majority of New Englanders of the merchant class now launched in the Atlantic trade, they felt the time had come to extend political power to all substantial people. They wanted to align their business activities with English policy and English tradition.

Although they were treated with far more courtesy by the

authorities than were the Gorton group, they received a firm rebuff in Massachusetts, including a scarcely justifiable search and seizure of some of their property. The colony's agent, directed to counter their moves in England, did so by successfully contending that life in New England would be intolerable if justice had to await appeals to England. Moreover, he pointed out, Massachusetts was a corporation and could admit members in accordance with its rules.[48] Although the petitioners lost their legal battle, they did foreshadow a view that the restored Stuarts were to find sensible: English subjects should not form enclaves outside of English law and disregardful of English tradition. But the culture was for some twenty more years able to establish its own traditions, traditions that proved sufficiently hearty to offer a basis for resistance to the reduction of New England to English law even after the return of royal supremacy.

The ethic of a state and church ruled by Christ the King had sinewed an exterminating army and overcome the counterclaims of a vaguer ethic of Christian brotherhood and a precise legal ethic of English tradition. Puritan culture, however, had not in so doing overwhelmed the counterculture of Indians, or opinionists, or petitioners, so much as it had shaped those cultures to express themselves in the vocabulary and with many of the same perceptions of reality held by the dominant culture. Disenchanted Indian sachems sought to justify their opposition through direct submission to the Colonial Office in London or to act on their discontents through emulating the union the Puritans had achieved among themselves; dissenters advanced their own social vision by entangling themselves in considerations of the function of learning and the nature of magistracy; petitioners in opposing English laws to the New England code were compelled to operate from within the strictures of that code. And by the same token the triumphant culture was not to continue to grow without weaving into its fabric threads from the concepts of its opposers. Such threads would lie ready for the plucking by members of the culture when conditions suited.

CHAPTER FIVE

Winter's Discourse

Roger Williams and freedom of conscience—
The nature of the good society—The function of learning—
Prosperity's meaning—The dangers of love—Dominating death—
Emergence of a literary style—Cultural consequences

No one so much as Roger Williams comprehensively combined the aspirations and assumptions that had strengthened New England Puritanism with sentiments and practices that the culture had been unable to retain in institutionalizing itself. His family was of sufficient means to see him educated at Charterhouse and Pembroke, Cambridge, and he was so demonstrably gifted a young man that he was confidentially employed by the jurist Sir Edmund Coke. Although he came quickly to distrust the uses to which learning was put, throughout his life he was able to employ it on behalf of the unlearned without engaging in anti-intellectualism, and to assert the rights of the plain folk. Although he hewed steadfastly to the theology of predestination as expounded by John Calvin, throughout his life he manifested a sense of the civil rights of the sinner. The awesome gap between grace and nature that he accepted indicated to him that, since the world was of nature, all men had equal rights in it; the crucial distinction made by the Holy Spirit was one that had consequences in eternity. This perception led him to an impatience bordering on the querulous when he confronted the Puritan establishment's mixture of assertions that the division of saints and sinners was absolute and that, nevertheless, it had application in the world of man and could serve as the basis for civil rights and civil distinctions. The eternal rewards of the saved, he believed, were to be experienced hereafter and it was outright tyranny to offer them as solace to the disinherited and rationale for the advantaged.

Williams, however, did not believe that the saints were not to differentiate themselves from the sinners. Rather, he held such differentiation was vital but limited to worship, and, most important, to their willingness to suffer for Christ, because to believe in Him was to be His witness.[1] The ethic of love was central for Williams. He saw the life of Jesus as a model to be imitated. Christ's kinghood was a metaphor of His inimitable godhood. In His human and imitable form, Christ was a "beggar's brat laid in a manger and a gallows-bird,"[2] a supreme example of the dispossessed and a certain sign that the saint was not to concern himself in this world with possessions and power over others.

If Williams had held the supreme importance of sainthood as a liberating force without also believing that this entailed a witnessing for Christ, he would have been like the Antinomians who found refuge in his Rhode Island. But in his insistence upon the imitation of Christ he stood well apart from the intent of those saints who felt that a triumph over nature should be theirs in this world. Their triumph resided in freedom from the laws that bound sinners, and in a consequent power to treat nature—lands, Indians, resources—as without inherent right to resist the divine motions within them. Williams' ethic of love led him to feel that nature was to be suffered in this world and testified against by the saint's lack of interest, rather than conquered with a consequent self-aggrandizement. Love meant loving the creatures of the Lord and seeking their good, rather than banding against them in a fellowship that possessed superior rights in the world.

If Williams had held the ethic of love as a special possession of the extraordinary saint fitted above others to suffer the ways of the world, he would have been outside politics and content to let men do what they would in this sphere. But he felt that the conditions of God's dispensation were such that, this world being of nature, and all men possessing natural parts, all nature was theirs to share. Men had an equal right to political power regardless of their religious beliefs. An important part of the witness he bore was directed toward establishing a commonwealth in which freedom of religious expression was guaranteed.

Although Roger Williams lived for nearly eighty years, his guiding ideas were formed early in his life and remained unchanged throughout his career. He first arrived in New England in 1631, a man in his twenties with an English reputation for reformed zeal, and joined a circle of acquaintances who had known him in England and were attracted by his considerable personal charm as well as his fervor. At the time of Williams' arrival in Boston, John Wilson, pastor of that town's church, had returned to England to fetch his family to the new home he had established, and the Boston church gladly invited Williams to fill the temporary vacancy. But Williams informed Boston that he could not accept its claim that it was still part of the Church of England. Regarding the established church as corrupt and antichristian, he declined the post on the ground that he dared not officiate to an unseparated people, and he made his way to Salem, where he had reason to believe that the radical foundation of that first church in the Bay would better suit his temper. But within a year he discovered uneasiness at the compromises that Salem also made with the established church, and he took himself off to the avowed separatists at Plymouth.

By 1633, however, Williams was back in Salem, having had sharp disagreements with the Plymouth settlers over his insistence that the land they had settled belonged to the Indians and that, therefore, it could not be occupied by royal patent but must be acquired through purchase and Indian assent. In Salem he was invited to become pastor, but the civil authorities were now fully alarmed by the opinions he was announcing. In addition to his troublesome position regarding Indian lands, he was saying that the church and state were absolutely separate and that magistrates had no call to mix in matters of religion. Indeed, so severely apart were the two that he did not believe that the oath, a religious ordinance since it was a swearing to God, could be invoked in civil procedures. Under his teaching at Salem, John Endicott had even been induced to cut the cross from the English ensign so as to symbolize the difference between the two spheres. Salem resisted the civil pressure to divest itself of so forceful and attractive a young minister, but when the General Court proceeded to delay further land grants to that town and suspended Endicott's right to hold office, it thought differently about the matter.

Although Salem compromised, Williams did not. The predestinarian doctrine taught him, he felt, separation of the saints from the sinners in all religious matters. This meant not only a purified church but a state that was not concerned with enforcing religion, because all men, perforce, were in the state. Williams, then, asked for a strict purity in the church and toleration in the state, and he did so openly and articulately. The magistrates asked John Cotton and Thomas Hooker to deal with him in conference and correspondence, but they could not persuade him that his severe church views led to a dangerous splintering of religion if any who wished to declare themselves more purified than others within a given church could establish their own worship; and, indeed, in this area Williams was within a few years to abandon his faith in an institutional church and to see himself as a seeker who joined in religious communion only with those whom he believed were similarly enlightened. Nor could they persuade him that the welfare of their enterprise was crucially dependent upon the cooperation of magistracy and ministry.

The result, therefore, was civil banishment at the hands of men who liked him and who continued to correspond with him for the rest of their lives. John Haynes, the Governor who pronounced Williams' banishment, was later Governor of Connecticut and was to cooperate with Williams, a Rhode Island leader, in a number of matters. John Winthrop also was to continue a relatively amiable friendship and to be a partner with Williams in a land deal. Williams, in seeking his banishment, felt he was bearing witness to the truth of his beliefs, but this seeking did not mean the acceptance of defeat in the world in order to triumph in heaven. It meant, rather, the acceptance of the consequence of truth-telling in order to retain the right to continue to bear testimony. In the spring of 1636 Roger Williams stepped from his canoe onto the western bank of the

Seekonk River, and there, on land that he had purchased from the Indians, he founded the town of Providence and the colony of Rhode Island, the first tolerating state in the English-speaking world. Within his lifetime it was to fill with Hutchinsonians, Gortonists, Quakers, and Baptists, with most of whom Williams was to have very severe religious disagreements, but to all of whom the colony extended civil liberties. In 1643 Williams returned to England to secure a charter for his colony from the revolutionary Parliament, and again from 1651 to 1654 he was in England to have the charter confirmed by Cromwell's government. He was not adequately remunerated by his colony for either journey and he lived his life in relative poverty, farming and trading into an old age, but ever ready to oppose by oral and written debate the practices of the establishment in Massachusetts and the preachings of the enthusiasts in Rhode Island.

Williams' banishment from Massachusetts was a tranquil event, unaccompanied by the popular opposition that formed about Anne Hutchinson. His was a clear case of overstepping commonly accepted bounds. But it did raise a central issue that could no longer be postponed when some who believed as Williams did came to influence in the England of the 1640s. Massachusetts could have regarded toleration as a temporary aberration brought on by revolutionary times in England, and could have professed the adequacy of its way for all well-meaning Christians, had it not had in its vicinity Rhode Island and a Roger Williams who, from within the same theological philosophy that it professed, was ever vigilant to give it the lie.

Doctrinally the 1640s were a time for Massachusetts to explain itself. To a great extent its institutions had been arrived at pragmatically, but with brethren in England now planning a new commonwealth, Massachusetts was expected to show the validity of its way so as to indicate its involvement in the common cause, if not, indeed, to offer its theoretical structure as a blueprint for reformers in the homeland.[3] The ministry, most notably John Cotton, rose to the occasion and produced a number of thorough explanations of the Massachusetts church way that knitted it to the history of the true church and the habits of Englishmen. The handful of independents at the Westminster Assembly, called to settle the church polity in England, used Cotton's defense of New England ecclesiastical polity as their wedge to split the Presbyterian phalanx, and for the next fifteen years such men as Cotton, Thomas Hooker, Richard Mather, and John Davenport were to find ample employment in answering the Presbyterian counterattack, as well as replying to the new attacks from the liberated factions of the far left. Their treatises are major documents of the history of Congregationalism and of limited democracy in America.

But Roger Williams forced Massachusetts to express also the perceptions that lay beneath its institutions and to articulate a modified doctrine of the conscience and a worldly-wise view of the social value of the hypocrite.

In 1635, at the time he had been debating the relationship of the church and state with Williams, who was still in Massachusetts, John Cotton had received a treatise against persecution for cause of conscience together with a letter eliciting his opinion. He replied by making a number of distinctions that would allow him to arrive at the issue. If the erroneous opinions a man held were in circumstantial rather than fundamental matters of religion, he was to be suffered unless he grew to such boisterousness that his differences became a matter of disturbance of the civil peace. If the erroneous opinions were on matters fundamental to religion—counter to beliefs that were essential for salvation—he was to be admonished wisely and fully so as to see the light of the true beliefs. Then Cotton went on to cast the fluid matter of religious opinion into a mold: "If such a man after such admonition shall still persist in the error of his way, and be therefore punished; he is not persecuted for cause of conscience, but for sinning against his own conscience." [4] Such a doctrine, Roger Williams was soon to assert, was monstrous, but it served as the basis of security in Massachusetts in the revolutionary decades.

When he was in England in 1643, Roger Williams prepared for publication the treatise that Cotton had answered, Cotton's letter of reply, heretofore unpublished and, according to its author, unintended for publication, and a thorough attack on Cotton's position; together they form *The Bloudy Tenent of Persecution* (1644). It was a book that was at that date still regarded as so dangerously wrongheaded as to deserve burning by the public hangman, and it was so treated. Williams' demolition of Cotton's contention that persecution was never for cause of conscience but for sinning against one's own conscience was based fully on what is now called a belief in freedom of thought, although his terminology was theological. In his *Bloudy Tenent* Williams gave the first full statement to a view of the conscience that he was to continue throughout his life to proclaim, one seen most clearly in a second reply he wrote to Cotton, wherein he said: "That thing which we call conscience is of such a nature, (especially in Englishmen, as once a pope of Rome at the suffering of an Englishman in Rome, himself observed) that although it be groundless, false, and deluded, yet it is not by any arguments or torments easily removed. I speak not of the stream of the multitude of all nations, which have their ebbings and flowings in religion, as the longest sword and strongest arm of flesh carries it; but I speak of conscience, a persuasion fixed in the heart and mind of man, which enforceth him to judge—as Paul said of himself, a persecutor—and to do so with respect to God, his worship, &c. This conscience is found in all mankind, more or less: in Jews, Turks, Papists, Protestants, Pagans, &c." [5]

Conscience, in effect, was not conscience if it could be readily turned against itself, as Cotton maintained, and it was for Williams an especial teaching of the Marian persecutions that Englishmen were particularly steadfast in clinging to their beliefs. He saw the peculiar monstrousness of violating man's right to believe what he wished under the subtle guise not of opposing it but of punishing it in the interest of the believer himself, with the claim that since he had been enlightened as to his errors he was not asserting his conscience but sinning against it.

Massachusetts in accepting Cotton's distinction was not rationalizing tyranny after the fact; it was, rather, accepting an expression of one of its deepest cultural convictions. That conviction was that the entire social fabric is held together in this fallible world by certain undeniable truths. These truths are universal, else they could not serve as the basis for human society, and are to be made available to all men. Indeed, the process of socialization is the process of the inculcation of these truths. Freedom to disagree with them is not freedom, it is error. Every man has the right to differ in opinion from his neighbor, but no man has the right to wrong his neighbor. Freedom to express erroneous views on fundamental matters even after true views have been explained is freedom to commit social wrong and no society can abide it.

The debate over conscience was, both parties saw, basically a debate over the nature of the good society. Williams attacked the established view on the assumption that the good society simply was not of this world. He differed from other pietists, however, in refusing to see this perception as a basis for accepting the authority of the few over the many in favor of a reward hereafter. Rather, for him the perception meant that in the absence of a good society men should construct the best society possible, and this best society was one in which all were free to hold their truths peaceably and their political powers equally. The crucial separation of the wheat and the tares is to take place hereafter, since society is, naturally, a mixed field.

But for such as Cotton that field in the parable was not society; it was the church. Hypocrites were bound to creep into even the best-conducted church and it would be madness to maintain reforming zeal at such a pitch that one was forever judging one's fellow saint for true profession. Rather, the visible church would always be somewhat imperfect and its members would have to await their entry into the church invisible before finally separating from hypocrites. This did not mean, however, that society should tolerate manifest error, because its very foundation was the commonly accepted truths of the nature of man's relation to God.

Williams was untiring in pointing out that, therefore, Massachusetts churches were by their own admission corrupt. The reply was that there are degrees of corruption, and that the admission of hypocrites was guarded against as far as humanly possible so that the Massachusetts churches were, relatively, the purest that existed.

They could point out that with his severe views of purity Williams was unable to attach himself to any church for fear of being tainted by communion with hypocrites and in practice destroyed the fellowship of the church visible. In reply to this, Williams said that the church visible as held forth by his opponents was but another contemptible establishment tied to materialism in direct opposition to the example of Christ. Most of those who separated from the national church because they would not compromise with corruption, "I say most of them have been poor and low, and not such gainful customers to the bishops, their courts, and officers." Henry Ainsworth, for instance, who had fled to Holland to maintain his separation "lived upon ninepence per week, with roots boiled." But nonconforming yet unseparating Puritans, such as those of Massachusetts, "have had fair estates, been great persons, have had rich livings and benefices, of which the bishops and theirs (like greedy wolves) have made the more desirable prey." [6] Now they were up to their old acquisitive tricks again.

Underlying the debate on liberty of conscience, and, more specifically, underlying the Massachusetts view of the matter was the conservative belief that the godly had a right to a superior share of the things of this world, and the practical belief that the good society could exist if it recognized central truths and then accommodated human weakness. Mankind being corrupt, there would always be hypocrites in the church and drunkards in the poorhouse. The doctrine of the erroneous conscience was a secular doctrine in its significant reaches, not a religious one, and should the state eventually become secularized, it could be applied on behalf of political truths that a man would hold if he were true to his conscience. In these terms, the Puritan establishment's way rather than Williams' way was to be influential because it could serve with efficiency the as yet unborn god of democratic capitalism. Williams' tolerating state was one that was, ultimately, justified because it permitted those who were saved to imitate Christ, but in any well-run society the beggar's brat, as the Puritans knew, should be placed in a home, and the gallows-bird hanged or rehabilitated. Love has no political function.

The England that Williams revisited in 1643 and again from 1651 to 1654, an England in which he became acquainted with John Milton and Oliver Cromwell, seemed to him to endorse the theoretical possibilities of his ideas. But that same England, for most of his fellow Puritans, had documented the practical soundness of extending oath-taking and other religious ordinances into secular life. It was a matter of pride and a guide to future generations, its historian pointed out, that during the Puritan reign "there was hardly a single bankruptcy to be heard of in a year; and in such a case the bankrupt had a mark of infamy that he could never wipe off." [7]

Whereas Williams was invigorated by the abundance of diverse preachings in the New Model army, most Puritans reflected afterward what Massachusetts felt at the time, that those who set up for preachers "depending upon a kind of miraculous assistance of the divine Spirit, without any study or preparation" brought about the ruin of the common cause. "When their imaginations were heated, they gave vent to the most crude and undigested absurdities; nor did the evil rest there, for from preaching at the head of their regiments, they took possession of the country pulpits where they quartered, till at length they spread the infection over the whole nation, and brought the regular ministry into contempt." [8] Williams' enthusiasm for freedom of expression, encouraged at a time in England when polemics had to be permitted as a safety valve that would preserve the union of revolutionary forces, was seen by the more powerful members of the Puritan party as an aberration that would have to be checked as soon as this was expedient because the survival of society itself was at stake.

Learning did not mean new ideas; it meant the full exploration of existing ideas and the marshaling of them for the service of undeniable spiritual truths. "Some pretend that they must try all things," said Samuel Clarke in a collection of lives which had great popularity as a source of examples in Puritan sermons. "But they speak besides the book. Who will try ratsbane, or a sharp sword whether it will pierce into his bowels? Some think that they can withdraw when they see danger; but Satan is subtle: venom will get in before we are aware, and error will stick, and eat like a gangrene. What gets the fly that plays with the candle? They that nibble at the bait, shall hardly escape the hook. Again, jingle not with terms that be improper in matters of religion; they savour of singularity, breed rents and divisions between preachers and people, and take off the mind from things more essential." [9] Clarke summed up his view of scholarship by presenting the life of Richard Capel, clerk, who contained all scholarship "yet for all this, he had that great blessing, . . . he never set on foot any manner of new opinion." [10]

Such uses of learning confirmed Williams in his suspicion that it had become the tool of the oppressor. He respected secular education: "Among all the outward gifts of God, humane learning and the knowledge of languages and good arts are excellent, and excel other outward gifts as far as light excels darkness, and, therefore . . . schools of humane learning ought to be maintained in a due way, and cherished." But they must be cut loose from the ministerial establishment that would use learning as a club over the people. A school of divinity was a contradiction, because divinity was not learned in an institution but came from God's election, and those who mastered it at the university and called themselves scholars because of their superior knowledge of divinity rather than humane learning had assumed a "sacrilegious and thievish title, robbing all believers and saints, who are frequently in the Testament of Christ, styled disciples or scholars of Jesus Christ." [11]

With such insights, Roger Williams became part of an unconscious elite who pioneered in the linguistic consequences of a revolution that they perceived to be intellectual, while their contemporaries lingered behind, consolidating its political consequences and limiting its potential for a redistribution of goods. "It pleased the Lord to call me for some time, and with some persons," he remembered, "to practice the Hebrew, the Greek, Latin, French, and Dutch. The Secretary of the Council (Mr. Milton) for my Dutch I read him, read me many more languages. Grammar rules began to be esteemed a tyranny. I taught two young gentlemen, a Parliament man's sons, as we teach our children English, by words, phrases, and constant talk." [12] If common life could be clearly recognized as the school of divinity, then learning in the schools could be freed for humane interests, and techniques and rules subordinated to the goal of the learner rather than observed as fixed elements of discipline that subordinated the learner to the status quo.

So great an advance into the new language did Roger Williams make that his writings have an intelligibility and attraction for the modern reader that are unmatched by the writings of any of his New England contemporaries. It is not just that his doctrines foreshadow modern opinion, but that they receive an expression that is modern. In polemics he followed the contemporary style, repeated a great deal of what his opponent had said in the sequence in which his opponent had said it, and attempted an almost line-by-line refutation in the vocabulary and style they shared. But in letters and expository works he pursued a humane diction and syntax in keeping with his perception that learning was now freed for application to the secular aims of men. As a result, it is possible that he was misunderstood by his conservative contemporaries, as he, a very devout man, scorned the conventional use of pietistic and moralistic phrases when discussing, for example, politics.

In writing to Connecticut and Plymouth on a plan he had for settling their boundary disputes with Rhode Island, he said, "If you please to ask me what my prescription is, I will not put you off to Christian moderation, or Christian humility, or Christian prudence, or Christian love, or Christian self-denial, or Christian contention or patience." [13] These were habits in which he believed, but he was now talking politics and they were not relevant. He would cite the Bible because it was the source of images that were applicable to human situations, but he would not give his interpretation of a passage of Scripture as a rule that others must observe in secular matters. Characteristically, in secular matters his biblical citations run thus: "What are all the contentions and wars of this world about, generally, but for greater dishes and bowls of porridge, of which, if we believe God's Spirit in Scripture, Esau and Jacob were types? Esau will part with his heavenly birthright for his supping after hunting, for good belly: and Jacob will part with his porridge for an eternal inheritance." [14] The Bible provides examples of behavior for

Christians but it does not provide precepts for the commonwealths of men. "To be content with food and raiment: to mind not our own but every man the things of another; yea and to suffer wrong and part with what, we judge, is right, yea our lives, and as poor women martyrs have said, as many as there be hairs upon our heads for the name of God and the Son of God His sake. This is humanity, yea this is Christianity: the rest is but formality and picture." So Roger Williams would attempt to live. But in discussing an intercolonial arrangement he was not going to put off his neighbors with a call to Christian moderation; he would put forth a political solution.

Such sentiments in such language were explicable to his contemporaries only if they were referred back to the man who held them, and Thomas Prince, Governor of Plymouth, so understood them. He wrote stiffly to Williams in reply to his letter: "Who would expect to be any whit perfected or completed in matters appertaining to God's worship, by such as close not with any public worship upon earth that is known? Not I." [15]

Martin Luther had refused to make common cause with the prophets who had sprung up in his wake, and Ulrich Zwingli saw no room for visionaries at Zurich, nor would John Calvin abide them in Geneva. The Sermon on the Mount could not be put into the statute book. The imperfect state must rule on this earth, and its authorities were charged with rigorous and violent, if necessary, opposition to heresy.[16] But if this were so, and it was so in the New England that isolated Roger Williams' colony, then Protestantism had need of an authority to replace that which resided in the Roman Catholic Church in order to provide the rule by which men were to live and in terms of which the state would protect them. For the majority of the New England Puritans this authority was to be found in the Bible as interpreted by the learned. Every man was encouraged to read his Bible with his own eyes, but he was equally required then to bring his understanding into line with the judgments of the ministry as they were expounded from the pulpit. Society existed in a field between the pole of the law, the principal lesson to be garnered from private reading and discussion of the Bible, and the pole of the Spirit, the inspirational force of which was all but confined to the presence of the word in the pulpit. Such a situation was under constant attack from the days of Roger Williams on, but it was resilient and durable because, although it attempted to exclude outside influence, it contained within itself a dynamic interplay that was never fixed. If Anne Hutchinson insisted erroneously on the dominance of the spiritual pole and had attempted to seize it for the believers without due regard for its all-but-exclusive residence in the pulpit, she did, nevertheless, force a slackening of legalism on the part of the ministry. If any particular minister emphasized the free flowing of grace to the slighting of the legal conditions, he was in the interplay brought to adjust his teaching to the reading and realities of the daily life of his parishioners.

The concept of the covenant of grace defined the field of interplay, and nowhere within the field was there room for opinions that would deny the common bond of certain absolute truths. But the field was broad enough and the play free enough to permit individual expression in social and economic pursuits that would satisfy the new man and further the ends of the community. The principal dangers to the system resided not so much in outside doctrines, although these were dangers and were vigorously repelled, as in internal ailments economically or psychologically manifested.

Control was achieved early over the economic threat posed by the community's reliance on a large unenfranchised labor force. Open land held out some hope to these discontented; and regulation within families, where other dependents, such as children, were treated with some sincere show of equality, also limited discontent. The Puritans moved upon the wilds as a community, not as individuals. Civil authorities would not grant individuals the right to reside on farms outside the established towns until such time as they had a sufficient number of neighbors to found a new town, with a new church. Reliable servants were frequently employed, therefore, to reside on the farms in place of masters whose business confined them to the town, and when the new town was formed they acquired, at the least, the privileges of the resident. The voice of community was strong in a frontier village because that village could not come into being unless it had a church and a preacher. Absentee ownership was stoutly but, in the long run, ineffectively resisted because of the need at times to raise public capital from the sale of lands even when the purchasers were manifestly unable to improve them in person. But the ideal of seeing the new lands improved into townships rather than estates was not compromised. With specie habitually in short supply and the international market constantly in fluctuation, merchants found land the soundest investment.

For all the shortage in the actual availability of liquid wealth, the deeper trend was toward prosperity. Beginning in the 1640s, preachers found a constant theme in this trend, and their sermons, perhaps exaggerated for effect, pictured a community busy and contented with material acquisition. The internal perception was not one of a tyranny, such as Roger Williams saw, but of liberty, perhaps too much of it. "New Englands peace and plenty of means breeds strange security," Thomas Shepard told his auditors, "and hence prayer is neglected here." [17] In the same vein he said, "There is a number among us, young and old, of all sorts almost among us, that swarm up and down towns, and woods, and fields, whose care and work hitherto hath been like bees, only to get honey to their own hive, only to live comfortably with their houses, and lots, and victuals, and fine clothes, but not to live hereafter eternally." [18] He is, of course, concerned, but the threat he raises is no longer one to the society; the picture he paints is of happy men. The joys in the feast of preaching available are now subdued and some "wonder men preach so little, and yet so long." This argues contempt of the ministry, and Shepard corrects it with a revealing image: "Men cry not out of men when they are telling money to them many hours; and yet this is more precious." [19] And even when sermons are briskly attended, the motive, he suspects, is far from spiritual: "When a man comes to hear a sermon, there is a sermon and the market, there is a sermon and a friend to speak withal; and so many young people will go abroad to hear sermons. What is the end of it? It is, that ye may get wives and husbands, many of you." [20] Again, although the preacher's complaint is sincere, the picture he paints is of contented men. What he sees as a danger to the well-being of his fellow townsmen is not a source of division within the community, but something that is modifying the whole. His admonitions are now becoming professional in the narrow sense; it is his job to warn against security on the personal level, but there is little call for the community to make a significant change.

If some men of property were excluded from civil rights and civil offices, perhaps in their busyness they preferred it that way, preferred to let others do the communal chores. In November 1647 the General Court had to pass an ordinance requiring church members to accept public duties such as those of constable, juror, selectman, and surveyor, whether they were freemen or not. Four years later that body attempted to achieve some compromise between the community's allegiance to the zeal that had brought it out of a worldly England and the fact that economic health was, to some extent, tied to the increasing demand for luxuries: excess of dress, especially gold or silver lace and great boots, silk, and tiffany hoods, was, in general, prohibited, "though allowable to persons of greater estates or more liberal education." If these two exemptions did not cover all who justly claimed social distinction, the ordinance went on, at the risk of redundancy, to accommodate them: "Provided that this law shall not extend to the restraint of any magistrate, or any public officer of this jurisdiction, their wives and children, who are left to their discretion in wearing of apparel, or any other whose education and employment have been above the ordinary degree, or any settled military or soldier in the time of military service, or any other whose education and employment have been above the ordinary degree, or whose estates have been considerable, though now decayed." [21] At least one group clearly left out were servants, to whom a market in the second-hand clothes of the deteriorated gentry was presumably closed. Although all callings were equal in the sight of God, this did not preclude the distinguishing of the more consequential in the sight of men.

In 1652, in a reflection of the general fervor that had seized England, some sentiment developed on behalf of permitting gifted laymen to occupy the pulpit. But the General Court disapproved: "The humor of the times in England inclining to discourage learning against which we have borne testimony, this Court in our petition to the Parliament, which we should contradict if we should approve of such proceedings amongst ourselves." [22] Contrary to Williams' assertions, Massachusetts leaders held that advanced education was a specific requirement for the privilege of preaching, because preaching had an immense social function. It provided the needed counterforce to private study and was therefore not to be confused with it as it would be should laymen occupy the pulpit. The preacher, rather, through the very fact of his superior education, aligned himself with the conservatism of those charged with the welfare of the whole society, and balanced the pull of particular interest.

Psychologically the system attempted to wean men from the distractions of love of the creature. The ethic of love held out by such as Williams was anarchic, in its view, and an ordered society that justified itself through accepting the kingship of Christ and glorifying Him in its daily rationale was one in which natural affections were sublimated. New England Puritanism succeeded in great part in restructuring the psychological reality of its adherents, but in none of its demands did it visit such personal pain on them. Their everyday existence was meant to teach them that a surrender to or compromise with nature was an endangering of their souls and a crime against society. Too great a concentration on material things was a sad neglect of religion, but, at least, it was in the service of the state and correctly proceeded from the assumption that nature belonged to the gracious and could no more resist their control of it than Satan could resist Christ. But an indulgence in love of the creature turned men from their godly purposes, and they must learn to discipline themselves.

In pursuit of this ideal children, as has been seen, were frequently placed out in other homes for training so that natural affection would neither corrupt their upbringing nor compromise the righteousness of their parents. As was common in Europe, so in New England the mortality rate of infants was high, and Puritan diaries abound in reflections on the death of children, almost all of them directed against self-pity and addressed to the lesson the Lord intended for the living parent, the lesson that he must wean himself from love of the creature. It was not easily learned, and yet it was so assiduously and painfully studied that the conclusion is unavoidable: psychological reality would be intolerable unless the motions of nature were denied intrinsic meaning and brought under the control afforded by perception of a larger pattern. When Samuel Danforth lost all three of his children in an epidemic, he told his friends: "I trust the Lord hath done what he hath done in wisdom, and faithfulness, and dear love; and that in taking these pleasant things from me, He exerciseth as tender affection unto me, as I now express towards them in mourning for the loss of them." The dominion of death was denied through the application of its lesson to the living. "Doth not the goldsmith cast his metal into the furnace?" asked Danforth. "And you husbandmen, do you not cause the flail to pass over your grain, not that you hate your wheat, but that you desire pure bread?" [23]

Thomas Shepard's extended debate with himself on the death of his wife is an extremely eloquent document of the Puritan's need to overcome nature, and of his sense that the victory is not automatic, proceeds not from heartlessness but from disciplining the heart. It serves as an epitome of the Puritan psyche:

> But the Lord hath not been wont to let me live long without some affliction or other; and yet ever mixed with some mercy. And therefore, April the 2d, 1646, as He gave me another son, John, so He took away my most dear, precious, meek, and loving wife, in child-bed, after three weeks' lying-in; having left behind her two hopeful branches, my dear children, Samuel and John. This affliction was very heavy to me; for in it the Lord seemed to withdraw His tender care for me and mine, which He graciously manifested by my dear wife; also refused to hear prayer, when I did think He would have hearkened and let me see His beauty in the land of the living, in restoring of her to health again; also, in taking her away in the prime of her life, when she might have lived to glorify the Lord long; also, in threatening me to proceed in rooting out my family, and that He would not stop, having begun here, as in Ely, for not being zealous enough against the sins of His sons. And I saw that if I had profited by former afflictions of this nature, I should not have had this scourge. But I am the Lord's, and He may do with me what He will. He did teach me to prize a little grace, gained by a cross, as a sufficient recompense for outward losses.

But this loss was very great. She was a woman of incomparable meekness of spirit, toward myself especially, and very loving; of great prudence to take care for and order my family affairs, being neither too lavish nor sordid in anything, so that I knew not what was under her hands. She had an excellency to reprove for sin, and discern the evils of men. She loved God's people dearly, and studious to profit by their fellowship, and therefore loved their company. She could read my notes, which she had to muse on every week. She had a spirit of prayer, beyond ordinary of her time and experience. She was fit to die long before she did die, even after the death of her first-born, which was a great affliction to her. But her work not being done then, she lived almost nine years with me, and was the comfort of my life to me; and the last sacrament before her lying-in, seemed to be full of Christ, and thereby fitted for heaven. She did oft say she would not outlive this child; and when her fever first began, by taking some cold, she told me so, that we should love exceedingly together, because we should not live long together. Her fever took away her sleep; want of sleep wrought much distemper in her head, filled it with fantasies and distractions, but without raging. The night before she died she had about six hours unquiet sleep. But that so cooled and settled her head, that when she knew none else, so as to speak to them, yet she knew Jesus Christ, and could speak to Him; and therefore as soon as she awakened out of sleep, she brake out into a most heavenly, heart-breaking prayer, after Christ, her dear Redeemer, for the spirit of life, and so continued praying until the last hour of her death, "Lord, though I unworthy, Lord, one word, one word," &c.; and so gave up the ghost.

Thus God hath visited and scourged me for sins, and sought to wean me from this world. But I have ever found it a difficult thing to profit even but a little by the sorest and sharpest afflictions.[24]

Love is not denied, but it is channeled back to heaven rather than permitted to compromise the pattern God has set for men on earth. It is a personal rather than a social force, and the heart in which it properly resides is not the organ in the breast but the affective part of the soul. The pull of nature is strong and death is a moving event, but grief must be tempered by a perception of a pattern that is better than human emotions: "She was fit to die long before she did die."

Death was a matter for civil rather than ecclesiastical supervision. One minister explained it thus: "The celebration of marriage and burial of the dead be no ecclesiastical actions proper to the ministry, but are civil acts, and so to be performed, because those things are such as in the very nature of them belong not to the church alone, but to all people whether Christians or pagans. . . . Beside the tying of these things unto the ministers as ministerial duties, is a means to confirm the popish error in the one, that marriage is a sacrament, and in the other that prayer is to be used for the dead, over the dead." [25] Roman Catholicism in granting a hierarchy of grace descending into nature had, in Puritan opinion, falsely emphasized human love. With regard to death it had misled men into a refusal to relinquish themselves to God's glory through encouraging them to employ their natural love in acts of prayer that, it was taught, could affect God's disposition toward the deceased. But, for the Puritans, when the dead were called to their predetermined lot, the living were to reflect on their own mortal condition rather than indulge in personal weakness and futile attempts to alter what was eternally decreed.

With devotions over the dead blocked, the Puritan culture encouraged rational exercises in the wake of death. The funeral elegy became a favorite literary form. In submitting to the very discipline of meter and rhyme, the elegist was expressing a sense of order in the event. And by far the favorite form of elegy was anagrammatic, one wherein the letters of the name of the deceased were rearranged so as to reveal the message his life held for the living; so, for example, Governor Thomas Dudley's name yielded the thought, "Ah old, must dye," and elegists competed with one another, as it were, in the ingenious extraction of such meanings. Deep within the culture's overwhelming commitment to the certainty of words over commitment to ambiguous images, to the dominance of the pulpit over the altar, was a folk belief in the animism of language. The meaning of words on this level was not arbitrary but organically connected with the essence of the thing signified by the word. Adam had named the creatures of the earth after their kind, which meant that he did not indifferently call the leopard "leopard" and the ant "ant," but that he saw the leopardness of the leopard and named it accordingly.

Pun as well as anagram therefore flourished in New England writing: was Shepard not indeed a shepherd; did John Cotton,

Thomas Hooker, and Samuel Stone, essential preachers all, not indeed afford their people the spiritual essentials of life even as the essential materials were cotton for clothing, hooker for fishing for food, and stone for building shelter? Wit, so severely confined in other areas of life, was indulged in verse and other shapings of language. Here reason and pattern were called upon because such were the proper tools in the psychological conquest of nature. The ponderous punning and puzzling of the Puritan elegy is a ludicrous testimony of the culture's concerted battle against the inherent value of emotion. If to modern eyes it betrays a tastelessness it also betrayed the same to contemporaries outside of the culture, but the imbalance it symbolizes was a source of social cohesion in the face of a nature that appeared particularly chaotic and cruel in the wilderness and therefore called for the severest discipline from those who would master it.

Sexual love existed in the world, the culture maintained, in order to move men to conjugal love. Marriage kept sex from being irrelevant. Should a spouse die, prompt remarriage was the soundest course. Thomas Shepard after the death of his Joanna, so vividly described in his memoir, took another wife. And since sexual motivation was given man in the interest of family, propagation was a duty, one made sharper in New England by the need for more hands and the sense of conquest through community. Just as men were not permitted to reside permanently on farms outside of town until they had established a new township, so this communal conquest of space was matched by a communal conquest of time manifested through the family. Numerous progeny were the soundest assurance of cultural continuity. If in actual fact New England did not come to exceed other sections of America in a disproportionately high number of families distinguished by intellect—Mathers, Adamses, Lowells—it certainly surpassed them in its awareness of possessing such because the culture was attuned to this form of control over the future.

New Englanders were bred to a distrust of love of their fellow man or of the opposite sex unless it served higher ends, and the result, to be noted in one diary after another, is anguished battle with desire. Michael Wigglesworth, tutoring at Harvard, complained to his diary in 1653, "Much distracted thoughts I find arising from too much doting affection to some of my pupils one of whom went to Boston with me today. I feel no power to love and prize God in my heart, my spirit is so leavened with love to the creature." [26] Cotton Mather expressed his battle against sexual longing, which he identified as impurity, in the same breath in which he expressed his fight against blasphemy and atheism. "These, even these, O miserable Mather, do follow thee with an astonishing fury," [27] he wrote, and he fell onto the dust on his study floor to implore divine aid against them. But such does not say that Massachusetts, especially in the port towns that received the sailors of the burgeoning Atlantic trade, did not have its brothels and its taverns. The social fabric, however, stretched to contain them even as psychologically the culture taught containment of natural affections.

Contrition, humility, and repentance, love, pride, and longing are terms as prominent in the Puritan vocabulary as in that of any other group of English-speakers. But in Puritan usage they are rarely applied to relations between men; they form, rather, the diction of man's communication with God. He faced his fellow men in the vocabulary of callings, duties, privileges, and respects. There exists more than one model of psychological health in terms of which such a strong repression of emotion is sick, but the models grew in a different social and economic context. What calls for emphasis is that such a cultural habit so well suited New England reality that it survived the decay of the churches and gave New England social life an almost legendary loftiness in the eyes of outsiders. Dispassionate restraint marked relations among members of the culture and potential disapprobation hung heavy over relations with strangers. Even when, centuries later, such New Englanders as Emerson and Thoreau sought to pierce the formalism of their townsmen they did so by relating the liberating flux of personal inspiration to an oversoul rather than asking that love be let loose in Concord. Even when Hawthorne scored the Puritan culture for its punitive treatment of Hester Prynne, he endorsed the checking of her perception that nothing that is natural can be wrong and her insistence that her act of sexual love was therefore right.

New England's most cherished verbal construct, the sermon, revealed in its form as well as its content the compulsion to overcome emotion with a reasoned view of a larger scheme. The usual format was one in which the preacher announced his biblical text, extracted a doctrine from it, and clarified the meaning of that doctrine by dividing it into numbered parts, following his explication of the doctrine with a series of numbered uses, practical applications of his message. The scaffolding of one, two, three, fourthly, fifthly, and sixthly, the four parts of the second point and the three parts of the latter use, remained in the sermon. They were aids to the note-takers, who would edify themselves in the following week by reflecting on and discussing the sermon, signals of the triumph of rational analysis over emotion. Feelings were to be addressed in the sermon because its primary function was to start or enforce the salvation experience and therefore to stir contrition in the hearts of its listeners, but the scaffolding was there to help the listener climb in an ordered way from his disturbed emotional state to a perception of his relationship to the divinity.

When the enthusiasm of the early years waned, and after the difficulties with Anne Hutchinson's group had proved the inconvenience of making the sermon the exclusive focus of religious fervor, the emphasis shifted to preaching that would cohere the sense of group identity and define the acceptable limits of individual reaction. Sermons came centrally to be exegetical. The emotional outlet they had once provided a community that denied itself such indulgence elsewhere came steadily to be transferred to another part of the service, prayer. In severe reaction to the dumb or reading ministry of the established church who preached infrequently and read homilies, the Puritan ministry delivered their sermons from memory and did not repeat them. Spontaneity, or at least its appearance, was crucial because the Spirit employed the live, not the written word; else reading one's Bible would suffice. Similarly, set forms of prayer were distrusted, indeed regarded as contradictions, since when one prayed he did so from an openness of heart that could not be sincere if it found a correspondent in a printed formula rather than in a spontaneous outburst.

"We dislike all reading of prayer in the act of praying, as inconvenient, yea directly contrary unto the act," said John Robinson. "In prayer we do pour out matter, to wit, the holy conceptions of the mind, from within to without; that is from the heart to God: on the contrary, in reading, we do receive and admit matters from without to within; that is, from the book into the heart." [28] When the sermon increasingly became an instrument of socialization, therefore, prayer became the vehicle for emotional outlet. In a settled society that no longer brought to its church gatherings a keen sense of itself as embattled, the sermon became a teaching and the prayer was that which vividly expressed their emotional condition.

John Norton, who succeeded John Cotton as the teacher of the Boston church, was a preacher and polemicist of the driest and most rational sort. But he revolutionized the style of praying: "It even transported the souls of his hearers to accompany him in his devotions, wherein his graces would make wonderful sallies into the vast field of entertainments, and acknowledgments, with which we are furnished in the new-covenant for our prayers." [29] Preaching, Norton saw, had to be addressed to social stability but prayer could serve the personal hunger for an experienced religion without disturbing the social balance. Since Norton's day, Cotton Mather happily noted, "our pulpits have been fuller than ever of 'experimental demonstrations,' thus the ministers of the Gospel may on all occasions present their supplications before God, in the discharge of their ministry, with more pertinent, more affecting, more expanded enlargements, than any form could afford unto them. New England can show,—even young ministers, who never did in all things repeat one prayer twice over." [30]

In shifting emotion to prayer, an act related to the individual condition of man or a congregation, from sermons related to the condition of mankind, the culture shifted from establishing to conserving itself. It also ratified a limited form of emotional self-indulgence that was to provide the opening in the culture for appreciation and practice of the literary art. Since emotion was confined, however, to the individual in his isolated turbulence, rather than permitted to affect collective views, its literary applications, when they developed in later years, would effectively be used to express psychological rather than social conditions. The great writers who flowered in New England soil were primarily concerned with the passion of the psyche not with the charged depiction of the social scene.

The Massachusetts Puritans' most accomplished lyricist was Anne Bradstreet. Daughter of that severe magistrate Thomas Dudley, and wife of another eminent civil leader, Simon Bradstreet, she was most admired by her contemporaries for her didactic verse: long rhymed disquisitions on physics, astronomy, and natural philosophy that imitated Quarles and DuBartas and relied heavily on sources such as Raleigh's *History of the World*, Plutarch, and Bishop Ussher, as well as the Bible. Today, however, her shorter and more personal verses speak most tellingly to the reader, verses in which she movingly develops the attractions of nature and brings them ultimately under the control of a divine pattern, not automatically but by contending with the obvious charm they exerted on her. Her most persistent theme in such poetry is time, "that fatal wrack of mortal things." [31] Like the great nature poets she does not condemn the changes brought by time, but, rather, expresses a deep longing to submit to them as if the beauty of seasonal rhythms was in itself divine. But finally she is compelled to confine the powerful influence of nature within a higher order. Her submission is complaint, much in the fashion of Thomas Shepard's contending with the meaning of his wife's death. In a stanza of a poem in memory of her "dear grand-child Elizabeth," who died in 1665 at the age of one and a half, she wrote:

> By nature Trees do rot when they are grown.
> And Plumbs and Apples throughly ripe do fall,
> And Corn and grass are in their season mown,
> And time brings down what is both strong and tall.

But plants new set to be eradicate,
And buds new blown, to have so short a date,
Is by his hand alone, that guides nature and fate.[32]

Natural order may be responded to with the feelings so long as divine order is assented to by the reason, and the extra foot in the last line emphasizes such assent even as it also signifies that it weighs heavily.

The perception of reality that the Puritan culture formed in New England was one that included not only rational justification for the common enterprise, but, more significantly, an emotional attachment to the environment in which it was conducted. The very climate of New England, so scornfully cited by those who preferred investments elsewhere, and first entered into almost by accident as the only place available, became for its inhabitants a metaphor of their sound condition. They first described New England as the land of the chosen people in rationalized reaction to revolutionary excesses at home, but it developed for them into more than a convenient location for their beliefs and became the absolutely right place for their principles. Their feelings structured its every condition into a metaphor of the inner condition of the saints. They became the land's and furnished it with the drama of their struggle. Unlike some other colonies, that which the New England Puritans inhabited was not only domesticated by their labors but also shaped by their imaginations into an emblem of their superiority. Roger Williams' courageous devotion to toleration stemmed from a profound Christian sense of the pilgrimage of Christ's followers and the ultimate indifference of the physical geography of that journey. Those who so calculatedly opposed him accepted the metaphor of pilgrimage in its loosest sense—life is a journey toward eternity—but in opposition to him made heavy emotional investments in the landscape across which they traveled.

More than two hundred years later, Henry Adams, a son of New England, reflecting on his childhood trip to the American South, analyzed the nature of his shock at that region. From the vantage of his adulthood he realized that he had been unconsciously trained to fuse physical and moral geography, to know that bad roads meant bad morals. The fusion was an unsolicited gift from the Puritans. Unsophisticated Edward Johnson described the fortunes of a band of his contemporaries who, stirred by Cromwellian liberties, embarked for the Isle of Providence off the coast of Nicaragua to establish there a tolerating state. When they found that the Spaniards had taken it, "the people some of them returned back again for New England, being sore abashed at this providence that befell them, that they would never seek to be governed by liberty again to this very day; yet others that were so strongly bent for the heat of liberty, that they endured much pinching penury upon an uninhabited island, till at length meeting some others like-minded with themselves, they made a voyage to another island. The chiefest part of their charter of freedom was this, that no man upon pain of death should speak against another's religion; where they continued till some of them were famished, and others even forced to feed on rats, and any other thing they could find to sustain nature, till the provident hand of God brought a ship to the place, which took them off the island and saved their lives: but upon this the winter's discourse ceased, and projects for a warmer country were hushed and done." [33]

More revealing than the gloating over these unfortunates is the imagination that now fuses heat with liberty, warmth with toleration, the south with indulgence of the flesh. Johnson described the would-be Caribbean colonists before they left Massachusetts: "It being a frequent thing with some after the novelties of a new land began to be stale with them and the sweet nourishment of Christ in the preaching of His word, began to dry up through the hot heady conceit of new conceived opinion, then they wanted a warmer country, and every northwest wind that blew, they crept into some odd chimney-corner or other to discourse of the diversity of climates in the southern parts, but chiefly of a thing very sweet to the palate of flesh, called liberty." [34] Escape from New England is an indulgence of the flesh, and Johnson's imagination is thoroughly representative in linking the physical facts of New England to the spiritual. The land had not staled with him because he absorbed its features even as it absorbed him, and made it a symbol of his superior condition, its very damp keeping him from hot and heady conceits. New England winters spoke of the foolishness of toleration every bit as much as did the minister in his pulpit.

The imaginative fusion of spirit and geography, morality and landscape, strengthened the culture beyond doctrine. When the nineteenth century brought the New England school of poets into their full, these poets—Lowell, Longfellow, Holmes, and Whittier, among others—were popularly called fireside poets: fireside because their collected volumes were published in editions called Fireside Editions and were to be read by the fireside during the winter, when the adverse climate limited outdoor labor and turned men inward to the domestic hearth. But "fireside" also in that these poets hymned the superiority of the controlled flame to the ravening sun, the superiority of right principles to natural indulgence, of restrained feeling to passion. In their expression of the symmetry of New England beliefs and New England scenery they were uneasy poets of the summer. The seasons they make memorable are the autumn of the gentian and the winter of the blizzard. They elaborate on a theme that the Puritan culture had made a part of its structure of feeling: New England nature validates New England ideals. When the Puritans entered into this perception they were no longer colonists emotionally, however much they remained so politically.

CHAPTER SIX

White Coat, Blue Coat

*Baptism and tribalism—Quakerism versus the total state—
Puritan violence—Restoration politics and commerce*

In 1646 the General Court called a synod to unify New England ecclesiastical polity against the opposing claims of Presbyterianism and left-wing sectaries whose polemic struggles in England were encouraging open expressions of difference within New England. One very sore issue that served as a focus for differences was infant baptism. The Presbyterians would baptize the children of all who attended the parish church, whether or not the parents were justified believers. The Anabaptists would baptize no infants but would reserve that sacrament as the sign of a person's having been called to salvation, and therefore would administer it only to adult believers when they joined the church fellowship. Massachusetts in practice had developed a way between these two procedures that under their conflicting pressures was in need of consolidation and theoretical support: children of believers were baptized as a symbol of the church's fellowship with their parents and its protective commitment to them until such time as they came of age and could evidence signs of their own belief.

Presbyterians and Anabaptists reflected a classic opposition within Christianity, but Massachusetts' middle way was seen by both as the kind of adjustment that, in effect, compromised not just the practical issue but Christianity itself. Constantine the Great had brought to Rome the Byzantine concept of the absolute sovereignty of the state, as opposed to earlier concepts of the principate, and in adopting Christianity as the state religion he sought to include all in the state under the church, even as he had brought the church under his authority. The model he went a long way toward establishing was one in which all infants in the state were baptized in the compulsory church, and it was a model built on by most of the reformed churches as well as by Roman Catholicism. Faced with Anabaptists who complained that such compulsory baptism mixed the impure with the pure, Luther had said, "It is the part of wisdom not to be offended at it when evil men go in and out of the church. . . . The greatest comfort of all is the knowledge that they do no harm but that we must allow the tares to be mixed in. . . . The *Schwärmer* who do not allow tares among them, really bring about that there is no wheat among themselves—by this zeal for only wheat and a pure church they bring about, by this too great holiness, that they are not even a church but a sect of the devil." [1] He could be comfortable with the Constantine model, as were the theorists of the Church of England, as were the theorists of Presbyterianism which had grown up as the state church in Scotland, and as, indeed, were all who sought to make the church coextensive with the state.

From its inception such a concept was challenged within Christianity by those who wished to emphasize and preserve the idea of fellowship based on personal faith and, therefore, to obstruct the drift toward a church including all in a given locality. Faith, they said, called men out of the world, and a national or regional church was self-contradictory. In Constantine's day the dissenting view was epitomized by the Donatists, against whom the synod of Arles ruled in 314 and against whom the Emperor himself ruled in 316. The thwarted Donatists, seeing that the root of their difference was the nature of the state rather than the church alone, attacked by promoting demonstrations against the state, so that Constantine was compelled to repress them with force. In this active civil disobedience they provided an example that conservative churchmen down through the ages never tired of citing in defense of the status quo: pietist groups had to be suppressed, they said, because history showed that they did not aim merely at the enjoyment of their opinions but also intended the overthrow of civil order.

Massachusetts occupied an uneasy middle in this classic confrontation over baptism. On one hand, it had accepted the notion of a church backed by secular power and therefore had accepted with it the worldly view that the institutional church would always contain some tares; hence the social basis of Cotton's reply to Williams and hence an inclination in Massachusetts to treat difference in religious opinion as civil rebellion. But, on the other hand, it also maintained that those in the church had come out of the world and, therefore, although it compelled all to church attendance it admitted only the chosen to church membership, administering baptism to their children only. Such a position was not the result of a pre-elaborated theory. It had contributed to social cohesion in the early days of settlement, when church membership and civil leadership were one, but after some fifteen years of settlement it was sorely tested as church members came to represent a shrinking percentage of the total population and economic conditions permitted nonmembers to prosper nonetheless. Presbyterians claimed that Massachusetts ecclesiastical polity turned a community against itself; Anabaptists claimed it tainted itself with the corruptions of this world.

The synod called in 1646 pronounced its findings in a platform of church discipline in 1648, but so vexed was the situation with regard to baptism that the platform sidestepped that issue. Rather it addressed itself to supporting Congregationalism as opposed to other forms of church organization, showing the logic and historical validity of the autonomous congregation of believers who covenanted with one another, elected their church officers, and communicated with other autonomous congregations as equals, but did not recognize the binding power of a synod although it relied upon such collective wisdom for its guidance. In practice, to be sure, the state was to be called upon to translate the findings of synods into civil polity.

Presbyterian polemicists said the platform was either mere democracy or horrid anarchy when they did not say it was both.[2] A hierarchical structure of national, provincial, and regional synods, they maintained, should ordain officers, discipline them and their congregations, and maintain a constant supervision over the church. In response, the supporters of the middle way of Massachusetts came to see it as being particularly English, just right for those raised within the civil liberties of that nation, and analogized Congregational Church government and English muncipal government. In praising Cotton's theory of New England Church government, the Independents at the Westminster Assembly said, "His scope is to demonstrate a distinct and several share and interest of power, in matters of common concernment, vouchsafed to each of these [the elders and the brethren], and dispersed among both by charter from the Lord: as in some of our towns corporate, to a company of aldermen, the rulers, and a common council, a body of the people, there useth to be the like." [3] When Presbyterians professed horror at the fact that the congregation in such a system voted upon excommunication rather than leaving such a solemn matter in the hands of the learned elders, the Independents reminded them that excommunication was the spiritual parallel of capital punishment in civil matters. Just as the English law sees that the power to condemn to death "is not put into the hands of an assembly of lawyers only, no not of all the judges themselves, men selected for wisdom, faithfulness, and gravity," but resides in a jury of peers, so is that spirit matched by Congregational policy toward excommunication. "And we of this nation use to admire the care and wisdom of our ancestors herein, and do esteem this privilege of the subjects in that particular [trial by a jury of peers] (peculiar to our nation) as one of the glories of our laws, and do make boast of it as such a liberty and security to each person's life, as (we think) no nation about us can show the like." [4]

With the liberties of Englishmen erected as a bulwark against the right wing of Puritanism (and in pointed reference to that body's Scottish allegiance), the left wing was met by a counterattack that equated the democratic freedom on which it insisted with papal tyranny, through a violent rhetorical twist of its own contentions. Those who insist on their liberties conceive, in effect, "though they will not profess it, the same of their own heads, which the papists do of their head the Pope, viz: that they cannot err, or be deceived: and this specially in such matters, as for which they have suffered trouble, and afflictions formerly, and so having bought them dear, they value them highly. But it is too merchantlike to strive to oversell a thing, which we have formerly over bought." [5]

The platform of 1648 thus proved a potent political document, but still the vexing matter of baptism was too touchy for even the platform's astute penmen to come to some statement on it. In this area Massachusetts clergy were in a narrow corner from which they had somehow to extricate themselves. Reservation of baptism to the families of believers was, after the early years, bad politics and bad logic. It denied the church direct supervision over an alarmingly large proportion of the infant population on the shaky ground that although salvation could not be inherited from parents, that presumption was, nevertheless, allowable until the child grew to consciousness. Logic seemed to call for restriction of baptism to conscious believers, in effect Anabaptism, rather than this weak presumption. And politics, as children so baptized came of age and yet failed to profess saving faith, seemed to call for a wider extension of baptism, lest those who were qualified to present their children all but die off. In the first two decades, for example, only one person baptized in the church of Boston sought and received admission at adulthood, and she was the daughter of the pastor, John Wilson.[6] Orthodox believers were thus increasingly faced not just with the social problem of unbaptized outsiders, but with the emotional burden of unbaptized grandchildren.

The issue was resolved—with a compromise rather than a solution—by a synod's declaring in 1662 that the children of those who had been baptized could also be baptized, even though their parents had not been admitted to full membership and could not therefore take the sacrament of the Last Supper. It was a singular decision because, although it was felt as a compromise by the culture, that compromise was, apparently, no more realistic politically or logically than the earlier policy it modified: the number of outsiders continued to grow, and the shaky presumption of the probable faith of the children of believers was made shakier by its extension to the children of those who had not made good on the presumption. The area in which the compromise was sound, however, was that of culture, the cohesion of the society. The source of stability, in the face of popular clamor and an abundance of new doctrine that logically extended the early promise of the Puritan revolution, was the powerful tribal sense that New England policy had bred, and this it now officially recognized and encouraged. Anabaptist and then Quaker doctrines were too firmly rooted in certain common Christian assumptions to be outargued convincingly, although the intellectual superiority of New England ideas could, its holders felt, be demonstrated, and they were untiring in such demonstrations. But the ultimate validation of New England's way for New England's community was to be sought in the extension of its crucial element, the family, into a tribe, membership in which dominated all other allegiances and held the individual to the established pattern. Continuity of belief, which had been the rationale for overthrowing a hierarchy that argued from the continuity of institutions and traditions, was in the 1650s too dangerously antisocial a soil in which to strengthen the growth that had begun in New England. The roots were sent down deeper into the subsoil of the Old Testament, where resided the pattern of the ever-troubled but ever-sustained folk of God. The road from the evasion of the issue of baptism in 1648 to its compromise in the Half-Way Covenant of 1662 is one along which the tribal sense was increasingly called upon to shape social reality.

Sixty-seven years of age in 1650, Peter Bulkeley of Concord allowed his mind to travel over the old days of Elizabeth and James in England and found that they weren't so bad after all. The persecutors were then in power, to be sure, but then the true believers were united and did not confuse their aspirations with mere democracy as now the common sort in Massachusetts seemed to do. "Shall I tell you what I think to be the ground of all this insolency which discovers itself in the speech of men?" he wrote John Cotton. "Truly I cannot ascribe it so much to any outward thing, as to the putting of too much liberty and power into the hands of the multitude, which they are too weak to manage, many growing conceited, proud, arrogant, self-sufficient, as wanting nothing." [7]

More affluent than most of the New England clergy because of the generous inheritance he had received, Bulkeley had himself attempted to insure a patriarchal development of the land in Massachusetts. Like Abraham, he was father of all those in his household who were godly. He severely disciplined his servants to his beliefs, but when they were eventually dismissed from his service he bestowed farms upon them, the orderly succession of grace thus being signaled by the orderly development of land.[8] His will also reflected this progression of faith, and, remarkably, he tied his children's legacies to their mother, so that if they proved vicious the legacies "shall lie wholly in the power of my said wife, their mother, to deal with them therein, as she herself in Christian wisdom shall think meet, either to give their legacy or to keep it herself." [9]

But in his advanced years Bulkeley perceived confusion where he had attempted to establish a pattern of order. "I am persuaded, that except there be some means used to change the course of things in this point, our churches will grow more corrupt day by day." He recalled the England of his young manhood, where, although professed believers were fewer, matters were better governed. What was the way out of the paradox? Perhaps an insistence on the original straitness should be reintroduced and "we should make the doors of the church narrower." But even as he made the suggestion, he recognized the vulnerability of such a response to a situation in which the "heady or headless multitude" refused to be governed by the wise and strong. There was warrant for stricter admission procedures in the word of God, but such a course "if it should be taken, would bring its inconvenience also in another kind." [10]

Bulkeley's widely shared bafflement was increased by the arrival in Lynn in the following year of three Anabaptists from Rhode Island, John Clark, John Crandall, and Obadiah Holmes. They held a private meeting with sympathizers on a Sunday morning, and, being detected, they were compelled to the public service in the afternoon and then remitted to Boston for trial. There they were fined by the General Court, and when they asked what law they had broken, Governor Endicott said they had denied infant baptism, and then, "being somewhat transported broke forth" and told the prisoners they really deserved death. The magistrates of Massachusetts, Endicott said, "would not have such trash into their jurisdiction; moreover he said, you go up and down, and secretly insinuate into those that are weak, but you cannot maintain it before ministers." [11] The Court's statutory ground was questionable, but its cultural ground was made clear by Endicott when he tired of legal haggling: the Anabaptists were trash, socially disreputable, and they were ignorant and preyed on the ignorant. Unable to cope with the learning of the ministry, they stirred up the discontents of others who were equally unlearned.

Obadiah Holmes elected not to pay the fine, although he knew that the alternative was whipping and imprisonment. As he awaited his stripes in prison, Satan came to him and urged him to pay the fine rather than make a spectacle of himself: "Remember thy self, thy birth, breeding, and friends, thy wife, children, name, and credit," [12] the devil in him said. For Holmes the voice of the tempter was that which spoke of family and worldly esteem, as it was for all who felt that religion was at odds with established society. In Massachusetts, however, birth, breeding, friends, wife, children, name, and credit were the temporal rewards of God's disposition toward His people. Holmes was struck thirty times with a three-corded whip and when it was over he told the magistrates, "You have struck me as with roses." [13] Two men were fined for coming up to him and congratulating him when he was cut from the whipping post. Roger Williams, hearing of the punishment, wrote his former Salem ally, John Endicott, underlining for him the monstrousness of the position he took against conscience and emphasizing the connection between powerlessness on earth and power in heaven: "The Lord Jesus Christ foretold how wonderfully the wisest of the world, should be mistaken in the things of Christ, and a true visible Christ Jesus! When did we see thee naked, hungry, thirsty, sick, in prison, &c. How easy, how common, how dreadful these mistakes?" [14]

Because the Anabaptists were of the lowest class and belonged to the whipped of the world, they figured in the imagination of the Massachusetts leaders as testimony not for Christ, but for the view that infant baptism was a doctrine that was particularly abhorrent to the refuse of mankind. By the same token it was for them a most important mark of a chosen group, and that group, because of the important civil consequences of church membership, was social. "Few things are said as plainly in the New Testament and as often," Leonard Verduin observes, "as that Christ's Church is not coextensive with any socio-political grouping or ethnic delineation, and that national boundaries are meaningless in it." [15] But to heed this message, as clearly the Anabaptists did, is also to believe that Jesus broke history in two when He appeared on earth. This was, in Massachusetts thinking, an illiterate procedure. Grace had been present on earth before the days of the New Testament, and Jesus had come to apply it to those who believed in Him rather than those who happened to be born Jews. While this changed the dispensation, it did not fracture history. Grace had a continuous chronicle. Even though its means had altered, its continuity from Old to New Testament was clearly perceivable to those blessed, as the saved must be blessed, with understanding.

Endicott equated Anabaptism with an ignorance that could not cope with the learning of the ministry because that learning, as it was acquired in clerical study and redistributed from the pulpit, was the indispensable cornerstone of Christianity. Without it any man could misread his Bible, and the ignorant would certainly do so, most frequently in the direction of a simple-minded literalism. An authoritative standard of interpretation must be asserted. The alternative was anarchy in essential matters. The Puritan revolution, powered by the common accessibility of the printed word, had developed a confidence in the intellectual ability of the folk, which, with the success of the revolution, broke into two parts. On one hand, that ability was improved by the more gifted, who taught their brethren how to build upon their reading and indicated the interpretive rules in terms of which meaning was to be discerned and literalism avoided. On the other, that ability was sufficient unto itself. Massachusetts leadership asserted that Christian liberty had been extended within a new order whose confines, although broader than those of the traditional church, were, nevertheless, discernible; dissenters maintained that Christian liberty was now absolute.

Obviously, the former view comports with the ideal of a Christian commonwealth, the attempt to make the folk and God's folk one, whereas the latter comports with the view of a secular state that relegates religion to the area of private opinion. An intellectual class became an inevitable component of the new Christian commonwealth, just as a strong strain of anti-intellectualism was developed by those who in the name of liberty and toleration opposed it. There were not many men like Roger Williams, who saw the compatibility of intellectualism with liberty through a confinement of scholarship to matters of this world alone.

The interpretation of the Bible that countered Anabaptist literalism was one that strengthened a sense of the people of Massachusetts as God's folk. The key argument offered against infant baptism was that the Bible affords no clear word for it by either commandment or example. The first lesson literalists had to learn, therefore, was that God delivered His will not only by command and example but also "by proportion, or deduction, by consequence." There is no commandment or example, for instance, for women to participate in the communion, "yet the proportion of the Lords Supper with the Passover, and deduction from such Scriptures as put no difference between male and female, make it to be received as the will and ordinance of Christ." [16]

The second lesson to be learned is that a conclusion of faith may be based on a syllogism the first proposition of which is found in the Bible and the second proposition of which is "found certain and evident by sense or reason." [17] And the third lesson follows from these: the Old Testament is sacred and instructive as is the New because, once read in accordance with proper interpretive standards, the Old Testament can also be seen to contain a record of the operations of the Holy Spirit on earth. The New Testament does not change the circumstances and ordinances of salvation "by way of abrogation or diminution but by way of accomplishment and enlargment," and therefore does not abrogate the rite of circumcision but extends it in the sacrament of infant baptism. "The greatest part of the books of the Old Testament hold forth the doctrine, worship, order and government of the New Testament to such who have not a veil laid over their hearts in the reading of the Old Testament"; [18] did not Paul profess publicly that he taught nothing but what Moses and the prophets did say should come?

The rite of circumcision was the ground for infant baptism. To bear its mark had been to bear citizenship in the Jewish state, just as to remain unmarked was to have been a Gentile. In Christ there may be neither Jew nor Gentile, but in Christ there was a new order of the chosen, and their mark was baptism. The Israelite model, although rationally cited as ground for a sacrament, clearly exerted a force beyond that and had special appeal because it spoke to a sense of identity in Massachusetts deeper than doctrine, a sense of common suffering, privation in a wilderness, and triumph over adversity by the commonwealth of the gathered. They too were a tribe, and when baptism had to be extended, logic and expediency would be governed by, and if need be even disregarded in response to, this sense.

Such a sense provided the basis for confidence in the extreme measures taken against the Quakers, whose assault on Massachusetts was felt as far more threatening than that of the Anabaptists. The tactics of the first Quaker growth in the 1640s and 1650s shadowed those of the Puritanism of an earlier period. Both built on moral earnestness that amounted to a passion for righteousness, both opposed the looseness of life that characterized the way of the world, both combated what they considered to be secular tyranny, and both hated a sacerdotal religion.[19] Each, of course, drew the line in these matters at a different point, and the Quakers, coming in the trough of the Puritans' wave, drew the line so as to exclude them. George Fox, the Quaker movement's founder, sought his initial audiences among those whose material lot had not been improved by the changes wrought when Cromwell came to power. In his first travels about England he not only preached commercial honesty, as had Puritan leaders earlier, but also spoke to the justices against the oppression caused by their fixing a legal wage for farm laborers below what was equitable, since they themselves were landowners. In the late 1640s he likened the new establishment in England, that of the Puritans, to commercial exploitation, as they had likened an earlier establishment: "When I heard the bell toll to call people together to the steeple-house, it struck at my life, for it was just like a market-bell, to gather people together that the priest might set forth his ware to sale." [20] And, like the Puritans again, once his movement made headway he reflected on its superiority for commercial purposes: "At the first convincement when Friends could not put off their hats to people, nor say you to a particular, but thee and thou; and could not bow, nor use the world's salutations nor fashions nor customs—and many friends being tradesmen of several sorts—they lost their custom at the first, for the people would not trade with them nor trust them. And for a time people that were tradesmen could hardly get money enough to buy bread, but afterwards when people came to see Friends' honesty and truthfulness and yea and nay at a word in their dealing, and their lives and conversations did preach and reach to the witness of God in all people, and they knew and saw that they would not cozen and cheat them for conscience' sake towards God:—and that at last they might send any child and be as well used as themselves at any of their shops, so then the things altered so that all the inquiry was where was a draper or shopkeeper or tailor or shoemaker or any other tradesman that was a Quaker: then that was all the cry, insomuch that Friends had double the trade beyond any of their neighbors: and if there was any trading they had it, insomuch that the cry was of all the professors and others, if we let these people alone they will take the trading of the nation out of our hands." [21] The Massachusetts Puritans looked over their shoulder to see that a hideous Doppelgänger was dogging their steps.

It was hideous because it so maddeningly mirrored them while denying the very essence of their belief. Anne Hutchinson had been, in comparison, a creature of light, because her insistence on personal revelation, although heretical, was made within some recognizable objective context. But now the chasm between spirit and nature they had bridged with the word of God and the enlightened interpretation of the Bible, the sacred record of a revelation that was finished, was reopened to be bridged again only by a supernatural light given to each soul. The church was a fraudulent show, a mere steeple-house, and the ministry penny-catching minstrels in that theater. As it entered the 1650s the Quaker movement began so rapid a growth in England that by the end of the century Gracechurch Street Meeting in London was made up of the richest traders in the city: Barclays, Gurneys, Hanburys, Lloyds, Osgoods, Hoares, Dimsdales, and Christys.[22] Quakerism had detached itself from a specific reliance on economic discontent and centered its converting effort on releasing the religious fervor that was seeking outlet from the psyche of the discontented.

Quaker missionaries thought of themselves as publishers of truth, and their technique was based on the observation, made early in the history of their movement, that the experience of light each had felt, the sense that his salvation was not an escape from the penalty of sin that others must pay but rather an escape from sin itself that others could achieve, was an experience that they seemed to have arrived at simultaneously but independently of one another. This meant that the publishing of truth was not so much a teaching as it was a releasing of what was already there. Consequently the missionaries would, when entering a new region, inquire of the godly people there and seek to identify one who seemed predisposed to their message. He was, in their terminology, the "live center" around whom another group could be gathered. England had an abundance of live centers after Puritanism had released self-mastery but contained its mystical flow, and New England too could be expected to possess them.

Moreover, in a world already habituated to seemly outward behavior and a stricter regulation of morals, the Quakers developed new badges of difference. The hat was not to be removed in the presence of authority, lest the blasphemy of honoring man as God be committed, nor was the formal "you" that argued distinction among men to be employed; rather the head would remain covered, and homely "thee" would suffice. And where the truth could not be published quietly and unopposed, as came to pass in New England, then there it was to be published dramatically by going into the streets in sackcloth and ashes to act out the lamentable condition of the people, or naked to symbolize the falsity of the pretenses of the opposing society.

The heralds of the Quaker movement in London were women, and again women heralded it in New England; their sex was predisposed to fear naught, once a release from the arbitrary usages of society was obtained through personal enlightenment. Barbados, a crucial port for the New England trade and a tolerating island, became the staging area for the invasion of the American continent. From there in 1655 Mary Fisher, a twenty-two-year-old Yorkshire servant, and Ann Austin, a London mother of five, took ship to begin the assault on Massachusetts. They were promptly imprisoned, stripped to the waist, whipped, and then shipped out within five weeks of their arrival. But the invasion continued, and Massachusetts, exhausting the lets of fine, prison, and corporal punishment, proceeded to the extreme of execution, hanging and sometimes a reprieve from hanging with the halter round the neck of the victim, who then asked to go through with the execution so that he might testify. The first executions took place in 1659, and the last in 1661, but before the capital law was repealed, the perimeter of Massachusetts was honeycombed with meetings gathered around live centers. The repeal of the capital law came at the command of the new Stuart King and was replaced by a cart-and-whipping act which in turn elicited the more dramatic of the Quaker demonstrations, such as public nakedness, which became more frequent in the period after capital punishment had been abandoned.

The horrible end of Quaker heresies, the ministry contended, was "to lead men into a pit of darkness, under a pretence of the light, and annihilate all the sensible objects of our holy religion under a pretence of advancing the spiritual; so that we must have no Bible, no Jesus, no baptism, no eucharist, no ordinances, but what shall be evaporated into dispensations, allegories, and mere mystical notions." This did not, they asserted, humble the creature and exalt God as the Quakers pretended. Rather, the orthodox said, in claiming for themselves an inner light the Quakers were exalting man above "Savior, Scripture, heaven, righteousness and all institutions." [23]

The Quakers too, then, raised the question of baptism, and far more than the Anabaptists they provided the impelling context for the synod that proclaimed the Half-Way Covenant. Their mysticism was more contagious than the Anabaptists' literalism, and the containment of mysticism became crucial. Revelation was completed, and its symmetry had to be asserted so as to expose its fullness and its total adequacy. That fullness necessarily included the Old Testament, which foreshadowed the society of grace and provided its regulations. The channel along which the Holy Spirit traveled was to be defined, and the definition, as has been seen, was tribal. On this level loyalty was instinctive rather than considered, and the outbreak of emotion encouraged by the experimental nature of Quakerism was checked by a reliance on the deep emotional sustenance to be gained from cohesion with a folk that had built a shelter for itself in the institutions of church, state, education, and family.

One crucial difference between the Quaker and the Puritan outlooks, which became clear only in the eighteenth century, but which was at work from the start, was that the Puritans thought of grace and intellectual enlightenment as cooperative but different. They therefore provided for continuity through preaching and education. The Quakers saw them as essentially the same. Therefore, in treating man as the receiver and transmitter of an oracular message available to all who would seek it, they made no major public provisions during their first one hundred years for other forms of intellectual training. Quaker schools were a later development.

Placing the emphasis where they did, the Quakers in an unopposing world prospered swiftly because there was no let to their thriving in the affairs of men, once they had attained the state of enlightenment. This itself was not to be submitted to intellectual analysis or directed toward institutional consequences. The discipline of the meeting, concerned only with reinforcing the oracular, released its members to focus sharply on success in the world. "Are Friends careful to live within the bounds of their circumstances, and to avoid launching into trade or business beyond their ability to manage?" asked the book of discipline adopted in Pennsylvania and New Jersey in 1719. And Frederick Tolles, examining that culture, concludes, "If a Friend were so imprudent as to find himself forced into bankruptcy, he stood in danger of disownment by the meeting." [24]

The Puritans' reliance upon election according to a closed revelation, upon the spiritual importance of intellectual activity and the right conferred by spiritual superiority over others in this world resulted in their bending all the institutions that human ingenuity had established to the culture's aims, rather than isolating the essential life of the elect to a discipline exerted in response to a world beyond their ultimate control. The identity of the Jews was tribal, but its outward manifestation was political; they constituted a total state. Such a comprehensive perception of culture, if it succeeded, as Puritanism did succeed, made its consequences felt beyond time and beyond the numbers of those who consciously assented to its explicit doctrines.

Such a comprehensive perception of culture also carried with it an awesome impersonality when the outsider was encountered. Because the culture was total, it accounted for the way in which emotion and idea were both to be put to public use, and in so doing it relied on the psychological inculcation of its pattern far more than on enforced submission to it. When that culture confronted the unchosen—not those who were reprobate but those who, unlike the culture's needed reprobates, could not perceive their condition in the culture's vocabulary—then it could react with a cold violence that in the view of the generality of mankind was scarcely human. Anne Hutchinson was tried for her opinions and was heard, if not heard out, but in the following decades Gortonists, Anabaptists, and Quakers were denied the basic dignity of being men with feelings as well as principles, who put their persons at hazard for their beliefs. Their professions were silenced by shouting down and insult in the court and by roll of drum at the whipping post and scaffold. They were publicly condemned not for the inner values that had placed them in jeopardy but for crimes against the state, and the contemptuousness of their social pretension was noted. Their offense was an offense against the discipline of the state and the ritual observances of community life, and it was granted no personality of its own. For this reason, Kai

Erikson notes in his study of deviancy in early Massachusetts, "perhaps the most terrifying thing about punishment in Massachusetts Bay, after all, was not its fierceness but its cold righteousness." [25] In other parts of the contemporary world, punishment was equally or more severe, but in Massachusetts it was administered with a unique impersonal certainty that lent it an overtone of inhumanity not found in the punishment of feeling men by feeling men.

In the abstract, an ability to concentrate on the spiritual issue when confronting human suffering was a virtue. Samuel Clarke in England provided examplary lives of good Christians in popular collections that, his admirers testified, served as "clouds of witnesses" to the true way of life. In praising James Andreas of Germany, he says that in 1550 Andreas "hearing of a Jew that for theft was hanged by the heels with his head downward in a village hard by, having not seen that kind of punishment, he went to the place, where he found him hanging between two dogs, that were always snatching at him, tearing and eating his flesh: the poor wretch repeated in Hebrew some verses of the Psalms, wherein he cried to God for mercy; whereupon Andreas went nearer to him, and instructed him in the principles of the Christian religion, about Christ and the Messiah, &c. and exhorted him to believe in Him; and it pleased God so to bless his exhortation to him, that the dogs gave over tearing of his flesh, and the poor Jew desired him to procure that he might be taken down, and baptized, and hung by the neck for the quicker dispatch, which was done accordingly." [26] The tearing of flesh that accompanies Andreas's preaching is in support of it; suffering is impersonalized for higher ends. The story is told as isolated example, but the perception of reality on which it is based came to structure an entire culture in New England and to be applied to whole groups of people rather than single individuals. Those on the spiritual side of the gap between grace and nature recognized no inherent rights in mere creation and were awesomely capable of treating human nature as they treated field and forest, as something wholly malleable with no intrinsic dignity.

The Mohegan allies had sensed this when they cried, "Mach it, mach it," at the Pequot slaughter and sought to contain the genocidal fury of the Puritan army. Roger Williams observed this attitude and ineffectively protested against it, offering Christ as an example of the persecuted. The Quakers, in reaction to this perception, exalted the dignity of common humanity, but for the Puritans this meant nothing other than the blasphemy of exalting the creature above his Maker.

The Puritan extension of righteousness from a personal to a cultural scope was to continue to condone the violence unto extermination in future Indian conflicts and was to add its dimension of impersonality to the history of race relations within America and to foreign policy when the foreigners were ethnically outsiders as well. Puritanism was not particularly violent in comparison with other cultures, but it clothed that lamentably common human resort with a doctrine of the rights of the wiser which made it acceptable to the learned as well as the unlearned. Other cultures exert acts of force against those who differ, but the Puritan legacy gives such acts a distinctive spirituality whereby the victimizer sees himself acting in a drama of beliefs rather than of flesh and sees the victim bleed bad opinions rather than blood.

On September 9, 1661, the restored Stuart King issued the missive that released all Quakers from capital charges, and a jubilant Quaker community promptly raised £300 for the chartering of a ship to convey the missive to Massachusetts in haste. That colony was now to face the meaning of its relationship to a royal England. In its response to the commercial opportunities provided by the impediment to trading ships from the ports of England during the Civil War, and to favorable tax legislation in the Interregnum, it had already made a vigorous entry into the Atlantic world, and the forces of society thus released were to become more important at the Restoration. In England, following Charles the Second's accession, conflicting economic interests soon produced a compromise between aristocracy and middle class for the better exploitation of the resources of an expanding society, and a similar cooperation between the Puritan autocracy and the Massachusetts merchants was already in the making in the colony.

Nathaniel Mather, son of Richard and brother of Increase, wrote to his family from London in the early 1650s, " 'Tis a notion of mighty great and high respect to have been a New English man, 'tis enough to gain a man very much respect yea almost any preferment." After discussing other matters in his letter he returned to this marvelous theme. " 'Tis incredible what an advantage to preferment it is to have been a New English man." [27] Nathaniel Mather was but one of many New Englanders who had returned after the defeat of Charles's army by the Scots in 1640, and who were enjoying preferments: they included Samuel Desborough, who was made Keeper of the Great Seal of Scotland, Hugh Peter, who became Cromwell's chaplain, Edward Hopkins, who took a seat in Parliament and was made Warden of the Fleet and Commissioner for the Navy and Admiralty, and George Downing, one of the nine original graduates from Harvard, who became Scoutmaster General for the English army in Scotland.[28] From the latter part of 1640 to his day in 1764, as Thomas Hutchinson wrote, "More persons have removed out of New-England to other parts of the world than have come from other parts to it." [29] A native stock came to suffice, but a native stock with familial as well as political and commercial alliances in Great Britain.

After the Restoration, the advantage to preferment frequently worked the other way, English experience providing a warm reception in Massachusetts. Increase Mather, after graduating from Harvard, joined his brother Samuel in Dublin. They had last met seven years earlier and recognized one another only after Increase produced letters of identity. He earned his M.A. at Trinity, Dublin, and after declining a fellowship there went on to a series of well-supported pulpits in England and the Channel Islands, finally returning to Boston in September 1661 after Restoration politics made his living in England insecure. Now, he found, an English background was the road to advancement: "Presently upon my return to New England being by reason of my 4 years absence become like a stranger, and people are apt to run after strangers though they have little in them of real worth, many overtures of settlement were presented to me. . . . I had invitations from no less than 12 places." [30] He accepted the offer of the Second Church of Boston. The saints of Massachusetts as well as the traders were anxious to explore their relationship to the wider English community.

But this exploration was conducted cautiously. What consequences did Charles's accession have for their church liberties and for the charter under which the magistrates enforced only that church way? The synod called in 1661 had in 1662 affirmed the Half-Way Covenant as a symbol of the fact that tribalism had carried Massachusetts through the turbulent period of the Interregnum when all manner of opinions were permitted in England. Not all the orthodox were happy with the pronouncement, but those who were most audibly discontented were those who believed that the baptism procedure should have been maintained in its original straitness, not made wider. Few within the church argued that it should have been made broader. A considerable body of minority opinion believed that the way to face the new monarchy was to stand united on original principles rather than to compromise. In effect, they saw no reason for alignment with the corruptions that were now in the ascendancy in England, and they drew their strength principally from those whose foreseeable future was tied to the land. Resistance to innovation in church and state developed principally among those who were being deeply and adversely affected by the growing dominance of the trader and the increasing governmental disregard of price regulation. Tribalism also meant first families, and such a consequence had less appeal in the relative democracy of the rural villages than it did in the seaports. Sumptuary laws continued to be passed as lip service to the rural people's sense of propriety, but were laxly administered under the realities of the stimulus to trade that luxuries provided and the returned sense of being part of the social community of Great Britain. Indeed, as the century wore on, trials resulting from the sumptuary laws in the Connecticut River Valley were more frequently trials of officials for failing to execute the laws than trials of offenders against the laws. [31] The advancement of Massachusetts as a commercial commonwealth and the political and ecclesiastical compromises that were its inevitable accompaniment raised a considerable undertow in those men whose economic destiny was tied to the land and whose distinction resided in their church membership rather than in their being carried to wealth and prominence by the new wave. They expressed their discontents most frequently by retarding attempts to accommodate the church to a changing social reality.

Trade and toleration were profitable partners, as the Dutch had shown and as the Quakers were beginning to show. Arguing on behalf of the Quakers' refusal to swear oaths in any civil or commercial matter, that movement's great apologist, Robert Barclay, pointed to the United Netherlands, where, "because of the great number of merchants more than in any other place, there is more frequent occasion" for entering upon oath, and yet the Dutch permitted those who wished to decline the formality, with the result of "great advantage to trade, and so to the commonwealth." [32] With the success of the masterless man who was as good as his word, the form of oath-taking was no longer necessary, although credit continued to be the blood of English commerce even after 1650, when, as the contemporary economist William Potter observed, Holland too had acquired sufficient specie to make brass or copper money the medium of exchange, as it was in Spain.

The David Brown who contributed commendatory verses to Potter's influential *Key to Wealth,* published in London in 1650, asked:

> What doth the Practice of Physick availe,
>   Though Doctors do in knowledge much exceede,
> If Persons sick, for want of means should faile
>   Bread to obtain, in their extreamest neede?

> So Logick, Grammer and Philosophy,
>   Arithmetick, and Rhetorick also;
> How fruitless, if such Learning never be
>   applyed, as meanes some further good to shew?

In his introductory remarks Potter went on to explain that "though heavenly things should beyond all proportion, be preferred before earthly, yet where they are both consistent, neither of them ought to be at all neglected; for as the earth since the fall, requires much skill and diligence to be improved, to the best advantage for outward subsistence, so until matters be ordered in such sort, as all men that are willing to take pains in an honest calling, may be put into a capacity of enjoying a livelihood thereby; no man can be excused, who (knowing any means tending thereunto) doth neglect either to discover the same, or endeavor the effecting thereof." [33]

Orthodox Massachusetts merchants had found heavenly and earthly things consistent, but not without some difficulty. Robert Keayne, Boston's richest merchant in 1639, had been called to answer to the Court for charging extortionate prices and had been made the subject of John Cotton's sermon in the church to which he belonged, a sermon in which Cotton admonished him from a social view that still saw the validity of the medieval concept of the fair price. But Cotton also endorsed a fervor the bounds of which Keayne had temporarily overstepped: "Though you may have a godly man busy in his calling from sun rising to sun setting, and may by Gods providence fill both his hand and head with business, yet a living Christian when he lives a most busy life in this world, yet he lives not a worldly life." [34] The admonished Keayne kept a more modest eye on prices until such time as the new mercantilist practice caused the older concept of fair price to lose its social force. In his advanced age Keayne valued his estate at £4000 and anticipated the question, "How could I get such an estate with a good conscience or without oppression in my calling, seeing it is known to some that I had no portion from my parents or friends to begin the world withal?" He answered by saying that his accomplishment came over a period of forty to fifty years through the "favor of God," whereby "though I had very little at first to begin with, yet I had good credit and good esteem and respect in the place where I lived so that I did ever drive a great trade not only since I came hither but especially in England." He reminded the hypothetical critic of his wealth that to accumulate £4000 in forty or fifty years averaged out to an increment of only £100 a year, and that this was no great matter for "any industrious and provident man." [35]

John Hull, who succeeded and exceeded Keayne as Boston's richest trader, had his way to wealth paved when the General Court ordered a mint to be set up in 1652 because the counterfeit coin that had flowed in to supply the want of specie had effected a stoppage of trade. All persons were given liberty to bring bullion, plate, and Spanish pieces to the mint to have them converted to Massachusetts coins, and it was forbidden to carry any of the minted coins out of the jurisdiction. From his commission as mint-master, Hull raised a fortune. His demonstration of the consistency of heavenly and earthly things is so complete that it arrives at self-caricature. No stop in either thought or expression separates the two, for example, when Hull writes an English business correspondent: "It were better if you felt me at liberty at least sometimes but indeed it is hard to foresee what will be & therefore it is best willing to submit to the great governing hand of ye great Governor of all the greater and lesser revolutions that we poor sons of men are involved in by ye invoice you see ye whole amounteth to £405:16:3." [36]

A significant number of those driving trade were, however, without church membership and therefore without the franchise, and their pressure was consistently felt. Since the majority of freemen were still in agriculture, these merchants could not hope for elective civil office even if they were extended civil rights, and since ecclesiastical supervision tended to be in lag of civil supervision in its retention of a conservative view of trade, it is a fair presumption that exclusion did not rankle so much in the sphere of actual advantages they might have enjoyed as in that of the social recognition they were denied. So long as they were permitted to drive their trade, as they were, they prudently improved upon these conditions and bided the day when they could more fully assert themselves. The tavern and the counting house, essential centers for trade, also became their social centers. During the Interregnum they had developed the commercial pattern that was to dominate New England economic life until the American Revolution, and this could not but pull other patterns into alignment with it. They pursued the ideal of the merchant-gentleman and were alert to every opportunity to advance it through the support of liberalizing tendencies within church and state and particularly through the improvement of their contacts in the Atlantic community and in the alliance of traders and nobility in Restoration England. Members of the autocracy were also vulnerable to the attractions of membership in a wider world, as Increase Mather reveals; and, in addition to the surface alliance that existed between city and country among the orthodox in opposition to those outside the church, there came into being a subsurface sharing of values between the sophisticated orthodox and the sophisticated residents in opposition to the distrustful intransigence of the more rural. The return of royalty raised questions about the future of charter government in Massachusetts and its presumption of duplicating all necessary laws on its own initiative rather than accepting them from England. The orthodox aggressively banded together in defense of the established way, but the band was not sealed. Conflicting economic interests had flawed it.

The hairline thread in the band was observable well before the Restoration and was correctly identified with trade. In his almanac for the year 1647, Samuel Danforth offered these verses:

> [May]
> White Coates! whom choose you! whom you list:
> Some Ana-tolleratorist:
> Wolves, lambs, hens, foxes to agree
> By setting all opinion-free:
> If Blew-coates doe not this prevent,
> Hobgoblins will be insolent.

The white coats are the party for toleration, and the blue coats, with whom Danforth clearly agrees, the party for maintenance of the prevailing order in anticipation of anarchy should their opponents prevail. May is the annual election month. He then moves on:

> [June]
> Who dig'd this spring of Gardens here,

> Whose mudded streames at last run cleare?
> But why should we such water drink?
> Give loosers what they list to think,
> Yet know, one God, one Faith profest
> To be New-Englands interest.

The good old way of one God and faith is presented in a basic rural image of improvement of the land. The blue coats are associated with it in June, a month of planting, even as the white coats find their vocational association in the next month:

> [July]
> The wooden Birds are now in sight,
> Whose voices roare, whose wings are white,
> Whose mawes are fill'd with hose and shooes,
> With wine, cloth, sugar, salt, and newes,
> When they have eas'd their stomacks here
> Then cry, farewell until next yeare.[37]

With the Atlantic in its summer calm the trading ships arrive, their whiteness a reflection in the poet's mind of the source of the tolerating principles of the white coats. Fifteen years later one could not so readily cry farewell for a year; trading was a constant feature of daily life. The hairline thread of economic division was spreading and bringing its civil consequences with it.

When Charles II dispatched his agent to look into the state of his American colonies in 1664, he charged him to insinuate himself into the good opinion of the principal persons there and to make a full observation "of the humor and interest both of those in government and those of the best quality out of government." He cautioned him not to lead any to believe that the crown desired to change their form of religion, but added "our only exception being denial of liberty of conscience." [38] He acknowledged that although he would like all his subjects to be of one faith, it was unlikely that people who had left England for religious opinion would be willing now to come under the established church. In these early explorations Charles hoped that his commissioners could accomplish three things: prepare the people for a royal governor by encouraging them to nominate a slate from which he would be chosen; bring their militia under the command of royal officers, a militia of Englishmen without such commanders being contrary to the Massachusetts charter, which was, after all, issued to a corporation of merchant adventurers; and see that liberty of conscience was assured. For nearly twenty years further the Massachusetts government successfully evaded all three issues. Even though some may have seen the shadow of things to come, it was clear to most that the government would be abandoned by the people should it yield the degree of autonomy it had and surrender magisterial enforcement of the Congregational Church way. Some gesture could be made, however, toward drawing the wealthier into a union with the autocracy, and toward that end in August 1664 the franchise was extended to those over the age of twenty-four who could get a ministerial certificate of orthodoxy in religion and unviciousness of life, and who were freeholders of estates ratable at ten shillings. Not three in one hundred could qualify, opponents maintained, but the gesture was significant. There was some hope of drawing traders into an alliance with the Massachusetts government because the new Navigation Acts passed in 1660, 1662, and 1663 were defining a difference between New England's and England's commercial interests.

Such differences were pointed up in 1668 by Sir Josiah Child, head of the powerful East India Company, who argued in his *A New Discourse of Trade* that "the frugality, industry, and temperance of New England are unexcelled, but they are lacking in that paramount duty of every good man to regard the welfare of his native country as the first consideration." This touched sinner as well as saint. Child went on to explain that, unlike the exports of other colonies, New England's competed: "New England inhabitants participate in the Newfoundland fisheries, to the prejudice of the inhabitants of old England. They make returns to England in the commodities of the more valuable sugar and tobacco plantations, by sale to the latter of food commodities, but these would otherwise be purchased from England. This prejudices the rise of land values in England." He then asserted that under their charters New Englanders evaded the Navigation Acts and surreptitiously transported Southern and West Indian goods directly to European markets without first landing them in England for payment of duty, thereby depriving the King of revenue, the English seamen of employment, and the English merchants of markets. Child saw the greatest danger in New England's aptness for building ships and breeding seamen. Moreover, whereas the Southern plantations employed slaves, so that every Englishman in them made work for ten Englishmen at home, New England employed only Englishmen and was therefore draining the homeland rather than making possible an increase in population, as did other colonies. Child's indictment had one major qualification. In direct trade with New England the homeland was a gainer: "We export to them ten times as much as we import from them," and therefore any reformation of the New England government by the crown would require "great circumspection and tenderness." [39] Such influential views gaining force in England could not help promoting a degree of alliance among New England traders, regardless of their church allegiance, and qualify to some extent the eagerness of merchants outside the civil establishment to seek amelioration of their social condition from royal governance.

John Josselyn, who in 1663 began a visit of more than eight years to New England, reported that he found "the great masters, as also some of their merchants are damnable rich: generally all of their judgment, inexplicably covetous and proud, they receive your gifts but as an homage or tribute due their transcendency, which is a fault their clergy are also guilty of." In short, he perceived a unity of style that was more important for him than whatever differences in attitude may have existed between the prosperous saints and sinners of the ports. "No trading for a stranger with them," Josselyn complained, "but with a Grecian faith, which is not to part with your ware without ready money"; that is to say, credit was only for those who were established. He found them to be "great syndics, or censors, or controllers of other men's manners, and savagely factious among themselves," [40] but the nature of the factiousness, he leads his reader to believe, stems from business and social competition rather than civil or ecclesiastical affairs.

Josselyn also reported on conditions that served to widen the rift between the merchant, on one hand, and both fisherman and farmer on the other. Maine fishermen, he observed, engage in great bouts of drinking between voyages, a drunkenness that is financed, if not downright encouraged, by the merchant. "When the day of payment comes, they may justly complain of their costly sin of drunkenness, for their shares will do no more than pay the reckoning; if they save a kental [112-pound weight of fish] or two to buy shoes and stockings, shirts and waistcoats with, 'tis well, other-ways they must enter into the merchant's books for such things as they stand in need of, becoming thereby the merchant's slaves, and when it riseth to a big sum are constrained to mortgage their plantation if they have any, the merchant when the time is expired is sure to seize upon their stock of cattle, turning them out of house and home, poor creatures, to look out for a new habitation in some remote place where they begin the world again. The lavish planters have the same fate, partaking with them in the like bad husbandry, of these the merchant buys beef, pork, pease, wheat and Indian corn, and sells it again many times to the fishermen." [41]

In the first decade of the Restoration, then, the culture revealed lines of division that crossed one another, some running between economic points of difference and others running between ecclesiastical points of difference. Toleration might mean good trade, but the good trader, while he was willing to tolerate religious differences, was quick to exploit economic weakness. The old orthodoxy might mean cold punitive action against the outsider, but it also could mean an attachment to a village round that was in its daily exercise cooperative and democratic. Land was worked in great part through public harvesting, the sharing of beasts of burden, and the communal herding of farmyard animals. The great strength of the culture was that it could contain these forces. The old controlling poles of spirit and law were still operative, although the field between was no longer vibrating to a strictly theological terminology. The transformation was gradual, not radical, one that the culture underwent as a whole rather than one that changed its essential nature. The movement was one of an entire society which, at the expense of whatever idealistic energies and dreadful practices, had cohered.

CHAPTER SEVEN

Saint Pompion

Reaction to royal supremacy—Puritan drama—Indian relations—
King Philip's War and racism

From the sending of the first investigators in 1664 to the dispatch of
Edward Randolph in 1676, the royal government accomplished little
of direct effect in New England. The colonists had improved the
autonomous base of their society. By now it was both self-assured
enough to meet daily realities with procedures developed in practice,
and flexible enough to qualify, supplement, or oppose the demands
placed on it internally without alienating any essential element.
During the first fifteen years of his reign, Charles II addressed
himself principally to the role England would play in European
politics, and from this point of view New England was a tangible but
far from crucial part of the imperial scheme. Indirectly, however,
New England felt the effect of the new government and recognized
that the day of reckoning was not infinitely postponable. The fact
that they were part of an empire and yet did not have a resident class
of noblemen or royal officers acted upon the consciousness of the
settlers to promote an ambiguous sense of provincialism. On one
hand, the New Englanders, in the period when they successfully
evaded royal domination, were sensible of the repressive measures
taken against their dissenting allies in England and defensively
asserted their sense of having not a dependent culture but a different
one. The first days of colonizing were seen as the golden age of a
chosen people, and leaders in church and state increasingly elabo-

rated this rhetoric to promote a unified resistance to English control. On the other hand, political and commercial realities indicated that New England's privileged position stemmed ultimately not from its being in a mainstream that would carry it into a confident future, but from its being a backwater of history that would be joined to the mainstream as soon as more pressing matters had been settled. As a consequence of this ambiguous position, the New Englanders asserted the validity of their all-but-independent position and played greatly on the tribal sentiment. In so doing they also had to celebrate the triumph of the fathers in the wilderness and emphasize the necessity of hewing to the fathers' line. Even while asserting their own values, they were saying implicitly that these were anachronistic. The first stage of provincialism, that before the actual arrival of royal officers, was thus one of defending an enclave in the face of the wider world.

The signs from England were plentiful and ominous. In 1661 the Corporation Act prohibited nonconformists from serving their country in even the lowest offices of trust, and in the following year the Act of Uniformity silenced the nonconformist ministers throughout England and deprived them of their maintenance. The Conventicle Acts of 1663 and 1670 forbade all persons to go to any separate meetings for religious worship where more than five beside the members of one family were present, and specified punishment by seizure of goods as well as imprisonment. The acts could be executed by warrant from a justice of the peace without a trial by jury. Then, in 1665, the Oxford Act banished all nonconformist ministers to five miles outside any corporation that sent members to Parliament.[1]

Charles, in telling his commissioners to America in 1664 that he wanted to promote liberty of conscience there, was sincere. He would himself have been content to see the same situation prevail in England, but his Parliament was in full cry for revenge on measures its predecessors in the Interregnum had visited upon Royalists and conformists, and just as his father had been dependent on a dissenting Parliament, so was he on a conforming one. Not until 1672, when he decided to take the risk of war with a Protestant nation, the Netherlands, could he convince his legislature that it should support an Act of Indulgence toward nonconformists. Without this gesture toward them, the Dutch enterprise would fail for lack of English unity, though in point of fact, the Dutch war failed anyway. Parliament was unhappy with the indulgence, and the nonconformists were uneasy at a Protestant war. With its failure in 1673 the repressive measures returned with a vengeance, so that, from 1673 to the end of Charles's reign in 1685, dissenters underwent the severest period of persecution they had yet experienced.

Each ship that arrived in New England during this period carried letters from the brethren at home describing their desperate condition and, in the main, indicating that the correspondents believed New England to be blessed in being ignored. "Some think New England to be rich, & have no need," [2] ran the burden of one letter to Increase Mather, for example. The political stance taken by the nonconformists in their adversity was one with which the New England leadership could only sympathize, and yet one with which it could only be uneasy. In petitioning Parliament in 1675 for ease from the Act of Uniformity, the nonconformist ministers of London talked about the oath of subscription required of them, wherein they were to swear that they would not "endeavor any change or alteration of government, either in church and state." [3] They argued, "If every free subject hath fundamental liberty to choose knights and burgesses, and accordingly to inform them of their grievances, and petition them for redress, and in them, as their representatives, do consent to the alteration of government and laws (if there be any) as profitable to the nation. How can such an oath be imposed on him, that he will not endeavor any alteration, as this is?" [4] Thus far, New Englanders could agree heartily.

But their brethren went on with the same political realism into an area that implicitly contradicted New England as well as Stuart practice: "The advance of the nation, doth lie in the freedom and flourishing of trade; and uniting the whole body in the common benefit and dependence on the government. The one of these bespeaks an established order, and accommodation; the other bespeaks indulgence, liberty of conscience, or toleration; for while people are in danger about religion, we dare not launch out into trade (say they) but keep our monies, seeing we know not into what straits we shall be driven." [5] The Puritans in the colony were forced by such a stand into their provincialism because they had both to assert the justice of this cry for redress and yet to explain, as they were capable of doing, that such liberty of conscience need not be applied to New England, where the foundation was different. They had to elaborate a New England, therefore, that was apart not only from English politics but from the consequences of principles that dissenters in the homeland held as crucial to their survival. This latter situation bound them to the rationale of the chosen people.

Models abounded in the Old Testament. In 1658, for example, Edward Holyoke dramatized the encounter between King Solomon and Tirzana, a Moabite princess who was one of his queens. What is it you request, "my sweet Tirzana?" Solomon asked, and she told him that she wanted leave for her maids and herself to worship in their own way rather than that of Israel's commonwealth. "Your religion is very cross to man's nature and is urged with great terror and strictness," she complained; "your religion reproves thoughts, words, and most men's actions." [6] Tirzana went on to argue the greater antiquity of her god and the greater toleration practiced in her homeland and told her royal husband, "It is a pitiful thing that man of a noble and free spirit should be so tired with hard injunctions and heavy burdens as with bands, cords, and fetters; and, it may be, that reformation that your noble father endeavored, and yourself have prosecuted, would not and will not be so convenient, as due liberty, which would be a more noble design than rigid reformation." [7]

Solomon was tender but firm in his reply: his Lord forbade nothing but what was evil, "and whereas you talk of strictness, etc., you are to know, man by nature is born a wild ass colt, and there is no taming of corrupt nature, but by a strict course of holy laws, which to a regenerate and godly soul is an easy yoke, and to which he is willingly subject." [8] Far from being of a noble and free spirit, man is of a most ignoble one, prone to all kinds of viciousness. "All the reformation we can possibly attain unto by the careful industry of my royal authority and of our priests and prophets and schools will not come to the purity and exactness that the Lord our God requires." [9]

Tirzana was unconvinced, but fell to crying and "having her handkercher in her hand, with snubs of umphs and imphs" [10] renewed her request. Failing with sentiment as she had failed with reasoning, she resorted to expedience and called upon her brother, wise in the ways of statecraft, to carry this argument to the King. He spoke of the great advancements Solomon had made in natural philosophy and architecture and how this made him an important part of an international community: "All princes of the earth, that come to visit your majesty, and bring their physicians with them, will carry notes and writings home with them that shall stand all ages and people in great stead forever." [11] Consequently Solomon's church policy was also on view, and in this light he should be more flexible. But Solomon, in the short run, remained firm and in so doing provided the readers of Holyoke's drama with inferences so obvious he himself did not have to draw them. Israel's established commonwealth under Solomon was the just spiritual consequence of Israel's wandering in the wilderness steadfast in faith, and whereas others could argue the antiquity of their commonwealths and established religions, Israel could counter with the undeniable precedence of its relationship to the true God, so that once it came to an establishment it was not to be shaken by the compromises that other commonwealths had entered into.

The analogy that Holyoke developed at the close of the Interregnum was consistently advanced after the monarchy was restored. "That which is threatened as a sore judgment to the Jews, is in a great measure fulfilled among us this day," [12] preached Thomas Walley, and the healing of New England's troubles, like the healing of Zion's, consisted in steadfastness to the good old way. In 1675, on the eve, as it were, of serious royal intervention in the affairs of Massachusetts, Benjamin Tompson fixed his countrymen's image of themselves. Attaching them to a steadfastness of manner

developed in colonial isolation, Tompson developed this as the source
of resistance to accommodation with imperial reality. In *New
England's Crisis*, he wrote admiringly of

> The times wherein old Pompion was a saint,
> When men fared hardly yet without complaint.[13]

Faced with social distinctions that were now not so much the
result of innate superiority as of the subtle invasion of English
manners, Tompson played up the plainness of the original settlers, a
democracy in daily outlook that validated the autocracy of the state:

> 'Twas then among the bushes, not the street,
> If one in place did an inferior meet,
> "Good morrow, brother, is there aught you want?"
> "Take freely of me, what I have you han't."
> Plain Tom and Dick would pass as current now,
> As ever since "Your Servant Sir" and bow.[14]

The breach in happiness had been made by trade, because, as
Tompson says of the time he hymns:

> 'Twas ere the Islands sent their presents in,
> Which but to use was counted next to sin.
> 'Twas ere a barge had made so rich a freight
> As chocolate, dust-gold, and bitts of eight.[15]

The men of the time were not merchants but planters who could
slay adversaries with efficacious prayer. In short,

> These golden times (too fortunate to hold)
> Were quickly sin'd away for love of gold.[16]

Conventionally the appeal to a golden age is ambiguous in that,
although it normally offers a measure of one's shortcomings, it does
not provide a dynamic for correcting them. Tompson treated the

problem of the practical lessons a golden age held, not by placing that age in antiquity—even New England's very recent antiquity—whence all since was a declension, but by seeing it as the result of a reform of a previous sinful age. To seek its comforts, therefore, was not a turning back, but rather the continuation of an advance. The present hour was, in his rhetoric, balanced between adherence to true New England principles, which were principles of growth, and reversion to the corruptions of the world:

> New England's hour of passion is at hand;
> No power except divine can it withstand.
> Scarce has her glass of fifty years run out,
> But her old prosperous steeds turn heads about
> Tracking themselves back to their poor beginnings,
> To fear and fare upon their fruits of sinnings.[17]

The emphasis is on tribal loyalty to the fathers, adherence to the land as a daily round that reinforces the best in the culture, and a vision of the future as a continuation of these rather than the future as an accommodation to modern manners. Such accommodation would be a reversion to corruption. In standing firm on the truth of its churches and the love of the fellowship of the saints, New Englanders will be progressing rather than regressing. But the progress, clearly, is not one of advancing into greater and greater benefits: "Many imperfections and omissions and commissions will appear continually through the lusts of corrupted nature," [18] as good King Solomon told his Tirzana. Rather, it is the decidedly pre-modern progress of the maintenance of the best possible state once it has been achieved.

Such a state appears too static, from one point of view, to be more than a hopeless ideal. To be sure, history determined change for New England as it did for the rest of the world. But the ideal affected the nature of the change because it was rooted in the lives of the people rather than attached as an afterthought. A broad expanse of daily reality was sufficiently explicable in Tompson's terms to encourage the acceptance of that kind of identity. The all-encompassing static view was balanced by a dynamic within the society that recognized the appropriateness, indeed the need, for daily drama. "The war in our souls by reason of the darkness of the understanding, and the untractableness of the will and the affections," [19] as Holyoke phrased it, would continue, and sufficient change could be subsumed into the field of this conflict to make the culture flexible rather than wooden. This war clearly, for instance, found its correlatives in Indian conflicts as well as in relations with England. The ideal announced in New England after the Restoration and consolidated in the lull before direct royal intervention was one that, however utopian it may have been in its farthest claims, also had application to the contemporary situation.

The culture that awaited its direct confrontation with royal government was based on real achievements and manifested in vital institutions. In 1642 a Massachusetts law specified a compulsory minimum of education in order to advance full employment, check pauperism, and ensure the means of continued inculcation of religious and civil truths. In a 1648 revision, apprentices too were assured of book-learning, not just craft training. The other orthodox colonies followed suit, so that all New England, with the exception of Rhode Island, was under a system of compulsory education. Harvard grew in strength as the standard of learning in the culture, and after the death of President Charles Chauncy in 1672 the college was managed by its own graduates rather than by those who had been educated in England. In 1638 a press was established at Cambridge, and in 1674 another was set up in Boston. By far the greater number of works issued by the Cambridge press were religious books, but there were also almanacs, poetry, history, and biography. Studying the literary output of the period, Thomas Goddard Wright concluded: "The early New England colonists wrote more than they would have written had they remained in England, and the quality of their work was not lowered by their removal, or by any lack of opportunities for culture in the new home." [20] Explicit press censorship did not begin until the arrival of a royal governor.

After the sermon, didactic verse was the favorite form of literary expression. Almost every learned man practiced the statement of his thoughts in rhyme and meter, and most did so privately, as they kept their diaries, in aid of their self-examination. The mechanics of poetry assisted them to tame their meditations and channel them into a measure that would reflect their control of them, their acceptance of God's dispensation toward them, and their perception of it as ordered. The written word, which had begun the revolution in consciousness that gave birth to their culture, was still the central way of apprehending reality. As has been seen with regard to elegies, words themselves exerted a near-magical power. To control them was to control the essence of what they designated.

Roger Williams noted of the Indians: "They abhor to mention the dead by name: and therefore if any bear the name of the dead, he changeth his name; and if any stranger accidentally name him, he is checked; and if any wilfully name him he is fined: and amongst states, the naming of their dead sachems is one ground of their wars." [21] The Puritan culture was exactly opposite in practice, and yet for reasons curiously similar to the Indians'. Puritans too saw the name of the dead as significantly attached to the essential reality the dead represented, but whereas the Indians developed this connection into a dangerous invitation to death itself to intervene among the living should the name be called, the Puritans, in avoidance of ritual parting from the dead and ritual remembrance of them in prayer, which they regarded as superstition, comforted themselves with an almost ritual elaboration of the names of the dead in elegy, anagram, and pun so as to retain mnemonically the meaning the departed persons held for the living. They could, as it were, let go life more readily than they could the word that contained life's meaning, whereas their Indian neighbors, having taken a religious farewell of their dead, regarded further verbal communication with them as commerce with death itself. Unlike the Puritans, the Indians released their emotions on religious occasions. The Puritan view placed a burden on the verbal disproportionate to that placed on it by other cultures, European as well as primitive, and, as a consequence, excluded almost all ends other than the didactic.

By far the most popular Puritan poem of the century in New

England was Michael Wigglesworth's "The Day of Doom" (1660), which in dramatizing judgment day provided a vivid, memorizable account of basic predestinarian theology. Kenneth B. Murdock estimated that a copy of it "was sold for one out of every twenty persons in New England." [22] The poem's contemporary appeal consists in its convincing presentation of the culture's deepest view of the nature of daily existence. There is scarcely a word in the poem about daily realities, but the persistent tension dramatized by Wigglesworth is that between the absolute and statically fixed divine dispensation and the constant human struggle that this permits and encourages, so that the former's rigidity promotes a dynamic life rather than denying it, while the latter's volatility, rather than dissipating itself into meaninglessness, is constrained to a pattern. Wigglesworth's rare imagination confronted theological issues and vivified them rather than evading the apparently harsher consequences of predestinarianism for the sake of a smoother story. As a result, he at times was forced into what to the modern eye is ludicrous, as, for instance, when he represents the voices of infants and unborn babes pleading that they never lived to show their dispositions and therefore do not deserve damnation, and does it so convincingly that—in defense of doctrine and yet in recognition of the eloquence of the plea—he can arrive only at the nearly absurd solution of consigning them to the easiest room in hell. But what shows as weakness in this notorious passage is the result of creative insight that over the whole poem gives strength: the perception of doctrine as vital, though fixed, and the perception of life as dramatic, though predestined. "The Day of Doom" is a vivid testimony of the New England culture's capacity to coopt conflict.

In its confident manipulation of nature as the unresisting means of the gracious on this earth, Puritanism encouraged a level of scientific experimentation that was closed, to be sure, on the highest level of speculation, but that was operationally strengthened by the practical and methodical bent of the culture. In the Oxford that had been vandalized by the Puritans in Cromwell's day, as Royalists lamented, those same Puritans founded the Royal Society, and at the Restoration the royalist imagination parodied science as a badge of nonconformist ugliness, much as nonconformists used the theater as a sign of conforming society's corruption. A high moment in the restoration of Oxford to what the church considered its fit position came in 1669 when Archbishop Sheldon's Theater was opened. An observer wrote of the proceedings: "Dr. South (as University Orator) made a long oration; the first part of which consisted of satirical invectives against Cromwell, fanatics, the Royal Society, and new philosophy. The next of encomiastics; in praise of the Archbishop, the theater, the Vicechancellor, the architect and the painter." [23]

The Puritans accepted the associations. They consistently opposed the theater on every ground—moral, spiritual, and social. In response to the contention that man must have his pleasures, William Prynne, who wrote the definitive attack on the theater, provided the Puritans' answer: "Though men are deprived of stage-plays, of all other unlawful pleasures whatsoever; yet they have choice enough of sundry lawful recreations, and earthly solaces with which to exhilarate their minds; and senses: They have the several prospects of the sun, the moon, the planets, the stars, the water, the earth, with all the infinite variety of creatures, of fishes, birds, fowls, beasts, creeping things, trees, herbs, plants, roots, stones, and metals that are in them." [24] On a more domestic level, Prynne went on, they have "the pleasures that orchards, rivers, gardens, friends, kindred, wives, children, possessions, wealth, and all other external blessings God hath bestowed upon them." [25] And to cap all, there is abundance of honest and healthful recreations, such "as walking, riding, fishing, fowling, hunting, ringing, leaping, vaulting, wrestling, running, shooting, singing of psalms and pious ditties; playing upon musical instruments, sating of the bar, tossing the pike, riding of the great horse (an exercise fit for men of quality) running at the ring, with a world of such like laudable, cheap, and harmless exercises." [26]

Scientific observation of natural facts, technical improvement of the environment, and a variety of physical exercises all were encouraged by a culture that distrusted the visual artifacts of man and theatrical display as, respectively, idolatry and a celebration of natural corruption. The mind could be improved, material comforts assured, and the body strengthened without opposing the divine will but in keeping with its intention.

Opposition to the theater was not opposition to drama but rather to the falsification to the point of obscenity of what was to be acted out by each man in his own person rather than by a class of men in assumed roles. Drama, indeed, as Wigglesworth and Tompson among many others demonstrate, was of the essence of life. The center of the drama was man's soul, wherein God and Satan waged their battle, and this was externalized to a battle between the chosen people and Satan's minions. The latter were not customarily represented by the sinners within society, because they had been incorporated into it for economic purposes. As a result the Puritan imagination was always menacingly prone to seek actors who would personify Satan in opposition to it. In the first fifty years some isolated individuals offered themselves in this capacity. So, for instance, in the winter of 1671–1672 the reverend Samuel Willard was confronted by Elizabeth Knapp of Groton, who told him "that the devil had sometimes appeared to her; that the occasion of it was her discontent, that her condition displeased her, her labor was burdensome to her. She was neither content to be at home nor abroad, & had oftentime strong persuasions to practice in witchcraft, and had often wished the devil would come to her at such & such times, & resolved that if he would, she would give herself up to him soul & body; but (though he had oft times appeared to her, yet) at such times he had not discovered himself, & therefore she had been preserved from such a thing." [27] Elizabeth Knapp, bored to derangement with the round of life in Groton, was nevertheless a sound enough member of the culture to express herself in terms of the drama and to offer to play a needed role in it. Given sufficient ministerial attention, she responded to the presence of God on the stage and became possessed by Satan, who spoke from within her but in a voice not hers, calling Willard "a great black rogue." When Willard replied, "Satan, thou art a liar & deceiver, & God will vindicate His own truth one day," the arch-hypocrite changed tone and said, "I am not Satan, I am a pretty black boy, this is my pretty girl." [28] The drama had become more vivid when Elizabeth Knapp's sexual fantasies entered into it more directly, but finally Willard had the victory with no bloodshed. Recruits for the role Elizabeth Knapp played were to remain scarce within the culture for nearly twenty years more.

Such recruits were not in the short run needed, because in 1675 it became increasingly clear that the Indians, who as pagans were always to be considered as men given over to the devil yet potentially redeemable, waged war. The Puritans did not simplistically reduce the hostility of the tribes that rallied around Metacomet, King Philip, to simple satanic influence; they well knew the political and economic causes of the conflict. But King Philip's War did now convince them, in the face of considerable evidence to the contrary gathered during the war as well as before it, that the Indians were, on the whole, to be regarded in the mass as satanic. Such a stance toward them, especially in view of their negative economic significance, was a more expediential policy than that of the making of distinctions, which had been halfheartedly followed thus far.

Low down but nevertheless present on almost every list of reasons for colonizing New England was the conversion of the Indians or, at least, the bringing to them of the clear sunshine of the Gospel. But, added to the difficulty presented by the extreme cultural differences of the Indians and the many things the Puritans had to accomplish for their own survival, was the structural resistance of Congregationalism. An ecclesiastical polity that held a man was not a minister except when ordained by a congregation of believers did not develop a corps of ordained evangelists to pursue the task of conversion. Nor, when it did find some teachers for the Indians, could it well visualize how to accomplish a beginning without accomplishing the whole: which is to say, it relied so heavily on the presence of a nucleus of believers, a gathered congregation, on which to begin the work, that it possessed but a poor technique for addressing a group in total uncultivation. In opposition to hierarchical churches that had developed branches for propaganda and techniques to accomplish it, Puritanism was singularly unfitted for evangelizing those outside the forms of European society.

Cotton Mather later admitted that Roman Catholics on the American continent exceeded the Puritans in their missionary work, but he complained that they taught the Indians nonsense and baptized all who were willing, without examining into their suitability, thereby revealing the obstacle that Puritan insistence upon sainthood and hence upon intellectual preparation was always to present to efforts at conversion. Mather pointed to the poverty of the New England Indians as a sign that New England efforts, if less successful, were at least more sincere: "No such estates are to be expected among them, as have been the baits which the pretended converters in other countries have snapped at." [29] He saw it as a sign of "popish avarice that their missionaries are very rarely employed but where beaver and silver and vast riches are to be thereby gained; their ministry is but a sort of engine to enrich Europeans with the treasures of the Indies." [30] There is some point to this, but it also became clear that, in spite of the undoubted sincerity of Puritan teachers of the Indians, the society itself was not strongly supportive of their efforts once it was obvious, as it was before 1640, that the beaver trade was dead. Indeed, the principal financial and moral support for Puritan missionary efforts came from Great Britain, where the Indians could more readily figure in the Protestant imagination in an ideal capacity, as brands to be snatched from the burning.

The Roman Catholic religion, with its confidence in the church as a treasury of grace, pursued individual conversion prior to or without a central regard for acculturating the Indians to European civilization. But the Puritan view very early demonstrated to its holders the necessity of civilizing before converting. Puritan missionaries, therefore, in relative innocence of the profundity of cultural patterns, took on the task of settling the Indians into European patterns in their everyday life as a necessary prelude to saving their souls. The Indians were to wear European dress, till the soil, and organize themselves into little commonwealths whence a congregation could finally be gathered. In pursuit of this program Indian children were to be apprenticed to the colonists to learn both a craft and civilized behavior, and the more promising were to be schooled and sent to

Harvard, after which they could serve as teachers to their people. The strongest gesture made to the durability of Indian culture was linguistic: Puritan teachers taught in the Indian tongue, translated the Bible and devotional aids into it, and printed such Indian-language books at the press in Cambridge.

The history of these efforts is, in the main, a history of a double defeat: the failure of Puritans to win men to their God and the destruction of a people who could not otherwise be made to relinquish their culture. If it is marked by that peculiar impersonal cruelty of the Puritans, it is even more marked by an unknowing insensitivity to the bases of cultural difference. Ignorance is a strong feature of the double defeat, stronger than malice, although the latter lingers more memorably in the historical record. A major irony that plays over the history is that the Indians were actually receptive to news about the Englishmen's God and apparently willing to attach themselves to Him because they respected the results He achieved. They were prevented from doing so by a polity that insisted such attachments could not come prior to civilized church gatherings. As a consequence the Puritans found in amazement that among their enemies in King Philip's War were Indians who still, in apparent sincerity, prayed to Christ.

Those who approached the Indians in a frank desire to help them to salvation, much as they suffered from the limitations placed on them by their own culture, were nevertheless sensitive to Indian ways, even though such ways did not synthesize for them into a useful anthropology. Roger Williams, who for some time in Rhode Island had no neighbors other than Indians, learned the language and set himself to studying the customs. With his remarkable ability to separate the secular and the spiritual, he was able to conduct what can be called significant ethnographic studies, while at the same time he steered clear of too close an examination of Indian religion for fear of being corrupted. "For the temper of the brain, in quick apprehensions and accurate judgments, to say no more," Williams reported, "the most high and sovereign God and creator hath not made them inferior to the Europeans." [31] With accuracy and sympathy he described their sexual mores and domestic arrangements and their attitude toward the English, but confessed that so far as their religious practices were concerned, after one experience "I never durst be an eye witness, spectator, or looker on, lest I should have been partaker of Satan's inventions and worships." [32]

Williams' trustworthiness was so thoroughly demonstrated to his Narragansett neighbors that he became their political adviser, and his home was regarded as a sanctuary by Indian servants fleeing English masters. When he went to England in 1651, he carried with him the Narragansett petition to the sachems in England that they might not forcibly be removed from their religion, and Cromwell, fascinated by his description of the Indians, held "many discourses" with him on the subject. Williams took it upon himself to preach to his Massachusetts neighbors the same indulgence that Cromwell had shown and urged conversion through the setting of Christian example rather than through more direct or coercive means.[33] As a result of the trust placed in him by the natives, he gained a superior knowledge of Indian intentions that was constantly called upon by the settlers in Massachusetts. He unwillingly became the first notable example of that melancholy figure of American folklore who was to attain a mythological dimension in the works of James Fenimore Cooper, the man caught between cultures. By every instinct of his humanity he was fitted to sympathize with the natives and succor them, while by every tie of birth, intellect, and belief he was committed to the preservation of the settlers who carried God's plan. In trying to accommodate Indian and European to each other, he was consistently and tragically pushed into a position that earned him the daily distrust of the settler in uneventful times and yet committed him to support that settler in critical times. His very presence in the wilderness as a practicing Christian was both the ground of his attraction to the Indians and the ground of his inability to do other than support those who were at least nominal Christians in armed conflict. Williams' efforts to provide a peaceful solution were drowned in the larger forces at work, and in his old age he had to take up his gun in defense of Providence against the warriors of King Philip.

In Massachusetts the minister who most effectively accepted the call to convert the Indians was John Eliot of Roxbury. Unlike Williams, he was convinced of the rightness of the Congregational way, and he labored with some success to acculturate the natives in order to prepare them for the word. He was sufficiently observant of their lives to recognize that technical as well as moral benefits had to be bestowed upon them if his efforts were to succeed, and in matters of natural philosophy he even recognized that the Indians could teach as well as learn. When the Indians complained to him that if they left off powwowing they would have no recourse in time of sickness, he responded by teaching the principles of anatomy and by appealing to the philanthropic to establish a school wherein Indians could be taught not religion alone, but natural science. He recommended that "there might be some recompense to any [Indian] that should bring in any vegetable or other thing that is virtuous in the way of physic. By this means we should soon have all these things which they know, and others of our countrymen that are skillful that way, and now their skills lie buried for want of encouragement, would be a-searching and trying to find out the virtues of things in this country, which doubtless are many, and would not a little conduce to the benefit of people of this country, and it may be, of our native country also." [34]

Eliot's long experience among the Indians convinced him that they had a useful fund of practical knowledge. In suggesting something like a medical school in which some of them might be enrolled and to which they would contribute their knowledge, he felt he was proposing a needed corrective to European techniques. "Our young students in physic," he said, "may be trained up better than yet they be who have only theoretical knowledge, and are forced to fall to practice before they saw an anatomy made, or duly trained up in making experiments." [35]

The quality of unworldliness that made Eliot so selfless a missionary led him also to project for the Indians a commonwealth that was as unrealistic as it was mathematically perfect in its divisions: one in which each ten would be guided by a leader, the hundreds by a council of the leaders of ten, and the thousands by a council of hundreds, on up as far as the need reached. So consumed was he by his vision that he neglected to note that he had totally ignored monarchical government. After the Restoration the book in which he described this Indian Utopia was suppressed by the General Court as being justly offensive "in special relating to kingly government in England." [36] In the book Eliot had said, "Much is spoken of the rightful heir of the crown of England, and the unjustice of casting out the right heir; but Christ is the only right heir of the crown of England and all other nations also." [37] In April 1661 he recanted, professing his sincere attachment to monarchy as lawful and eminent. The open field provided by his Indian labors had carried him to an enthusiastic vision that was seditious. The future of the Indians was to be conditioned by the fact that they were English subjects; this rather than a theoretical projection of their need had to be the starting point.

In 1649 the Long Parliament founded the first English Protestant missionary society, the New England Company, with the aim of converting the Indians of New England. The principal pattern of support the company offered was that of shipping to its commissioners in New England arms and ammunition, for which there was a steady and relatively unfluctuating market, and the commissioners, in turn, sold these for agricultural products at current prices and devoted the proceeds to Indian work. Because so few could be found to act as missionaries, in 1657 the company was forced to appoint agents to assist in the practical management of Indian government and to encourage Indian industry. The agents succeeded to the extent that they reported, in 1674, that there were fourteen towns of "praying Indians"—the usual term for Indians brought under some degree of acculturation—with a total population of about 1100. William Kellaway, in his study of the company, believes the figures are on the optimistic side, and adds: "In any case there were never as many again for, in June 1675, the disastrous Indian war—King Philip's war—began." [38] Although Captain Daniel Gookin, the company's agent, was allowed to make military use of the Indians, English hatred of them was strong, and the entire missionary effort was held in popular disrepute. Gookin had armed praying Indians against hostile Mohawks, and now some so armed were presumed to be among King Philip's adherents.

Mary Pray of Providence wrote in indignation to Boston in 1675: "The Indians boast and say those Indians that are called praying Indians never shot at the other Indians, but up into the tops of the trees or into the ground: and when they make show of going first into the swamp they commonly give the Indians notice how to escape the English. Sir, we have experience of them that they are as bad as any other; and it is reported by the Indians themselves that Captain Gookin helps them to powder, and they sell it to those that are employed by Philip to buy for him." [39] More than a trace of wartime hysteria enters into Mary Pray's indictment, but it is typical of the popular view of the praying Indians, which is to say that in the crisis the English attitude became racial. The reasons of the would-be peacemakers, Mary Pray insisted, were commercial: "Divers great men, for their trade and gain-sake, deluded the council and say peace; but God I hope will reward their deceit, who if they have but their gain they care not what becomes of this country." [40] Her view prevailed, and in the same month that she wrote her letter to Boston most inhabitants of Indian towns were shipped to Deer Island in Boston Harbor, where they were maintained at a bare subsistence on that bleak rock in a sad foreshadowing of other concentration camps.

Although the war effectively destroyed the widespread effort to convert the Indians by any means other than the sword, that effort even in its best days was not notably successful. "The learned English young men do not hitherto incline or endeavor to fit themselves for that service by learning the Indian language," Gookin complained. The tongue is difficult to learn, they receive no encouragement to do so from their society, and "the poverty and barbarity, which cannot be grappled with, unless the person be very much mortified, self denying, and of a public spirit, seeking greatly God's glory" [41] is not commonly to be found. Ultimately, Gookin felt, the Indians would have to serve themselves, and toward that end the company established an Indian college at Harvard in 1654, but in

1658 only one student was reported. Even those Indians favorably inclined to the Christian message as it was preached them drew the line at parting with their children for either apprenticeship or more scholastic training among the English, and Gookin himself seems to have lost spirit when the two most hopeful Indian candidates for the ministry died within the same short space of time, one killed by hostile Indians and the other by the consumption that found a fertile breeding ground among the Indians gathered in towns. But the hardships encountered by the New England Company spoke, at least, of certain genuine attempts to approach the Indians as individuals rather than to lump them according to a racial stereotype. King Philip's War put an end to this, even though in the very heat of the war the English participants had ample opportunity to observe the differences among the Indians and to attach themselves to individuals. This they noted in their memoirs, but were unable to register in their consciousness. Future efforts were to be directed to the Indians as an undistinguishable mass.

On June 17, 1675, a week before the war broke out, John Easton, Deputy Governor of Rhode Island, and four other Quakers met with King Philip. They endeavored unsuccessfully to hold him to peace and thereby fed the suspicions of such as Mary Pray, who claimed they sought the continuance of their trade rather than the welfare of the country. King Philip told them that in spite of his father Massasoit's aid to the English, Massasoit's brother Alexander was poisoned by them, the Indian's word was inferior to English word in legal complaints, and the English sold too much liquor to the Indians. In short, he arrived at the perception held by Miantanimo of the Narragansetts after witnessing the Pequot slaughter: the Indians must unite because their total existence was threatened by the English, and they must assert themselves by force because they had no status under law.

King Philip was killed in the summer of 1676, and the war ended shortly thereafter, but not before the colonies had expended some £100,000 and many English as well as Indian lives. The aims of natives and settlers in the war were remarkably different. Whereas the English fought with the end of subjugating their neighbors once and for all by rendering them powerless, the chiefs that united in war fought individual battles autonomously and pursued separate policies rather than a united strategy. The Indian effort was not directed at driving the English back into the sea, but was rather an act of self-assertion that had no practical intent with regard to future English-Indian relations; it did not envisage extinction of the English or dominance of them. Rather, the Indians were proclaiming their identity in what appeared to be the only way left to them. In the absence of any goal, any clear definition of victory in the war, the Indians picked away at the more vulnerable settlements and accepted the temporary rewards of plunder. They took prisoners constantly, but always with an eye to ransom rather than in any belief that they could thus effectively reduce English strength or morale. The opportunities the war presented for immediate gain were all the strategy they possessed. Hunters by upbringing, they conducted the war as a hunt that was to be pursued episodically, with periods of pause to enjoy the rewards of the kill or capture before returning to the warpath again. In noting this pattern, Mary Pray urged pressing them when they rested and added another dimension to the Puritan meanings of seasonal imagery: "Hath not the Lord made winter for us, as well as summer for the Indians?" [42] Compromised by English matériel and English wealth, the Indians hunted these as they would game.

Mary Rowlandson, wife of the minister of Lancaster, was captured by the Indians in their assault on that town in February 1676 and was carried with them on their frozen, half-starved marches until such time as they could arrange her ransom. She comforted herself in her adversity by calling to mind passages from the Bible; the lessons of Job and the comforts of the Psalms were most frequently on her lips. Her remarkable narrative of her captivity is most remarkable in the many details of Indian kindness toward her she is able to record without apparently being once shaken in her dominating conviction that she is among a satanic people. Indians who had been Christianized approached her to pray with her or even, bizarrely, to discuss points of theology with her over the chewing of a kernel of corn in a snowbank. One praying

Indian, for example, "told me that he had a brother, that would not eat horse, his conscience was so tender and scrupulous, though as large as hell for the destruction of poor Christians, then, he said, he read that scripture to him, II Kings vi 25: 'There was a famine in Samaria, and behold they besieged it, until an ass's head was sold for fourscore pieces of silver, and the fourth part of a cab of dove's dung for five pieces of silver.' He expounded this place to his brother, and shewed him that it was lawful to eat that in a famine which is not at another time." [43] The triumph of Puritan Talmudism is stunning but neither such discussion nor the charity she received from many in the squalid and hard-pressed band, and from King Philip too, whose war party was encountered several times, could penetrate the structure of her racial attitude. Noting her distress, some would come to her and assure her that she would soon be ransomed and back among those she loved, and one said to her that if she were willing he and his squaw would run away with her to her home. It was, however, impossible for Mary Rowlandson, who had seen her child killed by the Indians, also to see a common humanity in these gestures or to recognize individuals within the race of heathens. Her greater need for psychological stability in severe travail was met by a perception of reality that excluded such considerations.

Captain Benjamin Church, who led the mixed band of Indians and soldiers that eventually killed Philip and brought the war to an end, was better able to feel a sense of respect for his adversaries. He repeated the experience of Captain Underhill, who had fought the Pequots, and perpetuated one of war's most ironic traditions—the community of spirit established between able foes in opposition to those in their own camps who lack the dedication to the code they come to share through fighting one another. But, he learned, that sense of community could not be acted upon. His band was paid principally in bounty, thirty shillings a head for dead enemies, and this assured the adherence of its Indian members. When Philip was killed by one of them, Church awarded him Philip's hand "to show to such gentlemen as would bestow gratuities upon him," and after the war "he got many a penny by it." [44]

Church put into the record the most eloquent of all realizations of the potential brotherhood of settler and native and the saddest description of the fact that it was not to be. After the killing of Philip, his band moved on a war party led by Annawon, Philip's senior, the most trusted of his leaders, and the man who in age, skill, and lore was the living chronicle of his tribe. Realizing that the war was, in effect, over, Church sent his Indian followers into Annawon's camp to persuade him of the futility of further resistance, and the old chief agreed. Church's group entered without a shot, stacked the arms at some distance from their captives, and awaited the next day before taking further action. Church, not having slept for two days, stretched out as soon as matters were settled, but he could not sleep. He opened his eyes to see all the Indians fast asleep except Annawon who was staring at him across the firelight, "and so they lay looking one upon the other, perhaps an hour."

Then Annawon rose and moved into the darker part of the camp. Distrustful, Church secured his arms about himself and lay down next to Annawon's son so that the old chief, if he procured a weapon in his rummagings in the gloom outside the fire, could not get a shot without endangering his son. Speaking in the third person, Church continues the narrative:

Lying very still awhile, waiting for the event, at length he heard somebody coming the same way that Annawon went. The moon now shining bright, he saw him at a distance coming with something in his hands, and coming up to Captain Church, he fell upon his knees before him, and offered him what he had brought, and speaking in plain English, said, "Great Captain, you have killed Philip, and conquered his country; for I believe that I and my company are the last that war against the English, so suppose the war is ended by your means; and therefore these things belong unto you." Then opening his pack, he pulled out Philip's belt, curiously wrought with wampum, being nine inches broad, wrought with black and white wampum, in various figures, and flowers and pictures of many birds and beasts. This, when hung on Captain Church's shoulders, it reached his ankles; and another belt of wampum he presented him with, wrought after the former manner, which Philip was wont to put upon his head. It had two flags on the back part, which hung down on his back, and another small belt with a star upon the end of it, which he used to hang on his breast, and they were all edged with red hair, which Annawon said they got in the Mohawk's country. Then he pulled out two horns of glazed powder, and a red cloth blanket. He told Captain Church these were Philip's royalties, with which he was wont to adorn himself with, when, he sat in state; that he thought himself happy that he had an opportunity to present them to Captain Church, who had won them, etc. They spent the remainder of the night in discourse. And Captain Annawon gave an account of what mighty success he had formerly in wars against many nations of Indians, when he served Ashumequin, Philip's father, etc.[45]

Within the scene the old warrior moves from foe to comrade, from Annawon to Captain Annawon, and Church enters into the spirit of the Indian community even as Annawon's English moves Annawon some way out of it. Here was an ending, but here could not be a new beginning. Church left the camp to report to the officials in Boston, and when he returned, "he found, to his grief, the heads of Annawon, Tispaquin, etc., cut off, which were the last of Philip's friends." [46] They were worth 30 shillings each.

Peter Folger of Nantucket, father of Abiah Folger, who was the mother of Benjamin Franklin, thought he saw the Indian wars as God's punishment of the Puritans' intolerance. In his homely *Looking-Glass for the Times* he applied his opinion in verse:

> Let Magistrates and ministers
> consider what they do:
> Let them repeal those evil laws
> and break those bands in two
>
> Which have been made as traps and snares
> to catch the innocents,
> And whereby it has gone so far
> to acts of violence.[47]

Is this a time, he asked the authorities, to draw the blood of those who are really neighbors and friends as if you had no foes? The plea for tolerance was addressed to a commonwealth whose General Court had, at the outbreak of King Philip's War, issued a proclamation attributing the conflict to God's punishment of them for their permissiveness toward heretics, especially Quakers. Although he saw the folly of this, Folger did not disagree with the Massachusetts tribal sense, but, rather, hoped to turn it against intolerance:

> New England they are like the Jews
>   as like as like can be;
> They made large promises to God,
>   at home and at the sea.
>
> They did proclaim free Liberty,
>   they cut the calf in twain,
> They part between the part thereof,
>   O this was all in vain.
>
> For since they came into this land,
>   they floated to and fro,
> Sometimes, then, brethren may be free,
>   while hence to prison go.
>
> According as the times to go
>   and weather is abroad,
> So we can serve ourselves sometimes
>   and sometimes serve the Lord.[48]

Tompson saw permissiveness as the turning back to a corruption that had been reformed, and Folger saw intolerance as this turning back, but they both argued in the imagery of a chosen people. The greatly devastating war had demonstrated to the majority of the Puritan settlers that they were still the focus of God's attention. Experience had taught them Mary Rowlandson's lesson, that the Lord was indeed their comforter, and the comfort was there to be felt in a psychological certainty that sustained the people in adversity and carried them to victory. If some, such as Captain Church, had learned other lessons, these would have to be subsumed into what seemed to the majority to be a truth that had been lived. The basis for opposition to royal dominion was not a slogan based on a nostalgia for the days of the first founders, although it drew upon the strengths of the mythic power that men such as John Winthrop and John Cotton were beginning to represent. New England doctrine, rather, had been validated by New England experience because it allowed room for drama and interpreted it instead of simply asserting an ideal in opposition to the reality.

CHAPTER EIGHT

Courtly Pomp and Decay

Advent of provincialism—Dissension in church affairs—
Synod of 1679 and rise of professionalism—Religion sentimentalized

Provincialism is a term customarily descriptive of the relatively countrified and simple attitudes of a people as compared with the ways that prevail in the centers on which they recognize their dependence. The provincial follows fashions that are out of date among the sophisticated and defensively asserts their superiority, while at the same time making a semiconscious and belated adjustment to newer modes which, by the time he has absorbed them, are also outdated. New England in 1676 was not markedly provincial in this manner because its differences amounted to a cultural attitude distinct from that which prevailed in London rather than a retarded imitation of it. But that region was literally in the process of becoming a province, and its inhabitants did possess an unquestioned sense of the fact that they were Englishmen. The royal government that increasingly addressed itself to them was, in 1676, addressing a group which was more independent in outlook than it would be for some hundred years more; the colonists who revolted in 1775 were more provincial in the customary sense of the word than were those who opposed Stuart administration after the Restoration. The basis of provincialism, however, existed in powerful latency in New England in 1676 and resulted most obviously from New England's reliance on international trade.

The kind of rift among the faithful that would have profound provincial consequences was discernible in the internal affairs of the First Church of Boston as early as 1667. This was the most influential of the original churches and, in its controversy with Anne Hutchinson's group, it had demonstrated that its troubles as well as its triumphs were definitive. In 1650 the needs of a larger population in Boston caused a Second Church to be gathered, one at which Increase and Cotton Mather were to exert their leadership, and the First Church longed for a bold stroke that would emphasize its priority. Its original ministers had been John Cotton and John Wilson. Several years after the former died, he was succeeded by the eminent John Norton. After Norton died in 1663 and the venerable Wilson in 1667, the church was leaderless and anxious to call a minister whose fame was recognizably greater than that enjoyed by the run of Harvard graduates who were now filling the pulpits of Massachusetts. The First, accordingly, called John Owen, leader of the Congregational party in England, Vice-Chancellor of Oxford in the Interregnum, and theological apologist for the New England way in reformist debates in the homeland. It was Owen who as a young and prominent Presbyterian had read John Cotton's definitive defense of Congregationalism, *The Keys of the Kingdom of Heaven*, in order to refute it, and had instead been converted by it. In calling him, therefore, the First was not only calling a great man but affirming a Puritan notion of apostolic succession.

Owen considered the offer for more than three years, the conforming acts of Charles's Parliament making it attractive. But finally he declined, and the First, with an unquenchable thirst for eminence, cut across the unspoken protocol of New England church practice and invited John Davenport of New Haven.[1] He was the only man left who could clearly symbolize the First's adherence to its days of glory. A conforming minister of a prosperous London congregation in 1633, Davenport had secretly met with John Cotton when the latter was in hiding from Laud's pursuivants preparatory to his emigrating to Massachusetts. Davenport's purpose was to persuade Cotton to conform and remain in England to further the cause, but Cotton convinced him of the error of conformity, and four years later he too emigrated to New England, where he became one of the founders of New Haven. En route to New Haven he stayed in Boston in close association with John Cotton and entered the polemic war on behalf of the Massachusetts way, together with the luminaries of the first settlement. He assisted in the deliberations that determined the fate of Anne Hutchinson's group. After that his name became synonymous with New Haven. In calling him in 1667, the First Church was calling the last great survivor of the days of Cotton, Winthrop, Hooker, and Shepard to come to the center of New England church life and apply the truth of the first days against the dangerous drift of the time.

But in calling Davenport the First Church was also offering an affront bordering on insult to the New Haven church that Davenport had founded and ruled. Davenport would be receptive, the callers knew, because he was the leader of resistance in New Haven when that colony, caught between the rival claims of New York and Connecticut, finally was annexed to the latter in 1665. With unrealistic fervor, Davenport, who clearly abhorred association with so royal a province as New York, also sought to avoid annexation to Connecticut. That colony, he felt, was too unorthodox in its practice of permitting all inhabitants of a town to participate in town government, regardless of whether they were church members. Moreover, Connecticut churches took the lead in widening baptism, and Davenport was still unreconciled to the halfway measures of 1662. In spite of his unhappiness with the political disposition of New Haven, however, Davenport was its very personification as a separate community, and the New Haven church would not part with him. But the stern old man, seventy years of age in 1667, wanted the Boston post. He had every intention of going to the center and turning the tide back, not only reversing the widened baptism procedure but opposing royal dominance. He was one of the key links in the underground train of correspondence between the regicides William Goffe and Edward Whalley, who had fled England at the Restoration and whom he had hidden in his colony before sending them to a more secure retreat farther up the Connecticut River Valley, and he continued to serve as a postal link between them and their families in England. Not only had he been active in the first days, when the charter prevailed irresistibly; he still stood for the liberties and church restrictions of the charter and looked forward to waging battle against royal supremacy and against widened church admission in Boston with the same zeal he had employed in waging battle against annexation in New Haven—and also, a goodly number of Bostonians feared, with the same inflexible lack of realism. A substantial party in the First felt they could well do without this living anachronism.[2]

Failing to receive dismission from the New Haven church, Davenport could not immediately accept the Boston call. Congregational practice was firm in prohibiting one church from receiving a member of another church unless that new member brought with him a letter of peaceable dismission from his former associates. The church covenant was, first and foremost, a firm contract among believers. In May of 1668, however, Davenport visited Boston—for his wife's health, as he claimed—and there consorted with his supporters in the First Church, men already seriously at odds with a vigorous minority who opposed the call. Preaching to the First in July, Davenport gave a taste of his inability to compromise that confirmed both those who felt this was the tonic Boston needed and those who saw the hopeless unreality of accepting the leadership of an anti-royal, anti-halfway old zealot. Addressing himself to the insistence of the minority who opposed him that he receive a clear dismission from New Haven—this being their safest basis for opposition—he told them with regard to their stand, "It is evident Satan hath a great hand in it."

The minority regarded this as an intolerable insult, but the majority rallied around their choice and reacted by proposing to institute procedures of censure against the insulted minority. A council of outsiders was called to heal this breach and recommended that the dissenters, considerable persons in the community, be dismissed to form a third church in Boston. Meanwhile messengers returned from New Haven that summer to say that the church still refused to dismiss Davenport, and he, remaining in Boston, took the correspondence with the New Haven church out of the hands of his Boston supporters and applied himself directly to gaining a dismission. Finally, in October 1668, he received a qualified dismission, but one so grudging that there was good reason to believe it would not serve the turn when presented to the divided congregation of the First. The elders of the First, in collusion with Davenport's son, therefore, decided to doctor the letter of dismission, omitting all traces of New Haven reluctance, and present such a version to the church. On the strength of the altered letter, Davenport was called to office by a meeting of the church from which the dissenters were voluntarily absent 'on the understanding that their request for permission to withdraw and found another church was going to be considered. But as soon as Davenport was ordained in December, he led an attempt to squeeze the dissenters into conforming and continuing to contribute to the numbers and strength of his church, rather than honoring the understanding that their silent acquiescence to his appointment would procure them their withdrawal.

The scandal of the doctored letter broke in the summer of 1669, seventeen ministers bearing testimony against it. Davenport said he had nothing to do with the altering, although he did see the abbreviated version prepared by the revisers and believed that they had accurately extracted the substance of the dismission. The omitted qualifications of the New Haven church were superfluous, he maintained, and he sought both to be right in the matter and uninvolved by maintaining his insistence on the validity of the dismission while also claiming that the actual revision of the letter was none of his doing. Disputants in the controversy sought politely to exclude the venerable zealot, now clearly weakened by senility, from the issues, and, indeed, within a year he was dead. Although New England morale was to be rallied in terms of the faith of the founders, the event had proved that cohesion would come better from a rhetorical glorification of days past than from the actual presence of the last great clerical survivor. The living voice of the 1630s could in the 1660s bring only dissension.

There were other less famous but more consequential survivors of the 1630s in Boston. Of the twenty-eight members who broke from the First Church in dissent at calling Davenport and founded the Third Church, four were men who had been disarmed in 1637 as supporters of Anne Hutchinson, and two were the sons of men who had been so disarmed. Most were well-to-do merchants and tradesmen. The Third Church was joined at its founding in May 1669 by Sarah Cotton Mather, widow of John Cotton and of Richard Mather, and Mary Norton, widow of John, who donated the land on which the church edifice was built. They were far from unorthodox and they called as their minister Thomas Thacher, a physician as well as a preacher, who had gained a considerable reputation for his opposition to the Quakers. But they were, in the main, associated with the need to make further accommodations to the temper of the times than their opposed brethren of the First were willing to accept. An important undercurrent in the controversial founding of the Third is glimpsed in the letter its members sent to other churches in explanation of their step, "assuring you that however, we are traduced, yet we are not in the least alienated from the form of government according to patent under which God hath so long blessed this colony." [3] The affirmation was necessary, to some extent, because Davenport was so vocal a foe of the royal commissioners that those opposed to him were forced to clear themselves of collusion in any efforts to modify charter government. But it was most necessary because of strong and resistant discontent over the Half-Way Covenant. The members of the Third were announcing a critical distinction: it was consistent with adherence to the first principles of New England to modify church practice, because those first principles were embodied in the civil charter rather than in an unchangeable church admission procedure.

John Davenport had emphatically disapproved of the Half-Way Covenant. Those who had called him were pointedly attempting to reject the conclusion of the 1662 synod and to return to the bulwark of the original way, in practice as well as profession. The party that favored the First was popularly called Anti-Synodists, that in favor of the Third, Synodists, with reference to the synod that had adopted the Half-Way Covenant. The public clamor forced the greater part of the ministry, who had, of course, endorsed the halfway measure, also to endorse the Third. They were joined by the majority of the magistrates, although opposed by severe old

Richard Bellingham, the seventy-eight-year-old governor, last of the triumvir of anti-tolerating governors that included Thomas Dudley and John Endicott—"hard, harder, hardest," as James Savage characterized them.[4] The magistrates listened in disbelief as Bellingham convoked them and said "he feared a sudden tumult, some persons attempting to set up an edifice for public worship, which was apprehended by authority to be detrimental to the public peace." [5] The old technique of treating ecclesiastical differences as sedition seemed grotesque, especially when the quality of the members of the Third and of their supporters was considered. The deputies, however—representatives of the respective towns, in the lower house of the General Court, as opposed to the magistrates in the upper house, who were elected at large—took the alarm and accepted a committee report that said that the Third represented "a declension from the primitive foundation-work" and "an invasion of the rights, liberties, and privileges of churches." [6] They still chafed under the modification of original practice made by the Half-Way Synod.

At issue was whether the tribal loyalties that were increasingly to be called upon, as the colony wrangled with royal commissioners and fought Indians, were to mean loyalty to an unmodifiable church platform that was inseparable from the civil rights of the charter, or whether the church could grow with the times and loyalty be reserved for the maintenance of the charter alone. With the prevalence of the latter view, invocation of the founding fathers would in church matters be ritual rather than practical. The 1670 general election was fought in this context. Only twenty of the fifty deputies returned had sat in the General Court in the previous year. The freemen replaced the great majority of them in a clear assertion of support for the Half-Way Covenant and the Third Church of Boston; indeed, several members of that church were elected as representatives of towns from the western end of the commonwealth. The past was to be hallowed as a spiritual measure of the times and as inspiration for the future, but it was not to be applied as a brake to the practices of the day, however much it would serve as a source for deploring them.

In 1669 John Davenport had preached the election sermon, and the magistrates had flatly refused "to present their thankfulness in a solemn manner," because, as they said, in a resolution that one of their members had to put to the vote when Bellingham refused to do so, they conceived "many passages in the said sermon . . . resented by the reverend elders of other churches and many serious persons." [7] Now in 1670 Samuel Danforth was asked to preach the election sermon. His title was "Errand into the Wilderness." In the sermon Danforth provided a foretaste of the coming provincialism.[8] The ways of the founders were to be idealized—and eventually, after Danforth, sentimentalized—without their holding forth practical consequences. As very early the initiative had passed from ministry to magistracy, so now Danforth signaled the fact that it was to pass from magistracy to men of affairs. And the ministry, as Danforth unconsciously revealed, would in the process pass from close consultation in magisterial policy to the ritual role of sounders of the tribe's lamentation at its unwillingness to correct a drift it found too profitable to resist. Individual voices would continue to be heard in demand of more concrete applications of the founding faith, but the rift had opened.

In a sermon remarkable for its clarity and balance, Danforth referred in only the most guarded terms to the recent First Church controversy and did not take it upon himself to address that or any other issue. Rather he located the "cause of our decays and languishings" [9] in unbelief, and developed this general theme, in the main, by opposing hypothetical rationalizations for the lukewarmness of the times with quotations from the Bible. Thus, the rationalization, "Alas there is much variety and diversity of opinions and judgments that we know not what to believe," [10] is not opposed by specific opinions and judgments that should be believed, but by citations that demonstrated that the disciples knew what to believe. He linked prosperity with the falling off in fervor and went so far as to implicate sympathy with royalty in his criticism of luxury, calling it a love of "courtly pomp and decay," and again "courtly pomp and gallantry," [11] which was unsuitable to a wilderness. He made as sharp a point as he was to make and then hedged it by not proceeding beyond a quotation when he cited Zephaniah: "I will punish the princes, and the king's children, and all such as are clothed with strange apparel." [12] He mentioned the eager pursuit of private interests as a declension from primitive purity, but, unlike Thomas Shepard, who had raised this theme in the 1640s, he did not press it with descriptions of contemporary behavior that would find specific correspondence among his auditors. The sermon was passing from act to art, from a discourse that was to be validated by the consequences it set in motion to one that was to be valued for the progression of feelings it called forth and balanced in a self-contained whole.

The two years of war with King Philip were the most devastating in New England history, involving more suffering and a greater expenditure of life and wealth in proportion to the population than any other conflict ever fought on that soil. One in eleven in the militia had been killed, and one in eleven families had been burned out. Public debts were heavy, and the land had, in great part, been neglected. But the decade following the war was one of economic boom as farmers and traders vigorously redressed the balance. A report to the Colonial Office in that decade said, "No house in New England hath above 20 rooms. Not 20 in Boston, which have 10 rooms each. . . . The worst cottages in New England are lofted: no beggars. Not 3 put to death for theft." [13] Prosperity was flowing in, and wilderness was becoming metaphor. In 1662 there were fourteen keepers of inns, ordinaries, taverns, or victualing houses in Boston. After that year the increase was so rapid that by 1690 there were fifty-four such establishments, with the first coffee house opening in 1676.[14]

Ministerial salaries, initially paid by the church in accordance with a contract and in reaction against tithing, came increasingly to be met out of the town rates, and this, in turn, resulted increasingly in townsmen insisting on a say in ministerial appointments, whether or not they were church members. In 1675 the General Court had to enter into a controversy in Salem because the majority there wanted to retain Charles Nicholet as a second pastor to John Higginson, over the latter's objection to Nicholet's Presbyterianism. Higginson was upheld by the court on the ground that the invitation to the second pastor had been made by town vote rather than church vote and that this was an irregular and dangerous tendency. It was also a sign that those who did the paying would increasingly have the saying.

The churches were definitely losing influence, and the prosperity of the times was definitely the cause. But society was no longer so simple and united that ministerial concerns could result in immediate measures. Increase Mather had heard in 1679 from Abraham Kick, a former New Englander in Amsterdam, who had written, "Is there not in the land of our nativity, in the provinces & in New England, a growing lukewarm, & losing first love?" [15] This was the almost constant burden of the letters his brother Nathaniel sent from Dublin. However hard times were with him, Nathaniel saw no reason for New England to decline and was quick to protest in letters about any compromising measures taken by a commonwealth he envisioned as the bastion of true Christianity. Such letters from abroad were echoed by internal correspondence, but with a significant difference. New England clergymen conferring with one another about the deterioration in manners recognized the impracticality of affecting them directly and thought most often in terms of powerful rhetorical checks rather than of legislation; they yearned for a revival of faith, but accepted the reality that it would have to precede legal measures rather than accompany them. As one correspondent put it to Increase Mather, it is to be feared that many young people degenerate from their godly ancestors in practice, and while it is to be hoped that none degenerate in principles, "if you lay not too much stress upon external church privileges you are safe." [16] Here was a characteristically pragmatic recognition that the measures employed would have to be purely spiritual.

Intensifying the need to compromise rather than oppose was the attitude of nonconformists under persecution in England. To their advocacy of tolerance some were now adding the counsel of further adjustment to the world. Maybe it is not so bad, after all, even to attend the services of the Church of England, they said. God conveys knowledge of His mind to sinful man in four ways: through the creation; through suggestions to the conscience; through preaching; and through the church. The last may be considered apart from preaching so that even if the church is somewhat corrupt, nevertheless, it is "an undoubted moral duty, to attend the speaking of God in whatsoever way by providence brought unto us." [17] Bear in mind that moral duties are unlike things indifferent. The latter if they have a mixture of evil are wholly evil because they are not required of one, and therefore the evil is to be eschewed. But "what is morally good will remain so still, though mixed with evil." [18] No orthodox believer in New England would agree with this line of reasoning, but most were conscious of it and of the fact that they were caught in a drift that could very well bring it to bear on their own condition.

The government did, of course, pay attention to the outward manifestation of the drift. The cornerstone of New England polity had been the well-regulated family, but in 1675 the General Court recognized that heads of families could no longer be relied upon to do their moral duty unsupervised; it charged tithing-men with the responsibility of seeing that the Sabbath was kept and tippling controlled. After 1679, however, tithing-men were further authorized to interfere in all disorders that occurred in the families under their charge.[19] The General Court also attacked the problem of excessive drinking by a law of 1672 that forbade laborers to demand liquors as part of their wages. This was a reaffirmation of a 1645 edict, but with significant difference. The earlier law had forbidden employers to force laborers to take wine in part payment—it was moral in first intent. The later law said that the oppression of excessive wages was increased by the custom of demanding liquors, which in turn encouraged drinking and was therefore forbidden—it was economic in first intent.[20]

The decline from strict manners that had come to the seaport towns after King Philip's War was one that was tied to those towns' continual commerce with a wider world, continual exposure to English manners, continual servicing of mariners, and continual concern with royal regulations that were addressed primarily to trade. The decline in the back country was of a connected but different sort. The ravages of the war could be repaired by increased attention to the land, but this attention was paid with a corresponding-ing neglect of the learning and manners of the inhabitants. It was difficult now for the frontier settlements to procure teachers for their children, even when time could be afforded them for book-learning: centers of learning could not supply so great a number that some would perforce accept the unattractive conditions of the isolated country villages, nor could these villages compete for such services financially. In 1677 the government of Connecticut found that in the scattered settlements in its jurisdiction "the posterity of such, most of them, are endangered to degenerate to heathenish ignorance and barbarism," [21] and tried to prevent further settlements except in sufficient proximity so that they could protect one another and promote a social life. And in Massachusetts the General Court attempted to regulate frontier settlements by requiring that all assigned lands be occupied by assignees within eighteen months, be forfeited if not continually improved for four years, and be occupied only by inhabitants approved both by the majority of the group undertaking the settlement and a committee of the General Court. By law, fences were to be made and a home lot and meadow provided for a minister. But the short-range financial attractions of such agricultural undertakings were far weaker than their longer-range appeal to speculators, and new settlements were entered into more readily when absentee capital could be invested. This meant, in effect, that Massachusetts expanded less under charter government than under the subsequent royal officers, and when it did expand under the former it did so in some defiance of the laws.[22]

"God hath given me 4 living sons (of eight I have had)," wrote John Bishop, minister of Stamford in 1678, "& none of them brought up to learning to my great grief, though two of them in a good forwardness long since, but our Latin school failing, & my estate too feeble to send them forth, their progress also failed. I have one, now entering in his grammar, whom I would fain give learning unto, so far as able, & shall strain hard to school him near, or send him to Boston, if hopes may be had of attaining my farther end as to college learning." [23] The condition he describes is far from brutish igno-rance. His sons are literate, some even in Latin, and he complains of the want of learning in its most rigorous sense, but it is a sense that he had some reason to believe life in New England would meet. He records a relative decline, one that is echoed repeatedly, as when Thomas Hanford, schoolmaster of Norwalk, writes in 1682, "God hath given me 10 children, 5 sons & 5 daughters; but as yet I see not how to bring up one of them to learning. I am initiating my two youngest at home, *quoad passim*; but I know not how far I shall be in a capacity to carry them on." [24] Agricultural conditions called for many children to provide many hands, but the rewards were not such that the parents could acquire the money or the children the leisure for schooling. Striking is the reversal of the pattern of more civilized times, when the firstborn, at least, was dedicated to the father's profession. Now the best to be hoped is to salvage the youngest on the strength of the sacrifice of the older ones.

Such cultural reversals came about in a time of repeated external adversities: the heavy toll of the war; two calamitous fires in Boston (1676 and 1679); a serious smallpox epidemic; an unusually high rate of shipwreck in the latter half of the 1670s; and heightened pressure from the royal government. William Hubbard, New England's official contemporary historian, wrote of those times, "They conceived that personal afflictions did oftimes come only for probation, but as to public calamities it is not usually so, as they apprehended especially when by a continual series of providences God seems to be pleading against a people as He did against Israel in David's time; and as He had seemed to do with them for divers years." [25] Most of the orthodox shared this judgment, and nineteen ministers, led by Increase Mather, declared in a petition to the General Court in May 1679 that God had a controversy with New England and that a synod should be called to make full inquiry into its cause and state. The petitioners further noted that no joint profession of faith and polity had been made since the 1648 synod, and the time was ripe for fresh affirmation. The General Court assented and called the synod for September, charging it to answer the questions:

"What are the evils that have provoked the Lord to bring his judgments on New England? . . .

"What is to be done that so those evils may be reformed?" [26]

In answer to the first question, the synod compiled a list documented with biblical examples of and biblical injunctions against each of the evils cited: decay of the power of godliness, even among believers; pride manifested both in contentious spirit and in outward apparel—"servants, and the poorer sort of people are notoriously guilty in the matter, who (too generally) go above their estates and degrees";[27] slighting of the privileges of church membership, especially by halfway members who do not confirm the promise of their baptism; profaneness; Sabbath breaking; bad family govern-ment—"Children & servants that are not kept in due subjection; their master, and parents especially, being sinfully indulgent towards them. . . . In this respect Christians in this land, have become too like unto the Indians";[28] inordinate passions; much intemperance—"the proper end of taverns, &c., being for the entertainment of strangers";[29] want of truth-telling amongst men; inordinate affection to the world—"Farms and merchandising have been preferred before the things of God"[30] so that people leave church fellowship just for elbow room in which to cultivate more land, and traders sell at excessive rates while laborers and mechanics ask unreasonable wages; opposition to the work of reformation; and a want of public spirit. Since the evils were so clearly against Scripture and so manifestly widespread, God had full reason to send afflictions upon the New Englanders.

In answer to the second question, the government was urged to a stricter regulation of manners, one result being the extension of the tithing-men's duties that has been noted. But principally the elders addressed themselves to what was to be done in the churches, and local churches were urged, as most then did, to hold solemn meetings for the reaffirmation of their covenants. The Cambridge Platform was endorsed again, but not without debate. The usual procedure for admission of a professing believer was to have that believer give a testimony of his faith in the form of a spiritual autobiography delivered to the whole church, which would then vote on his admission. Women were generally excused from this because it was considered immodest for them to speak at length in public, and they were accordingly permitted to profess before the elders privately. As a result of the severe falling off in new members, however, the opinion had grown that faith, after all, did not bring articulateness, and that the requirement of a public profession inhibited too many otherwise worthy candidates. Indeed, the new Third Church accepted members who made their profession privately to the elders, who, in turn, communicated their satisfaction to the whole church.

Accordingly, when the Cambridge Platform was reconsidered, a debate arose as to "whether those professors of religion as are of good conversation, are not to be admitted to full communion, provided they are able to examine themselves, and discern the Lord's body." [31] Solomon Stoddard of Northampton advanced the affirmative against Increase Mather's negative, and it became clear that what was at stake, so far as Stoddard and his sympathizers were concerned, was not merely permitting private rather than public profession. Rather, Stoddard aimed at a wider basis of admission to the sacrament of the Last Supper by administering it to all who were of sincere and seemly behavior, regardless of whether they had arrived at a full stage of personal conviction of their justification. The communion was for Stoddard an ordinance that aided in the conversion of such members, rather than one that sealed it. He did not succeed in winning this point, too heterodox for that day, but he did succeed in having the synod modify the requirement of a personal and public confession of faith, repentance, and the works of God's spirit in the professor, to having the candidate make a confession of faith and repentance. Since this could be formal rather than autobiographical, and made privately to the minister rather than publicly to the church, Stoddard now had leeway to practice as he wished. The seemingly small change in wording did, in point of fact, open the doors wider, should local churches wish so to interpret it. The majority at the synod, however, and especially the seaport towns in contrast to Stoddard's relatively isolated rural area, simply took the change to mean that they no longer needed to insist upon public profession.

Other details of the Cambridge Platform were also changed before it was, in general, endorsed. Congregational principle had always held and continued to hold that a minister was no minister until ordained to the service of a particular congregation. But now the synod recognized his calling as also separate from his relationship to his particular parishioners by permitting him to administer the sacraments in other congregations also; by reducing the number of lay elders who would govern the church in conjunction with him; and by preferring ordination at the hands of neighboring ministers to that at the hands of lay brethren of the congregation he was to serve. The changes in detail are minor in view of the substance of what was retained, but they are significant because they are all in one decided direction—the clergy are now developing a sense of themselves as members of a distinct profession whose common interests are stronger than the interests each minister shares with his parishioners. Even the change from public to private testimony of faith was one that underlined their distinct professional competence. The clergy, who initially had stood in something of an organic relationship to their villages, as the chosen teachers and leaders of a cooperative band of the faithful, were separating into a class distinct from them. On the face of it the change in attitude was less democratic, the minister now insisting upon a privileged status that was conferred on him by others enjoying this status and that was applicable beyond the bounds of his congregation. But with this new professionalism he was also reacting to the spread of democracy. It was his defense in the face of the fact that towns were coming to hire and fire ministers by popular vote.

Indeed, the minister's assertion of himself as a member of a professional class even had trade-union overtones. The synod remembered that the original pattern had been for each congregation to have two ministerial officers, a pastor charged with the conduct of the congregation and a teacher charged with its instruction, although the distinction was flexible. So, for instance, John Wilson had been pastor of the First Church of Boston and John Cotton teacher. But now it noted a penny-pinching decline of this practice and urged the utmost endeavor in supplying all but the smallest churches with two ministers. And in assertion of the special qualifications that a minister should have, in assertion, that is, of his difference from lay believers, the synod emphasized the need for learning and therefore support of the schools: "The interest of religion and good literature have been wont to rise and fall together. . . . It is deeply to be lamented that now, when we are become many, and more able than at the beginnings, that Society [Harvard College] and other inferior schools are in such a low and languishing state." [32] Hard-pressed or careless churches were not to supply themselves with lay teachers.

The professionalizing of the clergy in reaction to the democratizing of the conditions of their employment drove a wedge between the ministry and the people the consequences of which can most readily be felt in the nature of the preaching in the last quarter of the century. It was the period of the "jeremiad," the stylized denunciation of the evils of the time, especially those brought about by prosperity, and the stylized reminder of first principles. It came repeatedly to be uttered as formula rather than practical teaching because its utterers were men whose rhetorical relationship to their audience had changed. From being the chosen leaders of a select band speaking to that band about common problems, they were becoming hired professionals doing a special job from a special position that could be regarded as incontrovertible so long as it was also aloof from practical consequences. The new minister should speak at length on the subject of riches, showing how uncertain they were and how secure in comparison was a faith in God, but he need not be talking to anybody in particular. His listeners assumed that as a minister he was charged with being their reminder of such truths on sermon day, even as they pursued their worldly ends during the week. And, isolated from the daily pursuits of his community, the minister, now not so inevitably a farmer or physician or schoolteacher also, accepted the role of being the lofty and unchanging vehicle of truths that had, like his new profession, become separated from the details of daily reality. The rural ministers who were still caught up in the daily round of life on the land used their sense of professionalism as a basis for resentment of their inferior treatment compared to colleagues elsewhere. They rarely regarded their own farming activities as a common bond with their parishioners. Variety in preaching was not so much pursued by adjusting the weekly truths preached to the weekly condition of the listeners as by embellishing the fixed stock of truths and making them more affecting. A good sermon was becoming one that was a moving experience in itself, and weeping preachers are now first heard of as men of special worth.

The kind of model the professional minister turned to was that supplied by such as John Flavel, the English preacher, who put forth a series of books teaching his readers how to "spiritualize" their daily lives: for example, *Husbandry Spiritualized* (1669) and *Navigation Spiritualized* (1671). In them Flavel showed how religious sentiments could be brought to bear on one's regular pursuits. "Spiritualizing" was the provision of uplifting morsels to those who labored in the world by one especially qualified to present them because he did not so labor but was professionally centered in a study whence he could classify the morsels into suitable categories. Flavel admitted that in spiritualizing husbandry "I met with some discouragement in my first attempt from my unacquaintedness with rural affairs." [33] But this he found no serious hindrance, since his task was not really to know these affairs, but to know what moving religious expressions existed that could embroider them. "I have shut up every chapter with a poem," he says, "an innocent bait to catch the reader's soul." [34] His method is to work down upon the condition of his readers from a superior position, offering them religious sentiments with which to comfort them in their condition, rather than working up from the facts of their existence and showing them how these are to be related to an aim larger than the sentimentalizing of the details themselves.

A half-century before Flavel, John Rogers had stood in the pulpit of a market town in England and said, "Ministers that would go to work indeed, must go with their tools, use both doctrine and exhortation; as he that would cleave a knotty log, must both use beetle and wedges, that one without the other would be to no purpose." [35] Practice is the life of all, he insisted, and he scorned those who sought elegance and said of such as he, "Oh, he is a plain homespun preacher, he may do well in a country town." No, said Rogers, "Christs sheep do otherwise." [36] Now Flavel sat in his study and told his country reader: "Methinks it should be a pleasure to you, when you come weary out of the fields from plough, or any other labor, to sit down in the evening, and read that chapter [of my book] which concerns that particular business, and refresh your souls, even from that which hath wearied your bodies. Were your hearts but heavenly and more time allowed for spiritual husbandry, your inward comforts would be much more, and your outward gains not a jot less." [37]

Flavel's works were popular among the ministerial class in New England because in New England too the specializations of modern life were separating the preacher to a set task, that of moralizing and sentimentalizing over the lives of those who pursued other special-ties. The jeremiad may, as Perry Miller says, have met the special needs of the New England communities,[38] but it did not so much consciously address those needs as it was a manifestation of how economic reality had divided society and allotted the minister the ritual role of lamentation. So long as he fulfilled it, others could concentrate on their roles. As a body, the clergy were keepers of a flame no longer needed in the daily community. As the literary class of the community, they instructed it in sentiment because the truths were Sunday truths, and in such confinement the emphasis shifted from practice to feeling. The conditions of life of the folk were such that as a body they no longer were expected to cultivate the intellect and the sensibility but assigned those tasks to a class, even as that class recognized its dependence upon the various practical pursuits of the members of the community and generalized over them rather than interfering with them. When industrialism arrived, with its consequent acceleration of specialization, certain readjustments would be made whereby the community reclaimed in part its intellectual interests in order to serve the demand for technical achievements, and whereby the clergy reclaimed in part its interest in daily activities by extending its moral concern into the supervision of Sunday schools, young people's clubs, and visitation of parishion-ers. But these were adjustments within a pattern of specialization that was signaled by the 1679 synod.

Thus, while the civil authorities and the men of affairs maneu-vered after 1676 to reject, qualify, or compromise the effect of increased royal dominance of the colonies, the culture itself was already responding to the same economic factors that were causing public men to react more explicitly. The separation of the ministry into a professional class deprived the culture of an important source of difference from English culture and made it susceptible to the fashions in sentiment as well as dress, in thought as well as social intercourse, that arrived together with the bulkier freight of trading ships.

CHAPTER NINE

Jack and Tom

Colonial society—Political parties—History as identity—
Alienation of the ministerial intellect—
Issues of political dominion—Puritanism and liberty

In response to the first visit of the royal commissioners in 1664, the General Court prepared a petition to the royal government stating: "This people did at their own charges transport themselves, their wives and families, over the ocean, purchase the land of the natives, and plant this colony with great labor, hazards, costs, and difficulties; for a long time wrestling with the wants of a wilderness, and the burdens of a new plantation; having also now above thirty years enjoyed the aforesaid power and privilege of government within themselves, as their undoubted right in the sight of God and man." [1] For twelve years more they were indulged in the power and privileges they claimed because the concerns of Charles's government centered so absorbingly in Europe. Beginning in 1676, however, the royal government took a series of measures that resulted, in 1683, in the vacating of the charter and, in 1686, in the institution of a royal administration in New England. When Increase Mather, in London in 1688 to attain redress of administrative actions the Massachusetts men felt were unjust, wrote to publicize New England's case, he said, "Never was place brought to such a considerableness in so short a time; that which was, not long since, a howling wilderness, in a few years time, became a pleasant land, wherein was abundance of all things meet for soul and body, which can be imputed to nothing else but their religion." [2] He estimated that the immigration up to 1640 had brought 4000 to Massachusetts and that these were now "marvelously increased" to 200,000.

The theme that was consistently sounded throughout the days of the later Stuarts was that the Puritan colonies were different because they had been cultivated at the expense of the settlers, not of the crown, and that their religious practices deserved to remain relatively undisturbed because they had led to an undoubted success. And, indeed, New England did stand as a monument to the capability of the Puritan ethic. The declension into barbarism that threatened and at least partially overcame other English colonies that were governed by an appointed ruling class and disciplined by no religion other than the feebly maintained established one was strikingly countered in New England. Institutions of church, state, and education were developed swiftly and confidently; the general level of literacy was high—higher perhaps than anywhere else in the English-speaking world; the rhythm of daily life was marked by a set of manners that were distinctly European in contrast to native conditions. From the moment they landed, the Puritans developed and advanced their mode of civility, strengthened by an assurance of their own righteousness and a self-reliance born of their possession of the spirit. If one aspect of their achievement was the impersonal fashion they had of dealing with strangers, Indians, and the birds and beasts they found on the land—as well as the land itself—another was that in an amazingly short span of time they had established a civilization that in its institutions and manners was totally competent and showed the ability of such new men to regulate their own affairs. The declensions they themselves lamented increasingly after 1676 were slidings from the rigid standard of morals and manners achieved in the first fifty years, but they were not descents into brutishness. These, indeed, were feared and in some part experienced only after royal policy undermined self-determination.

The French to the north had established trading towns at royal expense, and it was but a step from the palisades of these towns to wilderness and a series of compromises with it: religion was a matter of administering the sacraments to those who would accept them, apart from the requirement of a standard of civility; schools and printing presses did not exist; mastery was the privilege of men appointed in France, and a broad gap existed between them and the people at their command. A Puritan captive in 1690 noted: "The gentry at Quebec are very courteous and civil and live very splendid only by their trade [in furs]; but they have abundance of poor among them; for betwixt the churchmen and gentry, they are oppressed, but in such a subtle way that the poor people are not sensible of the cause of their misery, neither dare they complain if they were." [3] He was also amazed that the troops in Canada were supported by the royal purse, as were all other public charges, "and there is no public duties paid but by the companies of the peltry, which makes me judge the income is great, where such public charge is expended." [4] The Puritan colonies, by contrast, developed a gentry that had risen from the freemen rather than one that was separate as a class. They had no class that could be called poor and if a man was oppressed he had enough learning to discern the source of the oppression and was usually articulate enough to call for relief from it. Public charges in New England were met directly by the settlers, principally through property taxes, and the policy of moving upon unsettled lands in communities rather than individually brought local civic responsibilities to all even if they were not freemen.

In the southern English colonies there prevailed a standard that reserved to a ruling class the privileges of civility. To the folk it permitted only obedience and such freedom as could be achieved by moving individually beyond the perimeter of settlement and authority, a freedom necessarily entailing compromises with savagery. Colonel Henry Norwood, a royal officer who decided to seek his fortune in Virginia in 1649 rather than undergo the rule of Cromwell, spoke of the miseries of his voyage to America, starvation so fiercely pressing those on board that "The infinite number of rats that all the voyage had been our plague, we now were glad to make our prey to feed on; and as they were ensnared and taken, a well grown rat was sold for sixteen shillings as a market rate. Nay, before the voyage did end (as I was credibly inform'd) a woman great with child offered twenty shillings for a rat, which the proprietor refusing, the woman died." [5] So doleful was the situation that when Christmas arrived Norwood and his friends were hard-pressed to find the means to celebrate. They managed to amass the scrapings of the meal tub: "Malaga sack, sea water with fruit and spice, all well fried in oil, were the ingredients of this regale, which raised some envy in the spectators; but allowing some privilege to the captain's mess, we met no obstruction, but did peaceably enjoy our Christmas pudding." [6]

Small as the ship was, Norwood was "credibly inform'd" of the plight of the starving woman, yet he did not witness it first-hand. His circle could and did claim privilege for their Christmas regale in the face of the starving commoners. The metaphor of society that was carried to Virginia is made clear in his account. Indeed, it may be remembered that Moll Flanders' last husband, the highwayman, could only with difficulty be prevailed upon to accept transportation to Virginia rather than hanging in England. He was, he insisted, of the gentry and could not abide the contemplation of being outside that rank in Virginia, even though robbery was his way of maintaining it in England. Common labor was abhorrent to him, and he accepted transportation only when it was made clear to him that his wife's means were adequate to have him treated as a gentleman.

In New England the gentleman was not quite of this sort. He was most often from one of the wealthier families that had been associated with the colony since its first days—Winthrops, Dudleys, Bradstreets, et al. These had risen to a privileged status while still having to seek power through their industry and through presenting themselves, not always successfully, for elective office. Carl Bridenbaugh notes signs of the influence of this native gentry, such as the favorable treatment they received in judicial penalties.[7] But each instance he cites is one in which the law was made to bear on the offender and the remission given was in the punishment rather than in the charging or trying of the accused.

When John Dunton, the bookseller, visited New England in 1686, he observed a society that struck him as both very much like the one he had left in London and oddly different in the greater severity of its regulation of manners. Like Josselyn before him, he noted the need for a "Grecian faith" in trading with the New Englanders: "He may get promises enough, but their payments come late." [8] Nevertheless, he found his voyage profitable. Among other things, he had come to collect £500 in debts, and while this serves as a testimony to the scarcity of specie in New England, it is also a sign of the literacy of the community that it could have run up such a bill with a single bookseller. Dunton's voyage as a bill-collector was made with another large freight of books, and these he sold profitably at a rented Boston warehouse. "The books I had with me were most of them practical," he said, "and well suited to the genius of New England, so that my warehouse being opened they began to move apace." [9]

On one hand, Dunton noted, "The laws in force here against immorality and profaneness are very severe," [10] but on the other hand, the women who visited his warehouse out of curiosity were no different in either apparel or flirtatiousness from those who walked into his London shop. His friend Mr. Gouge of Boston only pretends to live a bachelor: he is "no enemy to pretty women." [11] And one Mrs. Hicks had recently come to the colony "with the valuable venture of her beautiful person, which went off at an extraordinary rate; she marrying a merchant in Salem worth thirty thousand pounds." [12] Himself possessed of a wife who was bookseller, cash-keeper, and "managed all my affairs for me," [13] Dunton noted that many a merchant's wife in Massachusetts behaved the same, as for instance the wife of Green the printer: "I have heard her say, 'that when she married Mr. Green, she espoused his obligations also; and wherever her husband, either by ties of nature, or squeezing of wax, owed either money or love, she esteemed herself to be no less a debtor. She knew her marriage was an adoption into his family, and therefore paid to every branch of it what their respective stations required.' " [14]

The theorists of Congregationalism in New England had been long and sincere in their protestations that they abhorred democratic procedures in church and state. Nevertheless, the Congregational form of church organization was far more democratic than either

Presbyterianism, which, in setting up a synodical structure to govern the church as a whole, tended toward autocracy, or Episcopalianism, which was totally hierarchical in the chain of command that depended from the crown, through archbishops to bishops to clergy. The balancing aristocratic feature of Congregationalism on which its theorists insisted was that, once the elders had been elected, they possessed unquestioned power to rule, whereas the congregation, ideally, had liberty only to assent. But, as has been seen, when arguments were sought for the justness of this arrangement, the one that prompted itself most readily was drawn not from scriptural or patristic models, but rather from that of the incorporated English town, a model, it was frequently asserted, that best suited the spirit of Englishmen.

On this restricted form of democracy the Puritans had formed themselves, and in the course of time, as the financial support for the churches came increasingly from those who were not members of the congregation, the democratic spirit found ways of manifesting itself in response to the economic reality. The hiring of a minister became more and more a town rather than a church matter, since town rates were involved, and the ministry came more and more to be a distinct professional class. The mechanism of democracy was established and well lubricated in Massachusetts, even though it did not in the seventeenth century operate at full capacity. When a royal governor, Sir Edmund Andros, finally did arrive, he recognized the threat to his supremacy that the democratic habits of Massachusetts presented and he moved against their institutionalized forms. He ruled without a legislative assembly and he also forbade the local jurisdictions to hold town meetings more than once a year.

From 1676 to 1688 the push and pull between royal policy and New England policy separated public men in New England into two frequently opposed parties, the popular and the moderate. The former party was centered in the rural communities and found its voice in the House of Deputies; the latter, centered in the trading ports, found its voice among the magistrates. With no wealth other than ownership of the land, the popular party stood for no compromise with any royal demand that threatened the charter.

Land in Massachusetts was held under the charter, and should this become void, all assignments also became void, the land reverting back to the crown under the legal ruling that Henry VII and his heirs owned New England on the strength of John Cabot's discovery. Those who occupied it by a title issued under the voided charter would have, at the least, to pay new quitrents to the crown, if not actually to vacate the land. Common lands, such as those shared by the residents of almost every New England town, were especially vulnerable and were, indeed, the first to be confiscated under Governor Andros.

The moderate party, concerned centrally with trade, faced the impossibility of continuing a favorable pattern of commerce originating in New England ports, should the royal government be driven to a full use of punitive measures. Some compromise was called for before matters came to this extremity, its members felt, and although the charter was to be regarded as the most inviolate of all of the counters in the conflict, even that, eventually, had to be considered as negotiable, for fear of what would happen if there were no negotiation whatsoever.

The moderate party was most obviously the politically realistic one. To say this, however, is to say very little more than that New England's economic future was, in the 1680s, inextricably tied to its access to foreign markets on the best terms that could be acquired. The unrealistic obduracy of the popular party was not, however, without a basis in experience: the temporizing attitude taken toward Charles I's demands had succeeded in keeping Massachusetts independent until the Puritan revolution alleviated matters. A similar policy might well succeed until another turn for the better occurred in London. New Englanders knew they were not the only Englishmen who disliked Stuart supremacy. Less attached to England in their daily lives, more habituated to the simple democracy of village manners and the town meeting, and increasingly distrustful of the artificiality of social distinctions and the new-fangledness of manners in the trading towns which accompanied the rise in prices from which they suffered, the members of the popular party felt strong reason not to compromise.

As individuals the clergy were not so closely affiliated to a political ideal that they were unresponsive to the realities of their particular congregations, popular or moderate. As an emerging professional class, they stood strongly for the charter, the source of their own particular privileges and a bulwark against the establishment of the Church of England in their colony. Their natural conservatism, however, was not a simple matter. The popular party too was conservative in wanting to maintain the status quo, but the implications of maintaining it against royal demands were radical, whereas the implications of the moderate tendency to compromise were conservative. When consulted by the General Court, therefore, the clergy provided the rhetoric for standing foursquare on the charter, but also continually cautioned against rashness, said rashness being the refusal to continue the dialogue of negotiation. In 1683 Increase Mather spoke for the profession when in response to the *quo warranto* issued against the charter he said, "We know that Jephthah said, that which the Lord our God has given us, shall we not possess! And Naboth, though he ran a great hazard by the refusal, yet said, God forbid that I should give away the inheritance of my fathers. . . . We know that David made a wise choice when he chose to fall into the hands of God rather than into the hands of men. If we make a full submission and entire resignation to pleasure, we fall into the hands of men immediately. But if we do not we keep ourselves still in the hands of God, and trust ourselves with His providence and who knoweth what God may do for us?" [15] This was the high point of ministerial counseling to resistance and came in the heat of shocked reaction to the fact that the charter had, in effect, died, although New England was called to send agents to attend its burial. Thereafter, the ministerial class came more and more to see the status quo as best preserved by compromise and to develop its own structure of professional church government to substitute for the structure once provided by the magistrates under the charter. That structure was necessarily a near-Presbyterianism, and once royal government in New England became a digested fact, the thwarted democratic instinct was kept alive in individual protests against the power of ministerial associations, a less seditious exercise than opposing royal authority. John Wise was to have a consistently courageous career of protest from his unsuccessful resistance to Andros's taxes to his successful resistance to ministerial association.

Increase Mather and John Wise provide striking examples of ministers who were still men of the street as well as the study, native-born New Englanders who in entering the ministry were serving their towns and commonwealth in positions that they regarded as the most potent possible. But as a group the clergy were withdrawing from political affairs, and, indeed, from 1675 to 1685 the profession as a whole suffered such a decline that only fifty-two men qualified for the Bachelor of Arts degree at Harvard during that period.[16] Public affairs were passing out of ministerial hands, and the clergy accordingly developed a specialized relationship to politics: they saw themselves as the chroniclers and validaters of New England's claim to have a special relationship to divine providence and allowed others to pursue the practical matter of defining what New England's relationship was to be to the British empire. The economic argument that the fathers of New England had developed a wilderness at their own expense intersected with the spiritual argument that God through a remarkable dispensation of His grace had chosen a people to conquer American nature. The clergy as a class increasingly concentrated on documenting the latter event and left the implications of the former to men of affairs. The wilderness was common metaphor, but it was no longer a single theme.

The separation of the theme into two was recognized, for example, by John Higginson, minister of Salem and descendant of Francis Higginson, the leader of the first Puritan church established in Massachusetts. In response to threats to the charter, he wrote Increase Mather in 1683, proposing that a treatise be drawn up called "The divine right of the liberty of Christians in all things that belong to the Christian religion, according to the blessed Gospel of our Lord and Savior Jesus Christ." This, he said, was the cause that led our fathers into the wilderness. John Higginson said to Mather: "For though we are many ways obliged to do our duty to preserve our civil rights according to the charter of this colony, yet they are not to be confounded with, but distinguished from our religious rights, which we have (not from men, but) from the charter of the Gospel of Jesus Christ, and though good men differ in their apprehensions about the [wa]y and manner of keeping our charter, (as in the General Court,) [yet I] would hope there is not a conscientious minister in New England but will agree in the cause of religion as expressed before." [17] Not untypical of the members of his profession, Higginson was concerned for the charter, but that, ultimately, was not in his hands. What was in his hands was the cause of religion, and this was to be advanced by a theological treatise.

Although nothing was written that quite matched John Higginson's request, vigorous ministerial efforts were made to meet that profession's felt need for a documentation of the uniqueness of New England's relation with God. In 1679 Nathaniel Morton of Plymouth bewailed the declensions of the time and called for a general history of New England to be written for the ominous reason that not only was it a needed reminder of the core of the common identity but that it must soon be done, or all who were aware of the need for it would be dead.[18] He appears to have been mistaken. Those who had experienced the great days were indeed dying off, but the consequence was that their descendants were eager to see them glorified in histories. Morton himself had made a notable contribution in his *New Englands Memoriall* (1669), based heavily on Bradford's unpublished history of Plymouth, and in 1682 the General Court voted £50 to William Hubbard, minister of Ipswich, to encourage him in the writing of a general history of New England. Hubbard had in 1677 published an account of the recent Indian wars, but his general history, based heavily on Morton's superior work, did not find wide acceptance beyond the Court's initial grant, and remained unpublished until 1815.

The relative neglect of Hubbard's completed history, however, was the result of his lackluster technique rather than of unconcern with such projects. Another ministerial scheme was entered into far more heartily when a meeting of ministers in May 1681 put forth proposals for the recording of illustrious providences. "Inasmuch as we find in Scripture, as well as in ecclesiastical history," they declared, "that the ministers of God have been improved in the recording and declaring the works of the Lord, and since they are in divers respects under peculiar advantages thereunto, it is proposed that each one in that capacity may diligently enquire into and record such illustrious providences as have happened, or from time to time shall happen, in the places whereunto they do belong; and that the witnesses of such notable occurrences be likewise set down in writing." [19] All clergymen in the colony were urged to aid in compiling the records, for "such divine judgments, tempests, floods, earthquakes, thunders as are unusual, strange apparitions, or whatever else shall happen that is prodigious, witchcrafts, diabolical possessions, remarkable judgments upon noted sinners, eminent deliverances, and answers of prayer, are to be reckoned among illustrious providences." [20] Increase Mather was appointed as collator, and the collection, *Remarkable Providences*, duly appeared in 1684 with ample editorial protestation that the work had just begun and that many more examples remained to be gathered as well as new categories established.

Some instinct that may be called scientific is in operation in the book, because the divine events are to be verified by observation and so collated that some general principles of God's providence may be inferred. But the instinct is weaker than the desire to establish a special relationship with God, and, as Perry Miller observes, such work was undertaken "in the hope that science, by bringing home to the multitude the horrors and dangers of diabolical possessions and witchcrafts, would keep alive allegiance to the ancient ways of New England even after a foreign authority had commanded concessions to difference of opinion." [21] What further requires emphasis is that, in the call to record providences, "witchcrafts" and "diabolical possessions" follow the phrase "whatever else shall happen" as an all-but-conscious augury of delusions to which those in New England who wished to continue the external drama of God's special interest in them would be susceptible.

Cotton Mather certainly furthered this end when in 1689 he published his *Memorable Providences*. In it he taught the reader to use his father's *Remarkable Providences* as a checklist of how those possessed by the devil behave. It is clear that the Goodwin children, who were possessed in 1688 and his dealings with whom form a substantial part of his book, had behaved in accordance with a pattern taught them by his father's work. Cotton Mather encouraged the sense that the Lord's interest in New England could be regarded as of strong continuance just as readily by developing evidence of witchcraft there as by developing evidence of extraordinary blessings. Addressing his book, he said, "Go tell mankind, that there are devils and witches; and that though those night-birds least appear where the daylight of the Gospel comes, yet New England has had examples of their existence and operation; and that not only the wigwams of the Indians, where the pagan powows often raise their masters . . . but the houses of Christians, where our God has His constant worship, have undergone the annoyance of evil spirits. Go tell the world what prayers can do beyond all devils and witches, and what it is that these monsters love to do . . . and in this way seek a just revenge on them for the disturbances they have given to such as have called on the name of God." [22]

The ministers who signed the book's address to the reader also encouraged the notion that evidence of diabolical possession was evidence that the divine drama was still being enacted in Massachusetts. Angels and men, they explained, are not made for civil converse with one another. Communion with devils, however, although interdicted, is not impossible. "The secrets . . . of God's providence in permitting Satan and his instruments to molest His children, not in their estates only, but in their persons and posterity too, are part of His judgments that are unsearchable, and His ways that are past finding out; only this we have good assurance for, that they are among the all things that work together for their good." [23] The reference to men molested in their estates is a passing attribution of satanic inspiration to the behavior of the royal authorities. Charles Morton, minister of Charlestown and one of the signers of the address, had been tried by the Andros government in 1687 for preaching a sermon "containing several seditious expressions." [24] He had been acquitted, but not before his estate was severely reduced by the high expenses of his defense. The center of the ministerial concern, however, is Satan's operation on persons, and this is seen as a correlative of political events. Just as civil oppression confirms men in their sense of their true rights, so witchcraft is confirming evidence of the spirit of God among the people. This clerical interpretation of the special task the clergy had taken upon themselves was to have vivid consequences in the next few years, when their assertions served as stimulus and their documentation as guide to those whose discontents were too mundane to be given attention unless couched in a vocabulary of satanic drama now made available as an explanation of the adversities of real life.

Memorable Providences bears strong, if unconscious, evidence of the power of the religious education of children in New England. The afflicted Goodwin child who was taken to live with Cotton Mather so that he could observe the devil's operations more effectively could not, when she was under diabolic possession, read the Psalms in ancient meter, nor could she read from the Bible when it was presented to her. But at that time she could easily read from "a certain prayer book," which is to say that her training had taught her the wickedness of the Church of England's Book of Common Prayer. Mather's elephantine coyness rarely shows through more unpleasantly than in his reflections on this altogether predictable phenomenon. He had, after all, selected the books presented to the child, and in so doing he was articulating his own reaction to the presence in Boston of a priest of the established church, who ministered chiefly to members of the governor's staff. He improved the fact of the child's ability to read from the Book of Common Prayer when possessed thus: "But I make no reflections on it. Those inconsiderable men that are provoked at it (if any shall be of so little sense as to be provoked) must be angry at the devils, and not at me; their malice and not my writing, deserves the blame of any aspersions which a true history may seem to cast on a book that some have enough manifested their concernment for." [25] His desire to score a point in the pettier aspect of the struggle with royal authority overcame whatever prudence he had and provided a context for those who would use the belief in the worldly operations of devils to relieve the oppression they experienced in everyday life, even to the extent of seeing villagers hang for it.

The greatest monument of clerical withdrawal from the political scene into a position of commentary on its eternal implications is unquestionably *Magnalia Christi Americana*, the immense history of New England finished by Cotton Mather in 1702. In it his provoking habit of calling attention to his learning and to the particular accomplishments of his own family by ponderous indirection is writ large, but also in it are preserved the details of the lives of a large number of New Englanders and valuable records of their gatherings. Mather's antiquarian instincts were matched by his incredible stamina, so that in including much of what even in his age was regarded as trivial he did in effect preserve the details of daily conditions that, however much they were aside from his main purpose, now serve as a treasury for modern historians whose theories of causality differ greatly from his. The style is unique, echoing in part the compendious works of such metaphysically oriented writers as Robert Burton and Sir Thomas Browne, whose certainty and ingenuity of mind provided a durable scaffold in accordance with which the petty and the pedantic found lasting form. Unequipped with their natural eloquence, Mather was, nevertheless, equipped with their classical learning as well as a facility in a number of modern tongues, and had models aplenty in addition to the central one of the Virgilian epic. The *Magnalia* is a work symbolic to the point of caricature of the vast intellectual energy that resided in the New England clergy and that, after that class retreated from politics into the study, lacked an outlet with scope. In current terminology, it is a monument to the alienation of the intellectual from a society that no longer regards his interests as vital, and a demonstration of the validity of that social presumption even as it documents the power society has thereby deprived itself of. The import of a baffled sensibility of gigantic proportions that the *Magnalia* conveys is not unlike that conveyed by Herman Melville in *Moby Dick*, but in Melville's case the work that grew as a result of his withdrawal from society found a large audience among those who, after the passing of that society, were responsive to the emotional and intellectual expression of his criticism of it. Mather was denied such an audience after his time because his criticism of his time is not expressed in an integrated vision of history. Rather, as Peter Gay observes, "Over and over again Mather interprets critical moments in Puritan society as personal crises, social conflicts as the struggles of individual Christians with Satan. Mather dissolves history into biography." [26] His piety, strongly tribal, led him to glorify persons as examples of his theme. On the eve of the novel's birth, his was the stuff of novelists. In writing history he offered only history's shards.

Cotton Mather's peculiar unrelatedness to his society was recognized by many in his time, although they did not see in it a symbol of the shifting role of the clergy. "I am glad to see your son so well furnished with evangelical knowledge," a minister wrote Increase Mather. "I only wish he delivered truths in your style, in that plainness of expression which the Gospels teach & most conduce to edification." [27] But although Cotton was an extreme example of the unplain and especially of the unseasonable, he was not untypical. Increase, with his English experience and his undeniable political gifts, was, in his effectiveness, becoming untypical of the ministry in general. John Dunton, ever on the lookout for profitable manuscripts to publish, noted of his meetings with Cotton Mather, "There is abundance of freedom and familiarity in the humor of this gentleman. His conversation and writings are living evidences that he has read much, but there are many that will not allow him the prudence to make a seasonable use of it." With a sighing sound that may well be the seventeenth-century equivalent of a rejection slip, Dunton goes on, "His library is very large and numerous; but, had his books been fewer when he wrote his 'History,' it would have pleased us better." [28]

With his intellectual proclivities so alienated from his society, Cotton Mather tirelessly developed his energies in the direction of moral aims connected with his pastoral charge. Temperance societies, young men's clubs, schemes for moral watchdog associations, and schedules of home visitations proliferated in his study, and it was this half of the split in his energies that was to have the more notable immediate consequences. Living at Passy in 1784, Cotton's some-time parishioner Benjamin Franklin wrote to Cotton's son Samuel, praising Cotton's *Bonifacius*, or *Essays to Do Good* (1710), saying that it had an influence on his conduct throughout his life. "I have always set a greater value on the character of a *doer of good*, than on any other kind of reputation," [29] Franklin wrote and in so doing revealed that Cotton Mather had, indeed, been fragmented. Morality replaced piety for Franklin, whereas it stemmed from it for Mather, and the runaway apprentice to the Puritan tradition emphasized the market value of a reputation for morality rather than the thing itself. Franklin epitomized the fact that the school of hard knocks could well substitute for the learning of the Puritan tradition and yet comport with the social and economic effectiveness that was also ingrained in the tradition, and he fixed that perception in the anecdote he told Samuel Mather:

> The last time I saw your father was in the beginning of 1724, when I visited him after my first trip to Pennsylvania. He received me in his library, and on my taking leave showed me a shorter way out of the house through a narrow passage, which was covered by a beam over head. We were still talking as I withdrew, he accompanying me behind, and I turning partly towards him, when he said hastily, *"Stoop, stoop!"* I did not understand him, till I felt my head hit against the beam. He was a man that never missed any occasion of giving instruction, and upon this he said to me, *"You are young, and have the world before you;* STOOP *as you go through it, and you will miss many hard thumps."* This advice, thus beat into my head, has frequently been of use to me; and I often think of it, when I see pride mortified and misfortunes brought upon people by their carrying their heads too high. [30]

Benjamin Franklin's *Autobiography* is the record of what Puritan habits detached from Puritan beliefs were capable of achieving in the eighteenth-century world of affairs. The diary technique of soul-searching for signs of the presence of grace was adapted to a review of the day's external accomplishments, and the boundless belief in salvation through fellowship in a community of the saved adapted to schemes of social betterment through association. But the Puritan influence was not confined to formulas for worldly success. Puritanism had become a reflex way of perceiving reality: of how to engage in social intercourse, interpret the implications of daily events with a disciplined conscience, and retain a consciousness of one's identity as an individual and as a member of a people. It was, in New England especially, a way of life, the structure of which was more durable than passing events or changing opinions. This was manifested most obviously in the culture's manners, most profoundly in the creations of those gifted writers in the nineteenth century who were to produce the first considerable body of American literary works.

The growing influence of royal authority from 1676 was countered on a level beneath words by a culture that had developed habits of its own. The society was forced in great part to yield, but it was resilient beyond the yielding. In the period from the first appearance at Boston of the royal agent, Edward Randolph, to the Glorious Revolution, the men of affairs in Massachusetts were compelled to a more effective verbal expression of their political beliefs than they had previously accomplished. Since this was in reaction to a force stronger than themselves, their articulation took the form of specific argument rather than extended theory. Nevertheless, a distinct outlook is discernible.

Massachusetts had extended its political control over the settlements in New Hampshire and Maine principally through application of the same principle that had permitted it to bring the localities of such as Samuel Gorton under its jurisdiction: by accepting the submission of certain residents in those areas as definitive. Other residents resented what they regarded as usurpation, and Massachusetts procedure was, indeed, more blatantly illegal with regard to the eastern territories because the Gorges family seemed to hold a clear patent for Maine and the Mason family for New Hampshire. To these patents, however, Massachusetts opposed the principle that, in the absence of a secure government, residents could voluntarily submit to what government they chose, and also the rule of expedience, because the border with the French and hostile Indians had to be secured. Massachusetts was doing so at its own expense and was not, as the Canadians did, taxing the purse of the monarch.

In 1674 the heirs to the Maine and New Hampshire patents made forcible protest to the royal government and baited their request for assistance by offering to surrender the patents to the King in exchange for one-third of the customs, rents, fines, and other profits of the territory. This was the occasion of the first forceful presence of a royal agent in Massachusetts.[31] Edward Randolph arrived in 1676 to ask that Massachusetts send agents to London to answer the claims of Gorges and Mason.

At the same time English merchants and manufacturers were becoming increasingly annoyed at New England disregard of the Navigation Acts and were insisting on protection from what they regarded as illegal practices ruinous to them and the whole of Great Britain. They were especially formidable opponents because New England had traditionally drawn its political support in England from that class and now had its Parliamentary and pressure-group alliances seriously weakened. While Randolph was in Massachusetts awaiting reply to the request for agents to be sent, he took shrewd notice of violations of the Navigation Acts and began discussions with those who were unhappy with the General Court's procedures and well disposed toward compromise with royal demands. Indeed he was so diligent in these efforts that Governor Leverett accused him of going about to raise a mutiny.

The haggling over Maine and New Hampshire resulted, in the short run, in Massachusetts purchasing rights to the former and withdrawing from the latter, but this was only a beginning. Randolph returned to Massachusetts in 1681 as collector of customs, organizer of a royal party in the colony, and tireless reporter to the home government of abuses in Massachusetts. The wedge between moderate and popular parties drove firmly into the political life of Massachusetts. In 1683 a *quo warranto* was issued against the charter, the popular party insisting that it should be answered not by agents who were apt to be compromised once they were near the royal presence, but by a London attorney. In the following year the charter was vacated in the Court of Chancery. The General Court of 1685 was a feeble assembly, conscious of its impending demise, and after being provisionally replaced by a council of royally appointed moderates it was replaced permanently, it was presumed, when Governor Edmund Andros arrived in 1686.

Andros was an experienced and efficient administrator who even after the Glorious Revolution was to continue in posts of royal trust, although not in New England, and his immense unpopularity was the result of measures that were, in terms of his charge, entirely legal. He insisted that the Navigation Acts be observed, that all landholders pay quitrents, that his government be supported by property taxes even though the taxed were no longer assessed by an assembly of those they elected, that religious toleration be instituted, that the South Church provide accommodation for the Church of England congregation until it could build for itself, and that the members of his administration be treated as privileged members of the society. Andros did not seek to compromise with the more democratic habits of the people he governed because those habits, in his experienced view, simply were not conducive to the success of his mission, and he boldly moved to check them wherever they appeared in institutions. He ruled without legislatures, reduced town meetings to once a year, canceled the compulsory education requirements because they did not include compulsory religious training in the established church in agreement with English law, and appointed the officers of the militia rather than permitting them to remain elective. While countering the popular party in this way, he welcomed into his circle any moderates who were willing to assist his administration and encouraged in Massachusetts the development of a native group composed of those who could serve as executors of royal policy.

The political statements of opposition to royal supremacy were, at first, a confused mixture of emotional appeal to the faith of the founders and idealistic trust in the fact that the same providence that had undone Charles I would eventually undo his sons. The charter was not to be surrendered, the popular party insisted in 1683, because the sixth commandment was against it: "Men may not destroy their political lives any more than their natural lives." [32] In this initial stage of reaction, however, there was already peeping through the rhetoric a sense of the peculiar rights not of God's chosen people but of Englishmen. In 1683 such rights were still entangled in the rhetoric of biblical citation and were asserted to refute the import of the observation that the Lord's people had in the Bible been commanded to surrender in entirety to the rule of the court of Babylon: "He scarce deserved the name of an Englishman that should thus argue. Because those monarchs were absolute, must Englishmen, who are under a limited monarchy, consent to be in that misery and slavery which the captive Jews were in?" [33]

The colonists were not yet prepared for a republican insistence that the people always retain the supreme power in their hands and merely delegate it to legislature or monarch at their pleasure, but they quickly developed their experience with covenants into a sense that they had entered into a compact with their ruler that limited his authority, and that James in the assertion of his supremacy was in clear violation of it. Moreover, as they tirelessly insisted, there was now a precedent in Massachusetts for legislative government and a particular form of religion as the exclusive one. As Andros's administration took hold, however, the New Englanders began to abandon arguments drawn from their own history, however much that history actually fed their resistance, and to concentrate on arguments drawn from the rights they possessed as Englishmen rather than New Englanders. With the accession of the Roman Catholic James and the resumption in France of the persecution of the Protestants in 1685, they could, they felt, make common cause with those in England who proclaimed English rights and liberties, and they did not hesitate to couple their dislike of Andros's administration with a distrust of the encroachments of papism. Although unsupported by evidence, the popular belief in Massachusetts was that, just as James had a strong ally in the persecuting King of France, so Andros was scheming with the French and Indians in Canada to ruin Massachusetts. Royal interest in Maine and New Hampshire, many New Englanders felt, was really an aspect of an anti-Protestant conspiracy. Rabble-rousing rhetoric coupled Indian alarms with papal policy and Massachusetts with Magna Charta.

On a more reasoned level, however, Massachusetts public men

were forced to think in legal terms within the English tradition rather than to rely on a tribal belief in their privileged differences, however useful such belief continued to be in rallying popular support. Their sense of the particular identity of New England had to be phrased so as to meet the consistent legal view that centered on three issues: the difference between dominion and empire; the nature of legal acquisition of land in a colony; and the nature of expansion of settlement in a colony. They had to think about these matters as Englishmen because, as Andros's legal adviser coolly pointed out to them, they could cite the history of the true church and the practice of their parents forever, but all such amounted to legally was claiming certain rights and procedures by prescription, and "the colony hath not been long enough settled, to claim any advantage by that right." [34] English legal tradition challenged Puritan ahistoricity and relegated it to the pulpit and to remarkable providences.

A dominion of the crown of England, as opposed to the empire of the King of England, was the direct property of the crown, "subject to such laws, ordinances, and forms of government, as the crown shall think fit to establish," [35] with no such limitation on authority as existed in the empire, which owed allegiance to the King but was not part of crown property. New Englanders, in opposing the Andros administration, had to learn how to claim for themselves the rights of those in the empire rather than accept their being of the dominion, and if they cited Magna Charta they had to attach themselves to its guarantees by closer reasoning than the mere citation. The profession of the law, which had been distrusted and disregarded among the early Puritans as the profession that most clearly grew from the corruptions of human nature and was most obviously superfluous in a commonwealth of the godly, now had to be taken seriously. At no points in their colonial history did New Englanders more acutely develop their knowledge of English law and their sense of being Englishmen than at those when they wanted most to assert their differences from England. The period that immediately preceded the American Revolution represents the fullest example of this; then lawyers came to the fore as revolutionary leaders and rallied a people to resistance to England with the rhetoric of English common law.

In Massachusetts in 1686, the distinction between dominion and empire first raised the phenomenon, and thereafter the Puritan genius for theological distinction was permitted an outlet in the field of English law. This, in effect, permanently outdated any ministerial claims to political leadership. Increase Mather's embassy to the court in 1688 was the last example of such leadership, if, indeed, his position can be regarded as at all relevant to his selection for the task. Such a shift also prepared the grounds for the ministerial defense of the important daily consequences of their professional concerns that fed the witchcraft hysteria of the next decade. The witchcraft trials were the last occasion on which theology took precedence over law, and the air of insanity that hung over them was a sign that the precedence was already anachronistic.

The issue of the ownership of the land was settled, in royal terms, by the theory of dominion. In settling their land under charter from Henry VII's heirs the people of New England possessed a right to the land only so long as the charter was valid. That charter having been vacated in law, the land reverted back to the crown.

In opposition, New Englanders advanced a doctrine that was also with precedent in English law. In defiance of the pretensions of Spain and France in the new world, English policy had in the past recognized the right of occupation and purchase from the natives. Forced into debate on the matter by Andros and his councilors, John Higginson of Salem, after protesting that he was no lawyer, said that the New Englanders had entered into their rights in the land "partly as wilderness and *vacuum domicilium,* and partly by the consent of the Indians, and therefore care was taken to treat with them, and to gain their consent, giving them such a valuable consideration as was to their satisfaction." "I told them," he said, "I had heard it was a standing principle in law and reason, *Nil dat qui non habet*; and from thence I propounded this argument; he that hath no right, can give no right to another, but the King had no rights to the lands of *America* before the English came hither, therefore he could give no right to them. I told them I knew not of any that could be pleaded but from a popish principle, that Christians have a right to the lands of the heathen, upon which the Pope as the head of Christians had given the West Indies to the King of Spain, but this was disowned by all Protestants." [36] However superior the gracious were to the natural, their superiority did not extend to seizure of property. The earth belonged to the sons of Adam, not just to Christians, and their rights could not be usurped. New Englanders owned their land by right of purchase from the original proprietors, the Indians, rather than from any presumption that their King or his ancestors could own the land merely by proclaiming that they did. In elaborating this argument the settlers were elaborating a theme that Roger Williams had early entered upon in opposition to the policy of Winthrop's administration, which tended to lay claim to disputed border areas under the doctrine that they were the King's and Massachusetts Bay was the King's chartered government. The Indians' rights became a crucial legal principle in 1686, whatever the actual practice had been. Little hypocrisy was involved, since the colonists did believe that they had made purchase and since they were insensible of, rather than in knowing opposition to, the Indians' idea of what land rights meant. To the settlers, the forms of treaty and purchase meant right to possess, whereas to the Indians they meant the right to use.

With regard to the third issue, that of how unoccupied lands were to be developed, Andros's policy was impatient with the Puritans' cautious communal advance toward the frontier. "It cannot be consistent with the interests of new plantations," it was insisted, "that two or three hundred thousand acres of land should be taken up by a small number of people, who are not capable of improving one tenth part of it; and the rest be vacant under the notion of commons, when persons of ability, equally concerned, would improve it, but cannot, because they are less numerous than the poorer sort of the town, whose advantage it is that land should so lie, and who manage their affairs by majority of voices." [37] The playing with numbers was transparent; whereas Puritan policy was attacked as reserving lands to a small number of people, it was also criticized because the majority held land back from the few. What was envisioned in such an attack was the immediate award of town commons to gentlemen of Andros's party, and eventually the creation of large estates and the establishment of a landed gentry, if not an aristocracy, as a counterweight to the democracy of Massachusetts towns.

Although deprived of the legal argument of precedent for their pattern of settlement, the New Englanders could and did scathingly cite the difference between their prosperous, orderly commonwealth and those English plantations to the south settled in accordance with the principles Andros enunciated, "inhabited by a people who commonly cannot, or may not have any principles of honor, honesty, industry, or virtue, miserable subjects of oppression and slavery, deceit and violence; who instead of turning a barren wilderness into a fruitful field, have commonly turned a fruitful field into a barren wilderness." [38] With regard to this issue, the culture based on the ability of the masterless man to be his own master, and centered on a concern for responsible covenanting and the literacy requisite for such responsibility, was unhesitating in its assertion of human dignity. However much its picture of itself was blotted in detail by punitive action against dissenters, its outline emerged without falsification as one of a society of men who were free and capable far beyond the antiquated fantasies of those who longed for a hierarchical society. The magnificent vehemence of New England rhetoric on this issue stems from an amply perceivable matching of observed detail with a spirit of human rights that swallows distinctions of legal rights. The pattern royal supremacy longs for in the colony, says the proponent of New England, is well known from practices elsewhere in America: "A poor naked hungry governor comes usually from the court every three years with a troop of miserable, debauched followers, and for the most part guilty of one crime or other, whose debaucheries, ignorance and necessities, provoke them to innumerable practices of fraud and violence. They do that in some of the English colonies, which it may be was never done by any civil people upon earth, *for they buy and sell one another for debt*." [39] The outrage there is more than defensive; it is a cry, finally, on behalf of what Puritanism has demonstrated man is capable of accomplishing. "They have made their plantations prisons as well as dens of slavery;

for none can go out of any of them without permission from the governor for the time and place; and by this, they deprive mankind at once of the only valuable thing in the world, *precious liberty.*" [40]

The pamphleteer may have overstepped the theological boundaries in his final assertion, but if he did so it was merely an overstepping, not a destruction. His culture was now moving in the direction he led, and Puritanism in America was coming to terms with the political consequences of its doctrine. Freed from ministerial restrictions, political thinkers in developing their ideas saw that Puritanism meant liberty. For one heady moment during the Puritan Revolution in England, it also contained the promise of economic redistribution,[41] but if this had been thwarted in England and obviated by the frontier conditions of New England, the political consequences of self-mastery were nevertheless to find a congenial soil in New England once they had separated themselves from theology. John Wise, who was to take an important step in that separation, had been among the group of men from Ipswich who refused to pay taxes to the Andros administration because they were not levied by representatives of the people taxed. They testified: "The Governor Sir Edmund Andros said to some of us by way of ridicule whether we thought if Jack & Tom tell the king what monies he must have for the use of his government implying that the people of the country were a parcel of ignorant Jacks and Toms and that he & his crew had the immediate dispose of our fortunes and we were to be put to bedlam for mad men." [42] Jack and Tom had cohered into a consciousness of themselves as free citizens.

The first major adventure of royal supremacy in New England had, then, accelerated the separation into specialized concerns of that culture's components. Merchants and farmers were further polarized, and the ministry was confined to seeking influence through interpretation of events rather than leadership in them, through keeping alive the sense of divine drama in daily life and ritually lamenting rather than opposing its direction. Jack and Tom were coming to see that the political liberty of the people was consistent with the Christian liberty of the saints. The culture in which these specialized concerns were becoming marked retained coherence because it yielded to their separation and reinterpreted the self-distinction it held dear in terms of the wider world of politics—French and Indians to the north, subjugated colonists to the south, Whigs and Tories in the homeland. New England was still a special place.

CHAPTER TEN

This Monday

Social consequences of the new charter—
Anti-French policy and Sir William Phips—
Legislative reaction to Negroes and the poor—Witchcraft

In 1687 James II sought to gain the support of nonconformists by a policy of indulgence in pursuit of which he could also loosen the restrictions imposed on the practice of his own religion, Roman Catholicism. After a brief flirtation with the King, however, most nonconformists concluded they were better off uniting with their old foes in the Church of England in anti-Catholic measures rather than compromising with Roman Catholicism in cooperating with James's policies. When the news of James's indulgence reached Massachusetts, however, more than a gesture was called for. Ten churches prepared an address thanking the King for his religious policy and, Increase Mather recorded, "It was by sundry good and wise men judged expedient that some one should go to London with the address, who might there obtain an interest in such nonconformists as have the King's ear; as in special take care for the well settlement of the college." [1] He accepted the mission and left in April 1688, departing secretly because officers had been charged to arrest him on the ground that he had in his public pronouncements defamed Edward Randolph. Although there was some basis for the charge, it is equally clear that royal administrators in New England would just as lief not have Mather at the court in London.

Four years later Mather returned under very different circumstances. William and Mary had succeeded James in a bloodless revolution, and from being the bearer of thanks to his sovereign and the petitioner for a charter for Harvard College, Increase Mather had become the colony's agent in negotiating the terms under which Massachusetts would be governed for the remainder of its colonial life. When the news of the Glorious Revolution had reached Massachusetts in the spring of 1689, the people took to the streets and in a professed spontaneity that had something of design in it arrested Sir Edmund Andros and members of his administration and restored Governor Simon Bradstreet and the members of the General Court who had last ruled under the charter, against the day of a new election.[2] In spite of the new monarchs' being vigorous Protestants—indeed, this was the prime factor in their accession— many moderates such as Governor Bradstreet were uneasy about so anti-royal a move as the imprisonment of Andros and the resumption of charter government, and Cotton Mather, nervously anxious that his father should have the freest hand possible in London, was reluctant about the drastic measures also. But popular fervor against the Andros administration now had opportunity for release, and most responsible men recognized that the restoration of the 1685 government was prudent in the light of the larger excesses of which the people were capable in the loosing of their long-suppressed hate.

What Massachusetts most obviously wanted from William and Mary was a confirmation of the charter vacated in 1684, but Increase Mather in his diplomatic maneuverings felt he clearly perceived that such was never again to be. The popular party at home disagreed with him, after the fact and at a distance rather than from close experience with royal negotiations, and never forgave him for acting on his perception. But although he returned to a commonwealth that contained a substantial party that was ever to remain deeply resentful of his compromise, he clearly appears to have acted to obtain the utmost self-determination possible for Massachusetts and not to have compromised until he reached the limit of what he could achieve toward the conditions of the old charter. The elected General Court was restored, but the governor and his deputy were henceforth, under the new charter, to be royal appointees. Moreover, the franchise was now extended to property-holders without regard to church certification. Maine was again placed under Massachusetts control, and Plymouth finally lost its independence and was absorbed into the larger colony.[3]

The ground that the popular party could always improve against Mather was that, although New Hampshire now became a separate royal colony, Connecticut and Rhode Island had their old charters restored and enjoyed a degree of autonomy unmatched by any other units in the British Empire. Least involved in trade of all the colonies, Connecticut under its restored charter quickly moved to provide the kind of government longed for by the popular party in Massachusetts. A 40-shilling freehold was needed for admission to freemanship, and at town meetings each freeman made his own list of twenty nominees for the magistracy. The lists were sent to Hartford, and there a collective list of the first twenty-eight names was drawn up and returned to town meetings, where balloting for governor, deputy governor, and twelve magistrates then took place from names on the collective list.[4] But in its relative rural poverty Connecticut also had to relinquish town control over lands that were sold outright without communal approval, and, with speculators an increasing factor in Connecticut economic life, the tone of politics was harshly divisive.[5] As a consequence of civil politics developing so disputatious a character, church policy turned conservative, and ministerial association there amounted to Presbyterianism. The clergy assumed firm professional control of the churches, now that they were removed from direct involvement in civil politics through the removal of the requirement of membership for the franchise. The popular party in Massachusetts did not approve of a good deal of actual practice in Connecticut, but that colony did provide an example of where popular instincts tended: strict local control of civil government along democratic lines and strict professional control of churches along autocratic lines. In Massachusetts, however, the popular party had to contend with a far more mercantile economy than that of Connecticut, and the merchants, recognizing their dependence upon English cooperation and distrustful of the punitive measures that might be taken against them by a strictly democratic government, welcomed, in the main, the kind of arrangement procured by Increase Mather. Indeed, even as the popular party fulminated against Mather's charter for falling short of the original charter, a substantial if small group of the merchant class sought a greater degree of autocracy than that provided under the Mather charter on the condition that it would remain in their hands.

According to the new charter, the governor's council was to be elected by members of both houses of the General Court, but this was in fact reduced to a nominating power because the governor could veto their selections. Since the General Court represented the smaller property-holders, the main political efforts of the large merchants were addressed to controlling or at least influencing the governor. Their success was considerable because Sir William Phips, the first governor under the 1691 charter, was, among other things, a merchant, and his council was composed in the main of merchants. Although they were a weighty pressure group, the merchants did not as yet constitute a distinct social class. Notions of gentry, insofar as Massachusetts possessed them, were still tied up with first families, and these, in turn, drew at least part of their income from the land, even though many members of them had moved also into trade and industry. As Bernard Bailyn indicates, "In New England in the 1690's, as indeed throughout the eighteenth century, the occupation of trade, though it defined an area of common interests for the men engaged in it, did not delimit a stratum of society as it did in England. It was not so much a way of life as a way of making money; not a social but an economic activity. It was the most important single vehicle for social ascent. By the wealth and connections it offered as by nothing else could one traverse the slope of colonial society." [6]

The difference from England, where merchants were an actual class below the gentry, is illustrated by Samuel Richardson. His *Pamela*, seeking those who would help to release her from her Lincolnshire captivity, is told by the friendly curate: "We have here the widow Lady Jones, mistress of a good fortune; and a woman of virtue, I believe. We have also old Sir Simon Darnford, and his lady, who is a good woman; and they have two daughters, virtuous young ladies. All the rest are but middling people, and traders; at best." [7] In New England first families and traders were not so separate.

Richard Dunn records a revealing model of their growing alliance, for example, when he traces the history of the Winthrop family through three generations and shows how in Randolph's day the Winthrops could cultivate him for business purposes and yet retain local respect, and in the next decade could strengthen their ties with trade through marriage, even as the merchants were thereby acquiring social prestige. An epitome of provincial social distinction is provided by the letter of the royal Governor in 1708, Joseph Dudley. The occasion is a dispute within the Winthrop family over Connecticut property jointly held by Fitz Winthrop, former Governor of the colony, who had recently died, and his brother Wait, a member of Dudley's council whose son John had married Dudley's daughter Anne. Fitz had willed the land to his daughter Mary Livingston of Connecticut, but in a successful if unpopular suit in that colony Wait insisted that the will was invalid because he had an interest in the property, and in his interest Dudley, appointed Governor of Massachusetts, wrote to Gurdon Saltonstall, elected Governor of Connecticut: "You will give me leave to tell you that [it] is the first family in this province, more than the first in your colony. . . . We are some of us English gentlemen, . . . & we should labor to support such families because truly we want them." [8]

By Dudley's governing days Massachusetts had settled into the colonial pattern that was to mark its politics until the days of the Revolution: an unpopular royal governor starved by an uncooperative popular assembly with whom he warred and whom he scorned socially as well as politically; a governor who accepted the division between merchant and countryman and ruled by alliance with the former rather than by attempting to compromise differences. But the vision of those who supported the charter that Increase Mather secured was different at first, and the Dudley pattern did not come into being until that vision had been tried and found wanting.

The anti-Catholic fervor that accompanied William and Mary's landing in Cornwall and progression to London in 1688 was to become a matter of policy rather than mere sentiment during their administration. France now came to take up the role in English policy that had not been played so forcefully since Spain had acted it out in the days of Elizabeth: the menacing military arm of papal claims to domination over the civilized world and the damaging commercial rival in the extension of empire. The new charter was framed with a nervous eye on the French to the north of New England, and Maine was restored to Massachusetts control in great part because such a move would assure voluntary local defense of the frontier; at the news of Andros's imprisonment in Boston the militia sent to posts in Maine abandoned their positions. Polemical tracts against Andros and on behalf of the liberties of Massachusetts that appeared in London from 1688 to 1691 slandered the former governor for complicity with the French and played up the great military achievements that could be anticipated from so Protestant a people as the Puritans of New England, provided they could have their fierce spirit fanned by a confirmation of their ancient rights. The profit motive was advanced undisguised. The advocates of the restoration of greater privileges to Massachusetts correctly diagnosed that the Navigation Acts might be less stringently applied if the colony produced a correspondingly greater revenue from the injuries it visited on France's American possessions.

Accordingly the rhetoric played up the religious grounds of the war by citing the French reversion in 1685 to persecution of Protestants and coupling this with profit: "Whether it be not good husbandry, in a manner, to throw up all business and apply ourselves one and all to this French war," ran one query, "in which if God give us prosperity, we shall get more from our enemies by fighting than we can get of one another by trading?" [9] Such war is justified, clearly, because "the wheel of divine vengeance is now turning apace, upon the French papists for their late bloody and matchless persecutions: in which persecutions our French neighbors have had a very peculiar share: Why mayn't we hope to be the executioners of God's wrath upon them?" [10] In short, the crucial question to be answered distinctly in the affirmative is "Whether there should not be a great piece of policy as well as piety in such an undertaking?" [11]

Some attempt, patently unsuccessful, was also made to use the promise of the French war as a basis for drowning the differences between landowners and traders, and so another rhetorical question, also designed for affirmative response, asked "Whether an old opinion among us, that the generality of the merchants in Boston pursue designs which 'tis the interest of the gentlemen abroad in the country to be in all things thwarting of, be not a foolish and groundless imagination?" [12] The popular party continued, however, to be distrustful of the Phips administration, although, as another pamphleteer insisted, "Few or none should be ignorant at this day, that since trade hath flourished, she has made as many and considerable changes in the world as ever empire did." It should therefore either be energetically pursued or relinquished altogether, in which case the "country gentlemen" would have their disastrous way: "That is, to prohibit all converse with strangers, lay aside our shipping, eat our own bread, drink our own beer, wear our own wool, and so turn savages, and then we shall keep our money among ourselves, make wool dear, and consequently make lands yield a good price. A project fit for none but savages to propose." [13]

If his administrative experience was short, Sir William Phips's background was, nevertheless, one that promised some hope that royal government under the new charter might proceed by compromising faction rather than promoting it. He was a native son of Maine, illiterate into his teens, but skilled in the seaside craft of shipbuilding, the seaside business of coastal trading, and the seaside arts of swimming and diving.[14] Rising in the trading business, in which he captained his own ship, Phips had learned the knack of complying with the Navigation Acts when necessary and ignoring them when possible, and had also developed some knowledge and experience in the ways of privateers. In 1684 he had led his ship's crew in a street brawl in Boston, and when the case came to court Governor Bradstreet told him to learn to carry himself less haughtily, since everybody knew "what he was and from whence he came." [15]

Phips's rise to eminence came from his successful pursuit of the stories that sailing men like himself heard in the Atlantic trade, stories of sunken Spanish treasure in the West Indies. He was confident he had enough information to locate one such sunken treasure ship and sufficient skill to raise its hoard. He persisted in his confidence when he visited London to find backers, and was so convincing that Charles II provided him with a royal vessel for his venture off the Bahamas. Although the venture failed, Phips was confirmed in his beliefs by additional information he acquired while sailing those waters, and, back in London, he acquired the support of the influential Duke of Albemarle, who had headed the military expedition that put down Monmouth's rebellion against the new monarch, James. Back in Caribbean waters, sponsored by a company the Duke had formed for the purpose, Phips located the ship he sought, off the present Haiti. Employing the amazing diving skills of Indians from his native Maine coast, he lifted a fortune from the sea. He was the nine-day wonder of the court upon his return, and his share of the treasure came to £16,000 and brought a knighthood from the delighted James, who drew the largest share, £40,000 of the raised treasure.

Conscious of his ill-suitedness to court politics and desirous of improving the fantastic rise he had achieved, Phips's thoughts turned to New England and the profits there to be acquired from trading and privateering from a protected position. There too the prestige he could not hope for with his unfinished manners in England might be his. Accordingly, at the cost of some hundreds of guineas he applied for and received a patent constituting him Provost-Marshal-General of the Dominion of New England in the Andros administration. He was heartily unwelcome to that knight, who had designed the post, one promising in spoils, for one of his circle. The post, moreover, was one that called for some legal skill, and Phips's rudeness held no promise for Andros that he would be able to improve the legal machinery of Massachusetts.

But if Phips quickly fell out with Andros, he just as quickly fell in because of that falling out with the magisterial group who four years earlier had reminded him to carry himself less loftily. He was a ready participant in adventures that promised profit, and when the old charter government temporarily resumed power at the Glorious Revolution, Bradstreet approached Phips to take the leadership in the move Massachusetts planned against the French. Indians from the French territory were raiding into Maine, French cruisers harbored at Port Royal in Nova Scotia were badly disrupting merchant shipping, and Massachusetts's claim to loyalty with liberty could benefit from a voluntary show of spirit against the French. Phips entered such service at first by cruising the coast in order to counter French raiders and to take French shipping, and then in April 1690 as leader of an expedition designed to strike a decisive blow at Port Royal. He surprised the fort there, took spoils, sacked the town, and desecrated the church. Governor Meneval of Port Royal petitioned Massachusetts for redress in later years when Phips was governor, complaining that Phips had illegally taken his personal property also, but he was unsuccessful. He attributed his failure to the fact that, although some in Massachusetts agreed with him, they were in fear of Phips, "who is supported by the rabble, to which he himself once belonged." [16]

Phips's success was heady stuff. The people did indeed love him because they loved success when it was so bluntly achieved by one of their kind, heartily and unapologetically. On the strength of his seeming infallibility, the colony raised a naval expedition against Quebec with thirteen hundred riflemen aboard who would take that town while cooperating troops from New York pinned down the forces at Montreal so that they could not assist their assaulted comrades. But the expedition was botched. The New York troops did not execute their part of the plan, and an alarmed Quebec was reinforced from Montreal; the ill-provisioned expedition arrived too late in the year to live off the land; smallpox spread among the fleet and army; and Phips's subordinates in charge of land operations were cautious in their attacks to the point of dereliction. John Wise, who served as chaplain to the troops, quickly passed over the adverse signs of God's disposition in the disaster and centered on the cowardice of the officers who served under Phips as the major cause of defeat. "I do profess had we had a man that would have ventured his life"—instead of Walley the militia commander—he said, "his way had been to have stilled all noise got himself and army into a few hours sleep sent on board and had ready one biscuit cake per man and a good round dram and have put these into their bellies the next morning & in the heat of it marched up to town the army would I am satisfied by their valor have paid him in kindness in good roast meat for supper by the next night and a good feather bed to have lain on instead of boards or straw." [17]

Wise's virile version of the defeat agreed with other eyewitness accounts. A better-provisioned and better-officered expedition would succeed; Phips as commander-in-chief was not at fault. Popular sentiment was for a renewal of the designs against Canada: "For ye beaver trade of Canada brings in hundreds of thousands to France every year," as another veteran of the 1690 campaign reported, "which would all go to England if Canada were in English hands, & then Newfoundland also, would be entirely in our hands ye fishery whereof as also of Canada & Nova Scotia is of great concernment to trade." New England could claim a primary place in the imperial scheme if Canada were reduced, because "some that understand what they say very well, have asserted that the taking of Canada will be worth more than a million of money to England, & that it is of greater concernment than all the interest we have in the West Indies." [18]

New England, however, had been drained of resources by the unsuccessful venture and therefore, although popular feeling ran high in favor of another try, further efforts would require financial support from England. In pursuance of this scheme and with his small glory scarcely diminished, Phips returned to England, where he found Increase Mather, the negotiations for the new charter, and himself as the nominee most likely to please the merchant interests that he shared and the popular group whence he had sprung. He landed again in Boston in May 1692 as its first governor under the new charter.

The first native American example of local boy makes good, or from log cabin to governor's mansion, ended in litigation rather than glory when Phips died in London in 1695 while preparing his defense against the allegations of malfeasance in office that had summoned him back to the court. Although he always retained an appeal for the plain people, this did not extend to the deputies who represented them, men of the popular party who well remembered that he was the choice of Increase Mather, the man who, in their mythology, had sold out the old charter. They consistently opposed him in civil affairs, as they consistently opposed Mather in all affairs in which he had a hand, so much so that Phips was early compelled to revise the election laws that had traditionally permitted the inland towns to be represented by deputies who resided closer to Boston. Such men were the articulate bane of his existence, and he attempted to get around them by instituting a residence requirement for deputies in the towns that elected them. With the country party opposed to him, Phips lacked the tact to consolidate the moderates behind him. He continued his own commercial evasions of the Navigation Acts and his own adventures into privateering while governor, and he was not above enforcing his version of law with his fists as well as with arguments: he struck a captain of the royal fleet on the streets of Boston and physically assaulted a customs officer. Although he was a fellow merchant, therefore, he was hardly a credit to the profession or an example of the English provincial gentleman that many merchants sought to be. Joseph Dudley, once provisionally President of the Council for New England with Randolph's aid against the day that Andros arrived, had never surrendered his ambitious vision of what the model of such a royal governor should be, and in pursuit of an ideal that was every bit as much in keeping with the wider trend of English life as it was self-seeking, he opposed Phips and documented a list of his misdeeds, one that he finally presented to the authorities in London in 1694. Phips, he claimed, indulged in illegal trade; failed, at times, to reserve the King's share in forfeiture and prize cases; accepted bribery from pirates to whom he permitted sanctuary in Boston; privateered himself and sat as judge in admiralty cases concerning vessels his own ships had seized; prohibited the trade of arms and ammunition to the Indians for pelts, only to seek a monopoly in it for himself; and pressed men from the militia and the royal navy into his private service. Phips died before the Dudley charges could be adjudicated, and Dudley, after Bellomont's brief tenure, did become Governor and did, as his letter to Governor Saltonstall of Connecticut indicates, proceed to set the social as well as the political pattern. In the year 1694, as George Gooch's study shows, "The chronicle of democratic thinking in England becomes silent for half a century." [19] Dudley was the provincial result.

Harassed as he was both by country and port during his regime, it is to be presumed that the rough and ready Phips was never more happily employed than when actively adventuring in one of his frequent, if usually unsuccessful, campaigns against French and Indians rather than politicking at home. With the clear alliance between Indians and French, Indian-hating in Massachusetts was now unqualified, an inevitable concomitant of New England's part in the wars with France that continued with little abatement from 1689 to 1713. Cotton Mather, during one of the rare periods of halt, between King William's War and Queen Anne's War, noted that there were some nice people who scrupled at the justice of Indian war, and said "If ever those rattle-snakes (the only rattle-snakes which, they say, were ever seen in the northward of Merrimack River) should stir again, the most scrupulous person in the world must own, that it must be the most unexceptionable piece of justice in the world to extinguish them." [20] The Indians were no longer heathens capable of conversion, but vermin.

The wars with the French made so heavy a drain on the resources of Massachusetts that they finally forced the issue of fiat money, backed by Phips's pledging his own money as reserve and by Cotton Mather's venturing into the realm of economic theory with writings in support of the measure. Poverty and vagabondage had since King Philip's War grown to the dimension of a social problem, and the province in 1690 had been compelled to recognize it in terms that reflected its own provincialism. In 1690 the Bradstreet government provided for the suppressing of "rogues, vagabonds, common beggars and other lewd idle and disorderly persons" by ordering the establishment of workhouses to which they were to be committed and where they would work with materials provided by town taxes. They were to be paid 8 pence per shilling earned, the rest going to the town, and they could be punished, should they grow unruly, by whipping and the curtailment of food. The detailed categorization of the "other lewd idle and disorderly persons" indicates how far along New England towns were toward a provincial aping of Defoe's London: "Common pipers, fiddlers, runaways, stubborn servants or children, common drunkards, common night-walkers, pilferers, wanton and lascivious persons either in speech or behavior, common railers or brawlers, such as neglect their callings, misspend what they earn, and do not provide for themselves or the support of their families." [21]

The political and commercial lesson to be learned from Phips's adventures among the Canadians was that New England was, after all, to get rich not by plundering its hostile neighbors but by consolidating its mercantile interests. Governor Bellomont was more interested to observe that Boston alone had "in craft, above the size of herring boats, more bottoms than all Scotland and Ireland combined. . . . Codfish consists of three sorts, 'merchantable, middling and refuse.' The first grade went to all parts of the world, chiefly to Catholic Europe; the second was consumed at home or in their own vessels; the third was eaten by the slaves in the West Indies." [22]

From 1696 on, New Englanders rapidly expanded their interest in the slave trade, and although their principal markets were in the Southern plantations and the West Indies, the number of slaves in Massachusetts rose from the two hundred Edward Randolph estimated in 1676 to five hundred and fifty when Dudley made an estimate in 1708. Although their number was small, Negroes were presenting a social problem. Like the Indians, they had initially been regarded as fellow men, and laws designed to exclude freed slaves from privileges had reserved such privileges to Christians. Until 1670 the children of slaves had been regarded as free. But with the term "Christian" broadening in meaning so that it failed to be sufficiently exclusive, the statutes of Massachusetts became overtly racial, and in 1693, in addition to Negro, the law was compelled to distinguish mulatto as a separate category, in recognition of the fact that strict measures had failed to prevent a body of what was termed "spurious or mixed" offspring. The terminology used to identify those who were white, however, still clung to a distinction designed to show their separateness as a matter of nationality and religion rather than race—they were English and Scotch subjects or other Christians.[23]

Although racial anxieties did not form any conscious part of the witchcraft hysteria that seized Massachusetts in 1691 and 1692, they played their contributing part. The devil, conventionally, was regarded as the "black man," with reference to his residence in the outer darkness, his dark designs, and his preference for nighttime operations. The center of contagion in Salem Village, however, was Tituba, a black slave from Barbados, and the circumstance of her racial coloring certainly lent not only credibility but force to the rumors that flew.[24] But the witchcraft craze was most evidently fed by the baffled sense of powerlessness that came especially to the rural people of New England, whose lives were no longer of public consequence as the politics of empire took hold in New England, and who, in participating in the only drama that the split between ministry and men of affairs allotted them, could proclaim their importance. For all the changes in government and for all the professionalism at the head of the churches, they could show that God's chosen people were still the earnest, simple believers. Mere ciphers in the merchants' books, and country clowns rather than plain folk in the social pattern that provincialism was bringing, they still had the warrant issued them by such books as *Remarkable Providences* and *Memorable Providences,* and this they exercised.

The hysteria began with the most powerless among the powerless—children, females, and servants—and continued to be fed throughout by these overlapping groups. Before it ran its course, nineteen persons had been executed as witches and the jails were filled beyond capacity with others awaiting trial. From the naming of socially marginal neighbors as the witches that afflicted them, the possessed witnesses, principally girls, proceeded through accusing the more substantial of their acquaintances to naming prominent persons, such as Lady Phips, whom they knew only by reputation. Whether the majority of the people of Massachusetts believed witches were infesting them is an academic question. There is no doubt that a great and not entirely unpleasant fear had taken hold of them—fear either of witches or of being themselves accused—and in the grip of that fear they acquiesced in the lore of witchcraft that had been established in relative innocence but manifest bad judgment by such as the Mathers. To oppose the witch-hunt was to stand self-accused of the crime.

The clergy were a responsible body and, although their retreat from the political arena had prompted their promotion of the great interest the devil as well as God took in New England, they did not desire the lives that were sacrificed. They were unable, however, to disengage themselves from the consequences of a stereotype they had promulgated, without denying its validity, and this they were emotionally incapable of doing even when, occasionally, they were intellectually equipped to do it. The hysteria was to be stemmed only after it had run its course, because the society quite clearly lacked a receptive disposition for the only claim that would, once the craze had passed, put an effective stop to any repetition—the claim that there were no such things as witches. Those who were capable of such a claim were, perhaps, timorously self-protective in not making it public, but their influence would have been slight at best. The old charter had gone under, the dignity of rural labor had gone under, the unopposed superiority of the Congregational Church had gone under, and the legal protection of the agricultural producer through fair-price and fixed-wage laws in opposition to his being an involuntary victim of international market conditions had gone under. But the Lord had other ways of manifesting His special interest in His folk. To deny this would be to assert a more rational religion, and the denial tarried at the heels of the still unacceptable declaration of the rationality of the universal frame.

The concerned clergy, constrained by a pattern they themselves had promulgated, could assert their influence only as technical advisers. The chief legal defect of the proceedings against the witches was the admission into court of spectral evidence, that is, the acceptance of the assertion by the afflicted girls that they saw the images of the accused afflicting them as proof of the accused's guilt. Proof to the contrary was well-nigh impossible to establish because, of course, evidence of the accused's physical presence elsewhere did not contradict the fact that his specter had been operating as alleged.

Courage such as his apologists frequently assign Cotton Mather in this affair was a matter of advising against the acceptance of spectral evidence. Otherwise, while his father was about the unministerial task of negotiating a new charter in London, Cotton was, willy-nilly, improving the only publicly consequential ground left his profession. Increase Mather and Sir William Phips landed in 1692 to find the craze advanced beyond the point of stemming.

When Goodwife Corey stood before the court in the first wave of the hysteria, she faced her accusers and told the judges, adults like herself and acquaintances, "They are poor distracted children, and no heed to be given to what they said." [25] She was simply asserting an observed fact within the frame of manners that had been second nature in her society. Family government was the cornerstone of order in that society. Wives entered into a partnership with husbands in the management of family affairs, but were silent on public matters and, in the last analysis, acquiesced in masculine judgments. Servants and otherwise unattached single people were incorporated into the family government that ruled the children. The civil laws supported the authority of the head of the family and, when a declension in manners was felt, assigned tithing-men to assure the fact that the family governor met his responsibilities. The 1679 synod had again affirmed the need for strict family governance and singled out tighter supervision of precisely those groups whose members were to take the lead in the craze and who, in a fatal two years, were to have their fling at seeing their superiors hang on their every word. Goodwife Corey was not heeded in her observation because a cultural protest larger than individual volition was under way and, like other protests conducted within the framework of a threatened way of life, it was expressed in the reversal of the image within the frame: children, females, and servants now were keepers of the truth, just as in more modern versions of such protests the politically weak were to seem to lead those in power. In the witchcraft days this demonstrated the truth of the common lore that God had chosen the people and even the least of them was special, just as in a more modern time it demonstrated the truth of the common lore that the good life was intrinsically native and the common man's problems were brought about by outsiders—foreign agents, aliens in his midst, and traitors who served them. Within a frame that is considered to be nearly perfect, the powerless, chafing at their condition, revolt not by shattering the frame but by reversing the picture it holds. Temporarily they appear to strengthen the cohesion of the frame. But after the craze has passed the inarticulate source of the protest asserts itself on the very framework: religion becomes more rational, or political power becomes more abstracted. The folk return to being the affected rather than the affecters.

The witch-hunting fervor signaled the end of family government as an instrument of civil polity in favor of a society governed by holders of the 40-shilling freehold. A young man when he grew to the capability could become an autonomously governing and governed unit in the state. And it signaled the end of a religion based on unmediated contact with the spiritual world, or, what comes to the same thing, on such a contact mediated only by a mythology of the special relationship enjoyed by the folk. A particular way of perceiving reality, a distinct cultural community, did not disappear, but the direct manifestation of that culture in the institutions of society was severely qualified. When he learned on December 4, 1685, that the old charter had been vacated, Samuel Sewall wrote, "This Monday we begin palpably to die." [26] Through his service as special judge in the witchcraft cases to his recantation of his complicity in the executions after the fervor had passed, Sewall acted out his culture's initial protest against and ultimate acquiescence in that death.

Puritanism had been powered in its formative years by a reliance on the printed word operating in conjunction with the word itself as manifested in the sermon. The pulpit in its revolutionary days was firmly opposed to the altar; the operation of the divine will in the universe was verbal. Iconoclasm was the negative expression of a deep distrust of the ambiguity of the nonverbal image as a vehicle for communion with the divine intent. The relationships between men and the relationship between God and man were to be fixed, debated, and altered if necessary in words, and the development of the human capacity for verbalization and the establishment of interpretive rules was of the essence of the movement. Only in this way could the believer establish control over the church and over his destiny. Should the nonverbal image be admitted or should the altar that contained the mystery beyond words of the body he accepted as central, then the existence of a church that was larger than and ultimately separate from the believers would be a necessity, because a grace that flowed along such channels could be controlled only by its assignment to an institution whose priests presided over the flow. To permit such grace to influence the folk without the recognized superiority in grace of the priestly class who served the church, the dispensary of grace, would be to reduce religion to anarchy. The Puritan cultural revolution was not anarchic because it provided doctrines of the informed conscience and widespread literacy as limitations on the newly liberated believer. But the witchcraft craze in Massachusetts revealed that the Puritan religion, in the formalism consequent upon its success and the professionalization of its clergy consequent upon its adjustment to a changing economic world, had too severely delimited the individual believer's sense of his direct access to the divine will. The verbal pattern that had been established as liberation now confined him. Reason would, indeed, soon replace other guides as a way in which God spoke to man, and the fellowship of believers would soon be signaled by their common participation in the rituals of the church rather than by their continuing assertion of their being a gathered band, each of whom had experienced God's particular regard for him. On the eve of such changes, felt but not articulated, the people, in indulging in the lore of witchcraft, indulged themselves in a final unchecked thronging of the avenue of immediate access to the spiritual world. And in the depth of its reaction to the abstraction of verbal formulas, the culture briefly and uncharacteristically sought to do without the word.

The children who had been afflicted by witches were regarded not merely as victims, but as privileged members of the community who had been selected in particular to have direct knowledge of divine intent. If any were not accorded the powers of intercession given those saints in the Roman Catholic Church who had come closer to God than their more mundane fellow Christians, they were, nevertheless, in the popular mind regarded as privy to the causes of affairs that were hidden from others. Thomas Brattle, who deplored the trials and executions, and whose letter, kept private during the hysteria, represents the best contemporary rational analysis of it, perceived that this use of the afflicted children was ultimately more indicative of a crazed culture than were the trials themselves. "That which aggravates the evil," he wrote, "and makes it heinous and tremendous" [27] is the practice of bringing distempered people to the afflicted children in order to learn what really ails them. Distraught parents with children whose physical ailments did not yield to the medical treatment of the day, troubled Christians whose loved ones failed to respond to the daily reality of the family but occupied a mental world of their own, were brought to the people who had contact with witches for the professional opinion, as it were, of specialists whose powers were qualitatively superior to those of the mundane practitioners of the society. Beyond the hanging of witches, the community appeared to be eager to surrender totally to a notion that its afflictions were unreasonable and therefore not to be remedied by practical effort. In a direct and fervid way its members rushed to improve the contact some had made with the invisible world and to substitute their findings for the procedures they had found ineffective in the visible world.

The men in authority, principally ministers, who had accompanied the change from the old days of religious fervor to the new ones of neglect of religion with an increasingly ritualistic lamentation of decline and exhortation to return to God's purpose in founding New England, now, for a space, had that return taken from their hands, and while most may have been alarmed by this, few could resist it. Brattle, in commenting on the use of those afflicted by witches as oracles, said, "As sure as I now write to you, even some of our civil leaders, and spiritual teachers, who, (I think,) should punish and preach down such sorcery and wickedness, do yet allow of, encourage, yea, and practice this very abomination." [28] The practice was the last widespread assertion of God's direct concern with New England, and it was, with the sensed awareness of its finality, the least verbal and the most orgiastic one. After it had passed, opposition to rational religion was the result of mere habit rather than conviction, and Cotton Mather was not in the majority when, in 1694, he expressed amazed consternation that in response to the latest professional appeal for further divine providences to be sent in, this time to him, for publication in yet another collection, fewer than ten communications were received. He had committed his personal importance to the wonderful working of witches in his neighborhood. In his first report on the craze, which had been rushed into print by Dunton in London as a very timely and profitable item, within weeks of his receiving it, Cotton Mather self-consciously announced that he expected buffetings from evil spirits because of his book against them, but that he had, nevertheless, set himself "to countermine the whole plot of the devil against New England." [29] But, as he had occasion to reflect in the next decade, if the devil buffeted him he did so only through visible agents such as the prosperous merchants who now proceeded to institutionalize rational religion through establishing the Brattle Street Church, and democratically minded fellow ministers such as John Wise, who opposed his scheme for a ministerial association. Otherwise the devil left him high and dry.

There was nothing in the events of 1691 and 1692 which began in Salem Village that ran counter to the pattern H. R. Trevor-Roper described when he studied European witch-hunts of the sixteenth and seventeenth centuries. His general conclusion was: "The stereotype, once established, creates, as it were, its own folk-lore which becomes in itself a centralizing force. If that folk-lore had not already existed, if it had not already been created by social fears out of popular superstition within an intellectually approved cosmology, then psychopathic persons would have attached their sexual hallucinations to other, perhaps more individual figures. This, after all, is what happens today. . . . And because separate persons attached their illusions to the same imaginary pattern, they made that pattern real to others." [30] Whereas the conclusion that social fears provided a collective outlet for individual fantasies is valid for New England also, and whereas, as has been seen, those social fears were held by relatively powerless people in a society adjusting from an autonomous role to that of being a small part in the imperial scheme, so that their inconsequence was even further increased, the witchcraft craze of New England was not the last fling of Puritanism, but rather the final outcome on a public level of the primitive relationship between God's intent and the Puritan believer. The new relationship, essentially in effect at the time of the outburst, was also structured by the cultural ideals of Puritanism, and the new order that emerged was no less the result of Puritanism than was the order asserted by those who were possessed by the hysteria.

Indeed, in temporarily abandoning the doctrine of the informed conscience and their confidence in the verbal as God's preferred means of communicating with them, the members of the culture were going against the grain of Puritanism in order to give vent to their anxiety about its future. With the restoration of calm there came also a restoration of faith in conscience and words. That Puritanism was in its general development more opposed to than in agreement with the witchcraft craze, and that such was a cultural aberration rather than an expression of the cultural standard, may be inferred from evidence gathered in an entirely different area of the culture. Allan I. Ludwig, in his valuable study of tombstone-carving in New England during that period, is concerned centrally with the history of an art form and not with the political or social events that may have affected it. Without reference to the witchcraft craze, he makes the following observation: "The Puritan did not care to dwell upon the triumph of Death, hence he was not apt to popularize the triumphant imps of death in his funerary art, although he momentarily tried them out between *ca.* 1690 and 1710. The fact that they were (after *ca.* 1710) excluded from the vocabulary of stone-carving is as important to remember as their previous inclusion." [31]

The beginning and ending dates of this sculptural excursion into a representation of death correspond with the beginning of the period in which New Englanders were compelled to assimilate the fact that the charter had died and its ending in the governorship of Joseph Dudley, who established the pattern of rule that was to characterize their province for the remainder of the colonial period. The imps of death leaped into sculptural being at precisely that period when the folk indulged their longing for adventures in the invisible world, and the conclusion that this indulgence was uncharacteristic of the deeper rhythm of their culture receives corroboration from Ludwig's informed conclusion that the imps were the fashion of a period but not characteristic of the development of the art as a whole. That nonverbal access to the divine plan was aberration rather than standard and that print was important to New England beyond any temporary excursion into other media are further illustrated by Ludwig when he contrasts English with New England practice in the art of sculpture: "No matter how provincial English carving became, a sense of nascent volume was almost always present while in New England the major movement was away from volume toward line and flatness as befits a tradition drawn from popular woodcut and engravings." [32]

In the main the literal third dimension of volume is missing from the Puritan perception of reality, just as the dimension of nonverbal mystical access to the invisible world is missing. The reassertion of the two-dimensional perception of reality came after the inarticulate expression of a deep sense of lost consequence, but it came in a terminology that was, ultimately, truer to the structure of life of the community than was that of the brief and bloody excursion into the third dimension. Purged of their fears, the Puritans became provincials.

CHAPTER ELEVEN

Loose Stones

Shift in sensibility—Samuel Sewall and Edward Taylor—
The politics of commerce at Harvard and Brattle Street—
Benjamin Colman, sensibility, and sentiment—
John Wise and democracy

On the night of January 2, 1686, Samuel Sewall had a very unusual dream. He saw Christ in the flesh come to Boston for a visit and take up His abode in the home of Sewall's father-in-law, the wealthy, orthodox merchant John Hull. When Sewall awoke he had two reflections on the dream: "One was how much more Boston had to say than Rome boasting of Peter's being there. The other a sense of great respect that I ought to have showed Father Hull since Christ chose when in town to take up His quarters at his house." [1] The adjustment of his daily reality to his deeply felt ideals was a constant source of trouble for Sewall. Heir to his father-in-law's business, he was acutely conscious of the potential inhumanity of trade as it affected the poorer folk and as it increasingly concerned itself with the enslavement of Africans. An orthodox believer and devoted amateur theologian, he was acutely conscious of the threat to religious purity represented by the dissolution of the charter and the burgeoning of doctrinal and practical differences between congregations now that the civil authority no longer enforced ecclesiastical uniformity. One of the wealthiest orthodox members of his community, he had the leisure to accept public responsibilities and the qualifications for having them offered him. He tried in his life to hold all together—merchant, judge, gentleman farmer, militia captain, moral writer, orthodox believer, and conserver of New England's values. From a somewhat cynical point of view his diary can be read as a comic document of a rather pompous man vainly attempting to keep whole what the world of affairs was rending asunder. The baneful effects of the new fashion of wig-wearing and of the vacating of the charter are treated in his diary with equally ponderous concern, and the former seems to give him more trouble. In his dream, at least, ideal and real came together as Christ recognized the propriety of the godly and Boston surpassed Rome as the world's spiritual center.

Sewall's competence as a merchant was adequate to conserve the fortune he had inherited, but his public and ecclesiastical concerns drained what innovative energies he had, and he was not a remarkably successful trader in his own right. He was a popular militia captain because his wealth permitted him to provide his men with treats; he never took the field at their head against an enemy. As a judge he proceeded barely on his frequently muddled good intentions and his native intelligence without special knowledge of the law.[2] The careers of others in his changing world reveal that Samuel Sewall's attempted combination of mercantile, military, legal, and ecclesiastical leadership was no longer tenable, and he was undistinguished in all endeavors because each was now becoming a profession that called for specialization. Sewall's diary is eminently readable because of its ample revelation of the manners of his time, such as the custom of courtship set forth in its most frequently reprinted pages, but little can be learned directly from it about the larger affairs in which Sewall consistently dabbled.

Beneath the changes in manners he deplored and beneath the details of daily spiritual concerns, Sewall's diary records the shift in sensibility that he was undergoing in common with most members of his society. Of this Sewall was relatively unaware as he picked and chose among the new fashions and, in the main, resisted most in allegiance to the plainer ways of the fathers. But his religion, the center of his conscious life and the metaphor of his dreaming one, while it remained orthodox in doctrine, altered in tone. In spite of himself, Samuel Sewall became an eighteenth-century gentleman even while eschewing wigs and deploring the declensions from the old way represented by the new churches founded by his fellow merchants.

In 1685, reflecting after the death of his newborn infant, Sewall echoed the frequent expression of the meaning of the event to be found in the writings of the earlier generation: "The Lord humble me kindly in respect of all my enmity against Him, and let His breaking my image in my son be a means of it." [3] The death was a lesson, doctrinal in essence, about the vanity of the things of this world, and the lesson was to be assimilated by the intellect, however much corrupt nature warred against it by pleading natural affection.

Four years later, during a visit to London, Sewall attended the preaching of John Flavel, the early sentimentalizer or, as he himself preferred, "spiritualizer" of the daily life, and was extremely impressed. Sewall himself was now inclining to a religion of sensibility, one that validated divine truths by the pleasurable effect they had on the feelings and that permitted a degree of self-indulgence in religious devotion. "Sung," he records during the visit to England, "or rather wept and chatter'd, the 142 psalm." [4] Death was undergoing a change, in his perception, from a severe reminder to wean oneself from the weakness of nature to an awesome opportunity for exercising the feelings by exposing them to the sublimity of an event greater than man's will. Its lesson was becoming secondary to the occasion it provided for an exercise in refined feeling. In December 1696 he visited the family crypt: " 'Twas wholly dry and I went at noon to see in what order things were set; and there I was entertain'd with a view of, and converse with the coffins of my dear Father Hull, Cousin Quincy, and my six children: for the little posthumous was now took up and set in upon another twice on the bench at the end, with head to her husband's head: and I order'd little Sarah to be set on her grandmother's feet. 'Twas an awful yet pleasing treat." [5]

Sewall is unaware that he is converting religion into a sentimental comforter and thereby imperceptibly compensating for its loss of force as a doctrine of life. The consequences of religious belief in the daily reality of Samuel Sewall were, however, changing. The capacity of belief not only to explain all things but in the explanation also to give a sense of control to the believer over what can be controlled and a sense of confidence in God's perfect plan in what cannot be controlled is less certain. Rather, the world of daily reality is fragmenting beyond confident doctrinal explanation: the unorthodox not only prosper but seem decent beings also; trade, law, or arms each has its own requirements not clearly comprehended under a single plan; and life's pleasures do increase with increasing prosperity and exercise a strong appeal, in spite of the observation that some abuse pleasure to the point of vice. Religion cannot explain, let alone control, these developments, but it can provide a sensible solace, and gradually, without any alteration in the doctrine of orthodoxy, religion becomes a matter of the sensibility that feels God's governance and delights even in the natural manifestations of it rather than an account of life in terms of which daily happenings can be explained.

So, in 1697, Samuel Sewall, unknowingly yielding to the attractions of sensible religion, was able to found his faith in the future of New England's saints on the natural signs that God had provided them rather than on an insistence upon the inviolability of theological or ecclesiastical doctrine. These he did not abandon and he had very decided opinions on right and wrong beliefs, right and wrong church practices. At a time, however, when the professional ministry was intent on haggling over these as the sole source of continuity of the tradition because they confirmed the importance of the profession, Sewall could reflect thus on New England's history:

> As long as Plum Island shall faithfully keep the commanded post;
> notwithstanding all the hectoring words, and hard blows of the proud and
> boisterous ocean; as long as any salmon, or sturgeon shall swim in the
> streams of Merrimack; or any perch, or pickerel, in Crane Pond; as long
> as the sea fowl shall know the time of their coming, and not neglect
> seasonably to visit the places of their acquaintance: as long as any cattle
> shall be fed with the grass growing in the meadows which do humbly
> bow down themselves before Turkey Hills; as long as any sheep shall
> walk upon Old Town Hills, and shall from thence pleasantly look down

upon the River Parker, and the fruitful marshes lying beneath; as long as any free and harmless doves, shall find a white oak or other tree within the township, to perch, or feed, or build a careless nest upon; and shall voluntarily present themselves to perform the office of gleaners after barley harvest; as long as nature shall not grow old and dote; but shall constantly remember to give the rows of Indian corn their education by pairs: so long shall Christians be born there; and being first made meet, shall thence be translated, to be made partakers of the inheritance of the saints of light. [6]

Sewall's distinction as it arises from this passage is based on the fact that he had become the land's far more than he had become, as he literally was, the land's owner. The pastoral rhapsody is made vivid and given strength because of the faith that lends it purpose without constraint. Mere nature is not indulged in the remarkable passage because, even before the saints in light come to furnish its completing keystone, the signs of human habitation are manifest in the telling use of proper names in conjunction with the habits of natural creatures. This interplay between the names man leaves on the land, as control, and the freedom of nature—further enforced by many proper names being taken from nature—results in a vision of dynamic harmony. Puritanism elsewhere in Sewall is crotchety, as it was, distrustful, as it was, demanding, as it was, and even cruel, as it was. In this passage it is also learning to become responsive to the natural world and pliant in its interchange with it; not relinquishing its insistence on control or the centrality of the saints in the creation, but distinguishing, after the abatement of its political dominance, between spiritual certainty and authoritarian exclusiveness.

When he was at Harvard, Sewall's chambermate was Edward Taylor, and the two began a lifelong friendship. A native of Leicestershire, Taylor had arrived in Boston in 1668 at the age of twenty-four, committed to a ministerial career that he felt was blocked in England by the policies of Charles II's government. [7] He entered Harvard, whence he was graduated in 1671, and, older than the average candidate for a ministerial post and without family connections in New England, he accepted a call to the frontier community of Westfield, nine men only forming the fellowship that invited him. The rudeness of the situation and the slimness of the fellowship made Taylor reluctant to remain in Westfield to organize a church, and King Philip's War further disturbed plans for a church settlement there, but finally, in 1679, eight years after he had arrived, Taylor gathered together the Westfield church. By that time, the year of the reforming synod, Taylor's most influential clerical neighbor, Solomon Stoddard of Northampton, was expressly advocating the admission to church membership of all who were not openly scandalous in behavior and the use of the sacrament of the Last Supper as a converting rather than a confirming ordinance. Such a procedure had strong attractions for the Connecticut River Valley settlements, which, in their isolation, strongly felt the need to cohere around the church. In the coastal communities a degree of civility had been achieved that obviated the need for the churches there to be comprehensive: other forms of social union were available. But on the frontier in an area frequently threatened by Indian raids, the villagers moved into a closer equating of residency and church fellowship.

This, however, was not what Taylor had fled England for, nor what he had migrated a further hundred miles into the wilderness for. He remained steadfastly orthodox, entrenched behind the two walls of the revolutionary years of Puritanism: the Westminster Confession of faith and the Cambridge Platform of church discipline. He allied himself with the Mathers, who, believing also in these bulwarks, were grudgingly retreating from them only under extreme pressure. But in Westfield, Taylor did not initially feel the political pressure that had built up considerable force in the older towns. He began and pursued his clerical career in unflinching opposition to the teachings of Stoddard, whose practices increasingly ruled the day in Taylor's valley. By 1700 Stoddard had organized the churches of his region into an association and was in open conflict with the Mathers because he was substituting associational approval for church covenant as the core of the governance of the corporation.[8] Taylor, too, opposed Stoddard both in practice and in a series of remarkable sermons that emphasized the high sacredness of the communion and the consequent necessity of limiting it to the saints lest it be blasphemed. In 1712 a faction had so far developed against him in Westfield that the church was threatened, but Taylor did not hesitate nor did he compromise. He underlined his belief in the awesome importance of the sacrament by exercising his authority to withhold it from the dissidents, and he carried the day. Under Taylor, Westfield was an enclave of orthodoxy in a region that was being developed and made secure by the new policy of association and broadened church fellowship extended to all who were not openly scandalous. He lived into his eighty-seventh year, unchanging in his views on the matter, and died in 1729. From 1723 he had an assistant in the pulpit, and, significantly, in 1726 his old foe Stoddard also took an assistant to help him in his old age. Stoddard's assistant, his grandson Jonathan Edwards, was to lead a revival that vindicated Taylor's practices after they had all but disappeared.

Taylor and Sewall remained friends and correspondents and agreed on the main issues of ecclesiastical polity. But while Sewall, from his unavoidable immersion in the currents of his day, was gliding into a religion of sensibility, Taylor in his isolation was unaffected. The difference in the sensibilities of the two men finally amounts to as significant a cultural distinction, in spite of their doctrinal agreements, as the difference between Taylor's policy and Stoddard's policy.

In the twentieth century readers discovered among the papers of Taylor's grandson, Ezra Stiles, a group of extraordinary poems. *The Poems of Edward Taylor* were not published in a complete edition until 1960, but in the more than two decades before that time, when selected poems began appearing in print, the general opinion had already developed that, in Edward Taylor, America had its major colonial poet and one of the more important poets in its entire literature. At the age of forty, it was discovered, Edward Taylor began a series of poems he was to continue for forty-four years, the *Preparatory Meditations*. Each month as he prepared himself to administer the sacrament he engaged in the devotional exercise of writing a poem on the biblical text on which he would preach on communion day. Together these meditative verses form his major work, to which he added strong miscellaneous verse, also on religious subjects, and a long poem, "Gods Determination," on the cosmological drama.

If one considers the poetry of Edward Taylor in terms of the great body of verse in English, the conclusion is inescapable that its modern fame derives in great part from the historical fact that nobody else in the America of his day produced verse of that quality, and the satisfaction to be derived from the discovery that, in a culture in which nearly every learned person wrote occasional and private verse, one such person, at least, wrote verse that lives beyond the occasion. But there can be small doubt that, in the larger English tradition, Taylor is a minor poet. Although the unevenness of his lines is explicable in terms of his method of syllabification rather than stress, and although the inconsistency of imagery is to be unified by a knowledge of the meditative process that gives the images connection rather than through an explicit consideration of the figures, the lines are no more fluent nor are the images more organic for such understandings. Writing without an audience, Taylor, well-read as he was, suffered the pattern that binds even the greatest primitive artists; although a development may be discernible, this development is not clearly from relative weakness to relative strength, but throughout his career he repeated certain weaknesses and repeated certain strengths. Writing regularly from 1682 to 1726, Taylor echoed a tradition he had known in his native England more than fifty years earlier, and the rude voice of his poetry sounds frequently like that of an unfinished George Herbert, but never like Dryden or Pope. To say this is not to insist that good poetry must be in fashion, but it is to note that the greatest literature communicates beyond its time because it is rooted in the reality of its time.

The reality in which Edward Taylor's poetry is rooted is that of the overwhelming importance of true church fellowship and the incredible miracle of communion. Taylor's strengths in his meditations come from his unceasingly powerful sense of the communion of the Last Supper as the entry of miracle into the common world. On this sense he based his opposition to Stoddard, and this sense elevates his verse. The communion is essentially mystical, and Taylor himself is mystical well beyond the Puritan standard.

Members of the culture, as a whole, in excluding the nonverbal had excluded the mystical in practice although not in theory and, in emphasizing the practical organization of the chosen people in order to establish and continue their existence apart from worldly corruptions, had discouraged too wide a flight of individual fancy. In his isolation Edward Taylor maintained his orthodoxy by opposing association with a personal, poetic vision of covenant, and by opposing broad administration of the sacrament with an intensely keen sense of its miraculous power. As a result, he stands as the greatest of the American Puritan poets, but also as a Puritan whose verse is in significant ways unrepresentative of the main thrust of his culture. In contrast to Samuel Sewall, who was feebler in a strict literary sense, Taylor indicates the way in which Puritan belief can have a continued meaning for the individual in a changing world through that individual's retreat into the mystery of Christianity at its core. But in a broader sense, Sewall represents the way in which Puritanism can continue to have meaning for people by adjusting to the shift in sensibility brought about by the shift in the economic world.

In 1725 Edward Taylor wrote his last meditation, basing it on Canticles 2:5, "I am sick of love," and concluded his address to God:

> Had I but better thou shouldst better have
>   I nought withhold from thee through nigerdlliness,
> But better than my best I cannot save
>   From any one, but bring my best to thee.
>   If thou acceptst my sick Loves gift I bring
>   Thy it accepting makes my sick Love sing.[9]

Two years later Samuel Sewall was attracted to a passage in the *New-England Weekly Journal* that was headed by a line from Pope, "And to be dull, was constru'd to be good," and copied it into his diary:

> This age is too polite, to bear the same ill-manners and roughness as the former. Then a man was thought the more religious for being a

clown; and very honest because he used no ceremony but downright plain dealing. But now the taste of mankind is very much rectified; and the world cannot endure the absurdity to see a man behave himself as if he were under the reign of Queen Elizabeth. It is certainly very decent to conform to the innocent customs of the times in which we live. This shews modesty and humility, and that we do not set up our private opinions against the universal voice and practice. Singularity in anything indifferent, shews a mistaken mind, and a high degree of pride and affection. It is an evident demonstration of a meanness of soul, which it is impossible should take place in a man of generous and enlarged sentiments. We are wonderfully deceived, if we think to gain a greater esteem by our abstractedness from mankind. For though some ignorant melancholy persons of the same character with ourselves, may be very lavish in our praises, yet all those gentlemen who have good sense as well as virtue, will look upon us with a secret pity, if not contempt; and be justly averse to our society, as we are unjustly to theirs.[10]

Doctrinally, Sewall could still see eye to eye with Taylor, but they had come to occupy sensible worlds that were farther apart than the hundred miles that separated them. In the year between the composition of Taylor's last meditation and Sewall's recording the citation from the *Journal*, Jonathan Edwards embarked upon his Northampton career. He was to give his life to the attempt to reunify the Puritan world through attaching a keen appreciation of the mystical relationship Taylor saw as the center of life to the psychology of the emotions that moved Sewall. He did so through unification of the predetermined universe and the scientifically verifiable universe.

The transformation of New England into a provincial English world in sensibility and manners as well as government endangered the preferred status of the clergy. John Cotton of Plymouth complained in a letter of 1688 that now that the old union between church and state was gone, "People being left to their liberty, maintenance of the ministry is likely to be brought to nothing very speedily." [11] He himself had been promised £30 less than what he had received the previous year, "and how much shorter the performance will be I know not." John Bishop of Stamford wrote in 1687, "The Lord rebuke that worldly, earthly, profane & loose spirit up & down the country & give us to be instructed before laid desolate." The people were not responsible to their ministry: "Many," he complained, "are gospel-glutted." [12] Changing governmental structure and heavy debts brought about by the wars with the French were leading the more rural folk of New England to disregard their ministers through undersupport of them and to use as a criterion for choosing a preacher the cheapest price at which he could be hired. Insofar as the individual church covenant was regarded as inviolable, the new political climate in which civil authorities no longer enforced a minimum church standard permitted those churches to neglect the better-trained candidates for the ministry as too expensive. Town democracy in the governance of the local church resulted, at the turn of the century, in a backsliding from learning into rustic crudeness. As riches were increasingly centered in trade, Boston ministers went on to higher salaries and Boston congregations exacted a level of cosmopolitanism from them, while country churches descended into coarseness and impostors began to appear in the ministry.

The clerical response could only be closer association for the regulation of the profession, but that association was difficult of achievement because to a people committed to Congregational principles it smacked of Presbyterianizing. Opponents of association could vigorously cite the pure, primitive practice of the New England churches in defense, among other things, of their continuing to hire the cheaper and the less qualified. The move toward association encountered other complicating factors also. Since it centered in the leading Boston ministers such as Increase Mather, who was, as John Dunton put it, "the metropolitan clergyman of that country," [13] it was distrusted by the popular party, who were unforgiving toward Mather and the moderate ministers of relatively prosperous congregations because of their fancied complicity in selling out the old charter. The popular spirit of democracy, baffled by the crown's assumption of governance in Massachusetts, jealously clung to local control of the churches. In Connecticut, where that spirit more readily found an outlet in politics under the old charter conditions, ministerial moves toward autocracy within the church met correspondingly with good success.

A further complication was added by Solomon Stoddard's successful establishment of an association on the frontier. Although the members of his association were within Massachusetts, their communication with Connecticut was better than with Boston because of the river, and the style of life in towns such as Northampton and Hadley partook more of the Connecticut mode. Stoddard had pushed association well beyond what the Mathers had deemed tolerable. He had abandoned the covenant as the indispensable core of the church and had broadened the administration of the sacraments. In contemplating association, therefore, the Boston ministers not only had to quell the fears of the popular party but also to dissociate themselves carefully from the extreme of the Connecticut River Valley group.

At the same time Harvard as the great training ground of the ministry became an important factor in the political controversies that were stirred as a responsible body of ministers moved to redress the neglect of their profession. The college was ultimately dependent upon the General Court for its support and governance and was therefore susceptible to the general drift toward nonintellectualism, if not anti-intellectualism, being experienced throughout the province. The young men there were attracted to the new, politer modes of religion and were caught up in the growing perception of their calling as a gentleman's profession, like an Episcopalian curacy, rather than as a way of life that called for distinctly superior intellectual abilities and a high vocation. If they were, in effect, to be hired for a job, then they wanted the best possible job. Their answer to the increasing control of the pulpit by the pews would be to assert a gentlemanly standard of life that was their social privilege.

John Barnard, who entered Harvard in 1696, describes a college scene that is not particularly different from that which was to come into being at far more secular colleges in the following times. "Upon my entering into college," he wrote, "I became chamber-mate, the first year, to a senior and a junior sophister; which might have been greatly to my advantage, had they been of studious disposition, and made any considerable progress in literature. But alas! they were an idle pack, who knew but little, and took no pains to increase their knowledge. When, therefore, according to my disposition, which was ambitious to excel, I applied myself close to books, and began to look forward into the next year's exercises, this unhappy pair greatly discouraged me, and beat me off from my studies, so that by their persuasions I foolishly threw by my books, and soon became as idle as they were." [14] The debonair Barnard was not, perhaps, typical of the average scholar for the ministry of his day, but he provides full evidence that the negligent could qualify for the degree. He is nowhere more revealing about his college career and the winds that prevailed in the 1690s than when he discusses how he came to arrive at his principles: "The pulpit being my great design, and divinity my chief study, I read all sorts of authors, and as I read, compared their sentiments with the sacred writings, and formed my judgment of the doctrines of Christianity by that only and infallible standard of truth; which led me insensibly into what is called the Calvinistical scheme (though I never to this day have read Calvin's works, and cannot call him master,) which sentiments, by the most plausible arguments to the contrary, that have fallen in my way, (and I have read the most of them,) I have never yet seen cause to depart from." [15]

Stunningly, Barnard had no need to read Calvin. He tuned his sentiments, which is to say the sentiments of the day, to the scheme for which he was fitting himself and called their happy conjunction the truth. Not only was learning falling off in value in the rural villages, but in the college it was becoming a matter of process rather than discovery: so much accomplished in books resulted in a license. A congregation in hiring a man who had gone through the process would be assured of hiring a gentleman, and if not exactly a scholar, at least one acquainted with some divinity through having read it, and most divinity through having heard of it. Even as they faced a growing anti-intellectualism in the villages, therefore, concerned ministers also were affected by the pleasant mediocrity of the average candidate for their profession, now that it had become another good job rather than a very special vocation.

Cotton Mather once debated with a Quaker, who told him,

"Therefore! therefore! *argo*! *argo*! Why, dost thou think religion is to be proved by thy *therefores*—by thy *argo's*?" [16] The view was no longer confined to Quakers. A religion of greater sensibility in the towns and of imitative adherence to established formulas in the villages would suit. The Boston ministers in 1699 issued advice to the country at large, warning against the impostors who were occupying the pulpits and insisting upon the high intellectual qualifications that should be demanded of a minister: "When the knowledge of the tongues and arts revived," they explained, "religion had a great revival with it: and though some unlearned men have been useful to the interests of religion, yet no man ever decried learning, but what was an enemy to religion, whether he knew it or no." [17] But in the popular mind learning was no longer linked with religion. It was linked, rather, with a certain ministerial class's attempt to dominate the local churches and drive up the price of their services. They wanted a minister who would assume his duties without fuss and provide what they were used to, leaving them free for other concerns. Lay eldership was no longer zealously sought because the status quo was not to be changed, and the congregation's control could therefore be asserted through the hiring of a suitably cooperative preacher and his firing if he did not cooperate. Joshua Scottow complained in 1694 that "brethren of low degree" did not care to serve as elders, but excused themselves by saying, "they know not the way of the Lord, they are of mean estates, and low capacities, their counsel will not meet with acceptance." He suggestively runs together property and capacity to influence a congregation. But if you went to the "brethren of high degree" because, as those of low degree insisted, "they know the Lord," then you found them telling you that "their occasions will not bear or admit of so mean an employ as to be a ruling elder." [18] The minister, in short, could have the management of the enterprise to himself. All the more reason why he should be selected with a high regard for his compliance together with a shrewd eye on price.

The popular party saw to it that the party of the Mathers was not going to use Harvard as an instrument for arresting the trend. Head of that college since 1685, Increase Mather had given greatly of his energies to it, soliciting acquisitions for its library and funds for its maintenance from English well-wishers, and encouraging the growth of science there. With a first-hand acquaintanceship, begun in his days in England just before the Restoration, with the Puritans who had founded the Royal Society, he saw no imcompatibility between such study and the fundamentals of religion he sought to maintain in their purity. Even as late as 1714, Samuel Sewall, who had yielded to sentiment, would balk at some science: "Dr. C. Mather preaches excellently . . . only spake of the sun being in the center of our system. I think it unconvenient to assert such problems." [19] Cotton was a Fellow of the Royal Society, and the Mathers' devotion to learning was comprehensive. The journey to England that eventuated in Increase's negotiating the charter of 1691 had begun with his seeking a far different kind of charter, one that would gain royal recognition of Harvard, although he came to be persuaded by English friends that the college was best incorporated under the Massachusetts government. Now that incorporation came to haunt him.

Increase Mather had made it clear that, however devoted he was to the college, it would be impossible for him to set aside his other affairs and reside there, devoting himself exclusively to its administration. No realistic person expected differently. But the popular party saw the occasion of his nonresidency as an opportunity to replace him, an especially sweet revenge in view of Phips's insistence that deputies reside in the towns they represented as a counter against some of their spokesmen. That party, therefore, became insistent that the president of Harvard reside at the college and drew from Mather the response they well anticipated, one based firmly on his sense of his own influential importance that, nevertheless, falls short of self-importance. "If I comply with what is desired," Mather told the General Court in 1698, "I shall be taken off in great measure at least, from my public ministry. Should I leave preaching to 1500 souls (for I suppose that so many use ordinarily to attend in our congregation) only to expound to 40 or 50 children, few of them capable of edification by such exercises: I doubt I should not do well." [20] The deputies pressed their insistence, and finally in 1700 and again in 1701 Mather spent three months in Cambridge away from his family before concluding that the continuance of such a life was impossible and requesting that the General Court choose another president. Then came the revenge of the popular party that left no doubt that it was directly aimed at Mather rather than the betterment of the college. He reported that "Thereupon the college was through the malice of Dr. Cooke and Byfield [leaders of the popular party] put into the hands of Mr. Willard as Vice-President who readily accepted the offer without so much as once consulting with me about it. Nor was he urged to reside at the college." [21] With so little to be expected from Harvard in the way of maintenance of standards, the Mathers as well as other orthodox-minded people turned to developing an interest in Yale, founded in 1701, as a bulwark against declension.

The loss of influence at Harvard followed close on the heels of another and more significant defeat for the Mather interests, this one represented by the establishment of the Brattle Street Church. Taken together, the two developments pointed clearly to the need for ministerial consolidation if the churches were not to deteriorate into autonomous and disparate units totally lacking in influence. Nathaniel Mather, Increase's brother, embattled in Dublin, who after the Restoration found hard going in his attempts to maintain his Congregational ministry, had drawn strength from the autonomy of the individual congregation because only in those terms could he oppose the superior weight of an adverse establishment and a hostile local population. For him the form of church organization that had initially been developed in a cell-like revolutionary fashion, difficult for its opponents to identify and root out, was still ideal, and he continued to maintain a particularized church structure that had lost its tenability in New England once such churches became, as it were, the establishment, and developed privileged interests and a class desirous of protecting them. "The company or body, as you call them, of professing believers throughout the world," Nathaniel wrote Increase, "are in truth no company, no body, having no compaction amongst themselves any more than the loose stones in the highways in Ireland & in France & in New England are an house or body of stones." [22] But it was not in the best interest of the clerical profession to accept such a view of the relationship of Massachusetts churches to one another.

The first association among New England ministers was organized in 1690 in the Boston vicinity and bore great and conscious similarity to the associations of Puritan ministers that had flourished in England in the Commonwealth period.[23] Its organizers announced it as a gathering at which professionals could exchange ideas and claimed it was without explicit political consequence. Every sixth Monday the members of the association met at Harvard for the purpose of promoting the Gospel and rendering one another mutual assistance in that great work. They discussed shop, as it were, helping out one another with difficult cases of conscience and listening to learned opinions on such topics as the power of synods or the power of elders, as well as indulging in rabbinical debates about legal passages in the Old Testament. The association left itself open to an extension of its influence by inviting churches or individuals to refer cases to it and by offering to enter into correspondence with similar associations as they were established. A perennial matter before the group was that of whether orthodoxy could not be advanced by the association's moving to assume supervisory power over the churches represented by its members. Although such a move had strong attractions, it was one to be approached in a gingerly fashion because of the fierce jealousy of independence inherited from the old days. When the Brattle Street controversy swept Boston it was finally settled with relative speed, although hard feelings lingered on for decades, because of the ministerial sense that it was more important to accept the new church with its influential and wealthy parishioners, provided that church would make common cause in asserting the centrality of the faith, than it was to alienate it into a position of greater heterodoxy. The Brattle Street Church, if it was too innovative in its practices and far too modish in its tone, was, nevertheless, a church made up of substantial community leaders, whose alliance was needed against the cruder tendencies now being manifested by unassociated congregations and the impostures being practiced in the pulpit.

If the controversy over the founding of the Brattle Street Church was of short duration, however, what that church came to stand for was of the utmost importance in New England life. Its founding was the explicit institutionalization of habits and attitudes that were widespread in the community but that were thus far still officially to be deplored from the pulpit on Sunday, while prevailing for the remainder of the week. Brattle Street Church set a pattern of church practice as consequential to the tone of daily life as was the pattern of government shortly to be established by Joseph Dudley.

In 1698 and 1699 a group of the wealthiest Boston merchants, including Simon Bradstreet, John Leverett, and William Brattle, all scions of first families, came together to establish Boston's fourth church, the Brattle Street Church.[24] They signified their adherence to the faith of the fathers by founding that church on the Westminster Confession of faith jointly entered into by Presbyterians and Congregationalists during the revolutionary period in England and adopted and reaffirmed by Massachusetts synods. But the church order they sought was one that, cleansed of the crudities of primitive Puritanism, would reflect the dignity of their stations and the politeness of their times. The public testimony of faith that still lingered in some churches was certainly too tastelessly personal and would have to go. The prejudice against set forms of prayer in favor of spontaneous prayer was also so consistently vulnerable to embarrassing personal excesses and to unlearned excursions that it could well be set aside and the Lord's Prayer introduced in its place in the service. And the prejudice against weekly readings from the Bible as a substitution of dead formula for the living word was also, in their eyes, an anachronistic clinging to the rudeness of a less polished age and was to be overturned in favor of a weekly listening to the language of the Bible. In short, what the merchants had in mind was a church that was distinctly predestinarian in theology but one that was responsive to an age in which sensibilities were more highly developed among the cultivated rich. Similarities with the best practice of religion in England were to be emphasized, even as economic, social, and political bonds with England were being reknit. English Protestantism now again under a Protestant monarch need no longer insist on the eccentricities of early Congregational-ism, but, its piety assumed, should distinguish itself through the fervent moral tone that was beginning to be its distinguishing characteristic. The church's objectiive existence, apart from the vagaries of any covenanted band that came together, should be manifested, the Brattle Street members felt, and an assured source of continuous provision of set prayers and biblical readings be estab-lished. If this approached Presbyterianism, such was only a term. What was really being approached, they felt, was a solid, refined institution that in a day of triumphant Protestantism did not hang back from its obligation to be a dispensary of religion simply from a prejudice in favor of a less objective church developed in reaction to issues that were no longer vital.

The merchants who founded the church had seen their profession come a long way in New England. They were no longer beset by the medieval principles of the fair price that Winthrop's early administrations had attempted to enforce, nor by a legally enforced doctrine of the viciousness of the trader as a nonproductive middleman. If merchants could not directly gain the popular suffrage at the polls, they could directly influence policy through their association with the governor's council. New England had come to accept their centrality in the economic life and had correspondingly yielded up to them the social prestige they claimed, reinforced by their superior access to the fashions that prevailed in London. At one time the question of whether or not a profit could be taken on a product by anyone other than the product's producer had been earnestly debated. Now New England culture had come so far into modern times as to recognize that even capital itself was a just source of profit. "Usury," as Cotton Mather explained, is "justified by the law of parity; there is no manner of reason why the usury of money, should be more faulty than of any other thing; for money is as really improvable a thing as any commodity whatsoever." [25]

But for all this a Sunday in most churches saw the minister take his pulpit to decry the concentration on wealth, to encourage a spontaneous expression of religious experience as something different from and superior to the daily world, to keep New England

Protestantism from the union with English Protestant sentiment that the age called for, and in that effort to confound coarseness and personal enthusiasm with fidelity to the original faith. The time was ripe, those at Brattle Street felt, for a church that was unapologetic about its consistency with the churches in England at which their social peers worshiped. This church would recognize that the moral code that had brought success to the trader by validating the credit system was at the center of religion. As men became more polished, this morality in its greater sophistication deserved a church form that would reflect it. There was no question of emulating the many rituals of the Church of England or of imposing a universal parish system upon the people. This would be a reformed church adhering to the purified faith of the Puritan movement and very select in its membership. But the principles of selection were, of course, to reflect the differences in the world from which the members were to be selected. If the established Church of England was corrupt in some practices, this did not argue that an insistence upon an order enforced by the ministry rather than democratically determined by the congregation was false, nor that the identification of certain rituals as central to the church's objective existence was blasphemous.

The brief but acid controversy that exploded upon the publication of the Brattle Street plans followed predictable lines. Increase Mather headed the unsuccessful opposition and took the occasion to tell some home truths. On one level his arguments were merely for the record, as when in opposition to the scheme for weekly Bible readings he affirmed: "It cannot be proved that that which some call *dumb reading,* or public reading of the Scriptures without any explication or exhortation is part of the pastoral office." [26] He threatened to withhold the right hand of fellowship from the ordination of the Brattle Street minister, but even while doing so revealed that the times were against him. His threat seemed hollow because that right hand of fellowship was not essential. In effect he admitted this when he said that he mentioned the matter not as a substantial obstacle, but "for the information of our young divines who being unstudied in the controversies of church discipline, are apt to think that the custom of giving the right hand of fellowship at ordination, is a novelty and singularity practiced no where but in New England, whereas it was used in other churches long before there was a New England in the world." [27]

If Mather's theoretical arguments had a dying fall about them, he did not mince words when he came to the core of the matter, even though he sensed that he was on the losing side. "To have power to choose their own pastors," he wrote, "is an invaluable privilege. For them to give or rather to sell that privilege away to all that will contribute, must needs be displeasing to the Lord who has bought it for them at so dear a rate." [28] Unlike the more rural ministers, Mather did not balk at the Presbyterian aspects of the Brattle Street organization, but he insisted that the common ground of Congregationalism and Presbyterianism should be observed and that common ground was "that no one shall be admitted to all special ordinances, but such as are not only free from scandal in their lives, but persons of visible godliness, making a credible profession of cordial subjection to Christ." [29] But who in the Boston of 1699 was finally to decide whether a substantial contribution to a church of Christ was not really a cordial subjection to Him? A sufficient number of influential men believed it was not to be Increase Mather, and Mather himself held open the avenue along which Brattle Street and other churches would communicate when he intimated that the new church might be tolerable if its ministers conferred with other ministers in weighty cases and were willing to explain their proceedings when requested. Always acute politically, Mather recognized that continuity was ultimately to be lodged in ministerial consolidation rather than in an enforced uniformity of practice.

The town satirists of Boston got directly to the home truth that Mather couched in a context of theoretical argument. One wrote:

> Relations are Rattles with Brattle and Brattle,
> Lord Bro'r mayn't command,
> But Mather and Mather had rather had rather
> The good old way should stand.
> Saints Cotton and Hooker, Oh look down and look here

Where's Platform, Way and the Keys?
Oh Torrey with Story of Brattle Church Tattle
To have things as they please.
Our churches cum Mico do stand sacro vico
Our churches turn genteel
Our parsons grow trim and trig with Wealth, Wine and Wig
And their heads are covered with meal.[30]

And a responding satirist did not hesitate to treat as mere words the sacred names that had been invoked:

Having heated his Noddle, with a dram of the Bottle
Then hey for the top of Parnassus.
He's so set on rhyming, bell ringing and chiming
The which for a grace to his rhymes take
That saints Hooker and Cotton, tho' both dead and rotten,
Must out from their graves for the rhymes sake.[31]

More important than any differences displayed by these virtuosos of the doggerel is their common cheerful acceptance of the social nature of the controversy and their common exercise of skeptical wit. A city in which couplets such as these could find author and audience was in a current of change larger than the stream of ecclesiastical polity, which, indeed, was now but a tributary.

The crucial factor in the success of the Brattle Street Church was its minister, the man who would have to oppose the Mathers in church theory and yet unite with them professionally, and the man who would have to strike a definitive balance between the authority of his office and the substantial nature of the congregation that employed him. The founders wrote to a Harvard graduate then resident in England, Benjamin Colman, offering him the post, and, in anticipation of the difficulties he would encounter in receiving the right hand of fellowship, advising him to receive, as he then did, ordination at the hands of respected Presbyterian ministers in London. From their point of view the choice could not have been better. Benjamin Colman brought to Brattle Street the urbanity, intelligence, and toughness his parishioners sought, and he brought them in abundance. He was precisely that combination of self-conscious New England Puritan and confident citizen in the society of international Protestantism that they sought. In him the provincial age of the New England churches found its man. Indeed, so perfectly was Colman of the age that, unlike many others who were in their time in New England less influential than he, he has faded into the shadows with provincialism.

Benjamin Colman's parents had arrived from England and settled in Boston the year before his birth. Trained principally by Ezekiel Cheever, he entered Harvard in 1688, was graduated in 1692, and then undertook some supply preaching before returning to the college for further theological studies toward the M.A. degree, which he received in 1695. With that degree he decided to visit and possibly settle in the native land of his parents. In embarking for England in 1695, he also embarked on a series of adventures that were to become the stuff of the first great English novels. His ship was captured by French privateers, and in his brief captivity in France he was played upon by the rakes among the English in his group, the whole adventure worth more than a chapter in a Smollett plot. Finally arrived in London, he engaged in the politics of patronage, coming to know such eminent leaders of Protestant dissent as Dr. Daniel Williams, and on the strength of the connections he formed began to serve as a supply preacher in English pulpits. During the course of this activity he had temporary care of a church in Cambridge and there encountered a congregation of the more primitive sort of dissenters, the kind whom he no longer in his increasing sophistication felt much affinity for, however close they may have been to certain New England groups. "They liked illiterate preachers," says Ebenezer Turell, Colman's son-in-law and biographer, and "they were also sadly tinged with Antinomian principles and his texts were too legal for them." Turell, writing in the 1740s, adds the note, "Like as this day in some places of New England." [32] Colman, that is to say, was learning to stress the due forms of proper worship and to distrust a pietistic fervor that was disruptive of clerical authority.

He received an unrivaled opportunity to advance himself and improve his social acquirements when he was offered the Presbyterian pulpit at Bath, where, as Turell notes, "Before he had lived among them two months he became acquainted with more families of fashion in London than he had done by living there two years." [33] The Bath post proved, indeed, as his worldly-wise advisers in London had assured him it would be, the best stirrup in England. The record of his adventures in Bath and in the inns along the road between there and London, where his chamber was entered by soliciting whores and where he met hanging judges and gentlewomen who were delighted to learn that in spite of being born in savage America he had learned to speak English, is the material of Fielding, but the definitive tone his career in England gave him was that of Richardson. Benjamin Colman educated himself in the just tempering of religious fervor by polite sensibility, the proper elevation of daily reality through the application of religious sentiments.

One important teacher of these lessons was Elizabeth Singer, a noted poet of religious sentiments, who under her married name, Elizabeth Rowe, enjoyed a fame among such poets of her day as Matthew Prior, with whom she exchanged commendatory verses, and whose elegy on her husband Pope both borrowed from for his own verse and reprinted as an appendix to "Eloisa and Abelard" (1720). Samuel Johnson later in the century noted that although "the attempt to employ the ornaments of romance in the decoration of religion" was first made by Robert Boyle, "the completion of the great design was reserved for Mrs. Rowe." [34] Colman became a frequenter of her father's home near Bath and there exchanged verses with her and engaged in long and moving conversations about the presence of the spiritual in their daily lives and the fine attunement of human sentiment and natural beauty that made up the divine plan.

Through his friendship with Elizabeth Singer, Colman developed close knowledge of the tradition of religious sentiment that he was effectively to advance in America, a tradition that was to be the instrument of civility on the nineteenth-century frontier until, in its final debased form, it received its quietus in Mark Twain's depiction of the poetic efforts of Emmiline Grangerford. The road that ended in Emmiline's "Ode to Stephen Dowling Bots, Dec'd" began with Mrs. Rowe's "On the Death of Mr. Thomas Rowe," and with lines such as:

> Ye muses, graces, all ye gentle train
> Of weeping lovers, assist the pensive strain!
> But why should I implore your moving art?
> 'Tis but to speak the dictates of my heart;
> And all that knew the charming youth will join
> Their friendly sighs, and pious tears to mine:
> For all that knew his merit must confess,
> In grief, for him, there can be no excess.[35]

Emmiline, Huck Finn tells us, "didn't ever have to stop to think" [36] but could write poetry as speedily as rhymes occurred to her, a lampooned version of Mrs. Rowe's admirable swiftness in composing the final two books of her *History of Joseph*, which, her laudatory contemporary biographer said, "I am inform'd, was no more than the labour of three or four days." [37]

In learning of how Miss Singer had first come to a sense of her election, Colman was rehearsing the genteel process that would replace the harsher transformation of personality insisted upon by an earlier age and still held forth by those who opposed the broader basis of church admission in New England. Conversion of the genteel sort would nevertheless allow Protestantism to retain its predestinarian loyalty. According to the best modern doctrines that Colman now encountered, conversion is a matter of religion's becoming the reigning principle in one's mind. Whereas some still believed that it was a "sort of instantaneous revolution in the soul, attended with an over-turning of whatever favourable sentiments persons had of themselves, and their condition before," that notion was mistaken. It had confusedly arisen from a failure to distinguish "between the change that the first converts to Christianity underwent, or which passes on those who having led a vicious life, enter at length into quite a new way of thinking and acting, which hath something of the violence of a storm in it; and that sense of piety which often silently steals upon tender and uncorrupted minds, like the light of the morning, hardly perceivable when it breaks, or in its gradual encrease, and yet shining more and more unto the perfect day." [38] In a modern age the latter process, Colman agreed, could much more properly be called conversion, and yet the former is still available for those whose earlier lives had been more dramatically vicious. In adopting such views and bringing them back to his influential pulpit, Colman was modifying predestinarian Protestantism to a form that would serve the needs of American westward expansion for more than a hundred years after his death, permitting the convert of the camp meeting and the daughter of the swellest merchant in town to share the same fellowship. He was preferring the superior claims of the refined mind and yet recognizing that the basis of that refinement was human sentiment which was universally accessible and could assert itself in the less sophisticated if properly awakened. Colman was equipped by taste and intellect both to move among the best families of New England and to welcome the Great Awakening as a confirmation of his perceptions rather than a threat to his status.

The first man in English dissent to bring the new gentility to the descendants of the Puritans was Dr. Isaac Watts, whose approval Colman frequently solicited in his career as preacher and writer. In words tinged with the patronage of his high-church allegiance, Samuel Johnson said that Watts "taught the Dissenters to write and speak like other men, by shewing them that elegance might consist with piety." [39] Watts spoke against running on at length in prayer, especially in a doctrinal way, and instructed thousands to "let the language of affection follow the language of our judgment, for this is the most rational and natural method." [40] He did not shy from the admission that his intent was to bring his fellow heirs of Puritanism into conformity with what general polite society regarded as the most decent behavior, while continuing to hold the particulars of their faith. His design, he wrote, is that the plainer Christians among the dissenters "might not expose themselves to the censure of talking without a meaning, not be charged with enthusiasm by their conforming neighbors." [41]

Establishing a tradition to be championed by Colman in New England, Watts turned to the Bible not just as a record of divine truth but as a standard for fine language, recognized as such, he said, by "the most authentic judge of fine thought and fine language our age has produced," [42] *viz. The Spectator.* Colman was in complete sympathy with the Brattle Street members' intention of having the Bible read weekly. Doctrinal matters aside, he relied on the sheer elevating power of its diction. His biographer notes, "He often made use of Scripture, not for proof and illustration only, but for the sake of the inspired language." [43] Watts and others in England, when they commented on Colman's treatises and sermons, "often observe with pleasure the variety of useful and beautiful thoughts, and just sentiments and fine address in them." [44]

In style Colman moved toward an exercise of his auditors' sensibilities through presenting them with allusions that engaged their fancy, rather than teaching truths that wearied the intellect and failed to develop a sensitivity to religion. If you take the fancy, he said, you fix the memory. As he began what is probably his most ambitious series of sermons, that on the parable of the ten virgins, he announced that he did not believe in analyzing parables so as to "force some divine truth out of every minute circumstance in them." To do so, he said, "is to press the stalk with the grapes; which wou'd but soak up some of the good wine, and spoil the rest." But while avoiding the ingenuities of his more scholastically inclined colleagues, he would not descend to the simple-minded bluntness of his less sophisticated colleagues: "In popular discourses, I believe we may easily be too shy and starch, if we bind our selves only to the first scope of the story, and wholly pass over many curious hints in it, which are both for use and ornament." [45] The unforced elegance of the stalk and grape image, addressed to those who were too baroque by half in their torturing of texts, and the telling force of "shy and starch," addressed to those who confused coarseness with honesty, were the hallmarks of a style that backdated the Mathers and reduced the ranters. Colman's was the tone of the finest strain of

Puritanism's eighteenth-century literature. His voice, superior to the hoarser repetitiveness of those still clinging to past models or the irritating pitch of voices that presumed to speak the learning that all men must hear, was the voice of a very high mediocrity indeed, but a mediocrity for all of that. Benjamin Colman provided a standard of sensibility at a time when his culture could no longer be unified by a doctrinal standard, and thereby gave his culture a tone suitable to its most provincial period. He provided the growth time between its rude and powerful economic and political sowing and its distinctive social and literary flowering. The Mathers were forceful reminders that Puritanism had a past, and Colman in his assertion of refinement and receptivity to emotion in religion was the ensurer of its future.

At Brattle Street, Colman took hold firmly and gracefully, and with him sentiment arrived for a long stay in Boston. Indulgence in the best instincts was both dignified and divine, Colman taught, and the battles with the flesh of such as Cotton Mather were made to seem a tortured anachronism. "I took my little daughter, Katy, into my study," wrote Mather, "and there I told my child, that I am to die shortly, and she must, when I am dead, remember every thing, that I said unto her." [46] This was a general spiritual exercise for Katy. He was not literally dying or about to die, but under the safe assumption that he would some day do so, he could further hypothesize that he was about to do so and use the hypothetical situation as an occasion for weaning Katy's affections from nature to God, from earthly to heavenly father. In the same period Benjamin Colman, writing to a woman whose betrothed had died suddenly, consoled her in the actual situation by inviting her to give way to her grief rather than combating it, and offered her a rationale for the indulgence: "Your soul is too great and just I know, to count it any indecency to be seen to mourn; you owe this honor to the dead, this justice to yourself." [47] Boston contained both men, and their common acceptance of the need to enforce the authority of their profession compelled them into a polite if chilled relationship.

The most radical break Benjamin Colman made with New England's past was one that went relatively unremarked at the time. His acceptance of set readings and set prayers was an attunement to his day, but its heterodoxy was muffled by his adherence to the central faith of the Westminster Confession. At the core of Puritan practice, however, far closer to its heart than its distrust of set forms, was the assertion of the democracy of the community of the saints, each man ultimately a priest in himself, and the consequent view of the minister as a member of the community selected to be its leader because of his greater learning and discernment, but not because of what was indeed impossible, his superiority in grace. Such a notion of the priest had developed, the original Puritans believed, in false churches that claimed an existence apart from the believers. In regarding the church as the eternally existing dispensary of grace, the false churchmen regarded priests as possessors of special grace and therefore the fit dispensers of it to the less gifted, who, in exchange, gave the priesthood their material support. Colman, however, found in the view of the superiority of ministerial grace the necessary leverage he needed to govern a wealthy congregation that had, as he well knew, hired him and that might, therefore, extend its material superiority into a challenge to his authority. The kind of church that Brattle and Bradstreet wanted, he sensed, was not complete unless the man who led it could eventually associate his power with something more potent than his having been hired for the job. In order to escape a dependence upon a fellowship of equals who, in point of fact, because of their wealth were not equal but more powerful than he, Colman came to insist that ministers' voices be more regarded than those of lay elders because ministers "may be modestly supposed to be their superiors in knowledge and grace." [48] What could well have been regarded as heresy was silently acquiesced in by the majority of his colleagues as a needed source of influence in what would otherwise be an unrestricted buyer's market for their talents.

In Connecticut, where a high degree of political democracy prevailed, ministerial consolidation proceeded relatively unchecked and was finally established firmly in the Saybrook Platform of 1708, which became the law of that land. The principal feature of the platform required "that the churches which are neighboring to each other [usually those of a county] shall *consociate* for mutual affording to each other such assistance as may be requisite, upon all occasions ecclesiastical." [49] Consociations were given the power to decide cases of scandal that arose within particular churches in their jurisdiction, and cases too broad for treatment by that local body were to be taken up jointly by the consociations. A church might refer the case of an offender to the consociation for settlement, but the individual offender could not make the same referral if his church was satisfied of its judgment without consultation. In addition, the Saybrook Platform established ministerial associations that were to assemble at least twice a year, function as professional societies in which learned opinions were exchanged on the pressing problems of the day, and serve as boards for the examination and licensing of candidates for the ministry. Such associations were authorized to proceed against ministerial heresy or scandal, on one hand, and against churches that did not settle an approved pastor, on the other. The Connecticut ministry thus achieved the associational benefits of both a professional society and a trade union and were able to do so most obviously because a population fully engaged in the divisive politics of local democracy felt its basic liberties unthreatened by the establishment of an authoritative hierarchy that presided over religion.

In Massachusetts, however, a large party still chafed under the loss of the privileges of the old charter, privileges like those Connecticut still enjoyed. Such people continued to guard jealously whatever degree of democracy remained. Politically this meant the never-ending battle between the royal governor, whose approval was needed for all civil measures, and the popular assembly that voted the government financial support. Ecclesiastically this meant that the autonomy of the local congregation took on the force of a political metaphor. In protecting the particular church's right to self-determination against the consolidating instincts of the more prosperous clergy, the village democrats were able to express their otherwise baffled opposition to reduced liberties and mercantile control of their lives. When, therefore, the Boston Association of Ministers at its meeting in September 1705 drew up proposals for a firm compulsory control of churches, an immediate adverse reaction to this infringement of the people's liberties promptly checked the scheme. Even opponents of the scheme were most of them concerned with such matters as the existence of pastorless churches and the increase of the unworthy in the pulpit, but any move to correct such abuses had too strong a flavor of Presbyterianism, if not downright papacy, for it to find acceptance. Massachusetts, in the main, had to yield to the drift toward an increasing gap between the sophistication of the wealthier churches and the rudeness of the poorer ones, and the leading ministers would, in the main, have to exert their influence through the maintenance of a style that they hoped would trickle down into the country rather than through the assumption of supervisory powers.

The good old way, in Massachusetts rhetoric, could be used to support two very divergent attitudes. On one hand, it was the way of the autonomous congregation threatened by the prelatical tendencies of association. On the other, it was the way of a faith based on the power of the word that came from a learned preacher, threatened by the centrifugal features of growth. That the former view eventually triumphed is an indication of the nature of the anxieties that most deeply moved the folk, anxieties about their ability to control their daily reality greater than anxieties about the uniformity of their religion. Distrust of associational control inevitably bred distrust of intellectualism as a tool of the ruling class, and a corresponding folklore of the superiority of plain ways and common sense.

The thwarted move toward association in Massachusetts was made most significant because of the response it drew from John Wise, "the furious man," as Cotton Mather called him, who emerged as the most eloquent spokesman of the people, "not only tenacious of their liberties," in Mather's words, "but also more suspicious than they have cause to be." [50] Although addressed to the 1705 proposals, however, Wise's writings against them were not composed before 1710 and they were not, therefore, a factor in the actual dispute. They stand, nevertheless, as the fullest expression of democratic thinking in the period, representative of the otherwise unexpressed beliefs of the people.

John Wise's father was an indentured servant, and John Wise himself was the first from such a background and the only one for some decades to have attended Harvard. After graduation he served in frontier pulpits in Connecticut and Massachusetts and as chaplain to Connecticut troops in King Philip's War. He moved to Chebacco parish within Ipswich, Massachusetts, in 1680 and was installed as pastor of the church he organized there in 1682, holding that post for the remainder of his life. During the Andros regime he was one of the leaders of the Jacks and Toms who were tried for refusing to pay their taxes, and he served as chaplain in Phips's first expedition against Quebec. It is clear that his chaplaincies were not construed by him as precluding his right to enter into the combat directly or to advise the commanders with whom he served more as colleague than as subordinate. His local reputation was great both as a minister who could pray the shipwrecked safely to shore and as the best wrestler in his part of the country. He recognized the central importance of trade in Massachusetts, but he also sought an accommodation for the depressed state of the farmer and was an early and strong advocate of land banks. John Wise, who presumed to speak for the people, was also of them.

Wise's writings, taking their occasion from disputes over whether the Congregational Church should give up a degree of autonomy in order to ensure general standards, are always unhesitating in moving between questions of liberty therein raised and wider questions of civil rights. "That government which sensibly clogs tyranny and preserves the subject free from slavery," he affirmed, "is the only government in the state to advance man's temporal happiness; and we in the country honor the resolve in civil affairs, and also affirm (upon great experience) that such a constitution in church government is (also) the only way to advance grace and man's eternal happiness." [51] He pointed to the history of modern churches that had yielded to a centralized authority and whose people found that the only liberty left them was "that they have had the liberty to be governed with a hook in their nose (like wild cattle in a string) by the mercy and pleasure of their drivers." [52] In his discussion he took up the pretensions of the civil monarch to be ruler of the church in terms that left no doubt about his view of the divine right of kings in civil affairs also: "Having seized all the keys of church power, they profess no dividend shall be made, unless it be to Christ Himself, as they pretend; tho' I believe thousands of them never expect to meet with Him, nor think that He will ever audit any accompt of theirs." [53]

Wise argued from natural rights as he understood them in classical texts, and in their development by Hobbes and Grotius as these were represented in his greatest single guide, Samuel Pufendorf, author of *De jure naturae et gentium*. Whatever clog natural corruption presented to the advancement of natural rights could be confined to theology, Wise insisted. In a discourse on church polity as opposed to a treatise on saving faith, he said, he would "waive the consideration of man's moral turpitude, but shall view him physically as a creature which God has made and finished essentially with many ennobling immunities, which render him the most august animal in the world, and still, whatever has happened since his creation, he remains at the upper-end of nature, and as such is a creature of a very noble character. For as to his dominion, the whole frame of the lower part of the universe is devoted to his use, and at his command." [54]

In 1772, nearly a half-century after his death, an edition of Wise's two tracts on church polity was published in Boston and sold out so rapidly that another edition was immediately prepared, more than a thousand copies of which were bespoken before publication. At that later time Wise's concern for Congregational order could be read as transparent metaphor for more vital concerns that could then be openly considered. In the same period the journalistic genius of Tom Paine was to intuit that political action could derive broad popular support by being made a metaphor for spiritual rebellion. As Wise in his day was anti-monarchical, but was compelled to express himself in anti-prelatical terminology, so Paine, who was anti-theistic, perceived that in his day the American people had reached the end of their patience with a predestinarian God, although they were not yet prepared for the blasphemy of saying so explicitly. His remarkable *Common Sense*, however, played on this impatience, stirring revolt against King George through a depiction of the history of royal rule as a history of the Calvinist fall of man. "Government, like dress, is the badge of lost innocence," he announced at the outset; "the palaces of kings are built on the ruins of the bowers of paradise." [55] And in a brilliant stroke of persuasion he urged, "Reconciliation is *now* a fallacious dream. Nature has deserted the connection, and art cannot supply her place." He clinched the argument with a citation, "For, as Milton wisely expresses, 'never can true reconcilement grow where wounds of hate have pierced so deep,' " [56] and did not bother to explain that the quoted sentiment was that of Satan faced with God's eternal decree.

John Wise in his advocacy of civil liberties was riding the broad current that carried along the very different Benjamin Colman of Brattle Street. The natural nobility of man, in spite of the fall, was a fact that could be used by him as a basis for advocacy of civil liberties, just as it was used by Colman as the basis for a religion of sensibility. Both men were predestinarians, but the consequences of that doctrine no longer called for a watchfulness in daily life against the corrupting tendencies of nature. Rather, corruption was a spiritual fact to be wrestled with psychologically, whereas God's plan provided nature for man as instrument and guide. Wise's doctrine extended to all mankind the rights over the natural creation that the original Puritans had reserved for the godly and restricted the superiority of the godly to spiritual matters. In the same way Colman's doctrine made the sensible pleasures of nature and the refinements of a society based on that sensibility the property of the godly as well as the worldly. Wise did not inhabit a world in which his doctrine of ecclesiastical polity based on natural right could be pushed explicitly to its civil consequences. Although he moved freely between church and state in his discourses, the former was his center and the latter provided illustrations drawn from historical regimes, such as those of the Catholic monarchs, that it was safe to cite disapprovingly. Colman did not inhabit a world in which the sensibility was its own excuse for being, and his application of his doctrine did not as yet permit extension into a *belles-lettres* centered on morals and manners exclusive of theological lessons. Wise was the best exemplar of the native source of the strength and independence of the folk, and Colman was the best exemplar of the force of civilization; socially they were in inevitable conflict. But they shared a high capacity to adapt beliefs they held in common to a changing reality, and their adaptations were to be definitive of their culture's perceptions and make negligible that culture's need to consolidate itself in more explicit institutions.

CHAPTER TWELVE

An Abundance of Artificers

Religion as civilizer—Slavery—The social pyramid and high culture
—The Great Awakening—Psyche versus society and literature—
Jonathan Edwards, Benjamin Franklin, and Puritan continuity

John Barnard, who became a Calvinist at Harvard without reading
Calvin's works, had difficulty finding a pulpit that would suit him
after his graduation. He was Boston-born, and not believing he could
be happy among a ruder people such as those of Yarmouth, who
issued him an invitation in 1705, he turned it down. In that same
year Benjamin Colman invited him to preach a sermon at Brattle
Street Church and in the following week invited him to dinner, after
which Colman apologized for not having sooner enjoyed Barnard's
preaching at Brattle Street. The reason, he explained, was that it
took time to convince his parishioners that Barnard, raised in the
Mathers' church, was not a "mimic and tool of the Mathers." [1]
Appreciating that young Barnard was a sensible man of the new age,
Colman talked to him about his travels in England, his friendship
with Mrs. Rowe, and his own poetical compositions.

But there was no suitable opening for urbane Barnard, and so he
accepted the post of chaplain to the 1707 expedition against Port
Royal, another colonial disaster in the draining war. Returned from
their defeat, the campaigners, according to an observer, were thus
greeted by the women of Boston: "Is your piss-pot charg'd
neighbor? So-ho, souse the cowards. Salute Port-Royal." [2] Boston
gentility had its limits.

Still without a post, Barnard accepted another chaplaincy, this in the Barbados fleet of 1709, and returned to England with that fleet. There, like Colman before him but with less success, he attempted to improve his relationship with the great dissenters of the day such as Edmund Calamy, and he served as supply minister in openings they provided for him. New Englanders, he found, were regarded as strange, if not downright savage, by all except the few merchants who traded regularly with their province. Barnard, accordingly, saw no reason not to conform to the best pattern of English manners. He dressed as a "small courtier" rather than a dissenting divine and attended Church of England services when he could conveniently do so. The results of his English travels, he felt, were that his civility was acknowledged to the improvement of English opinion of his native land and that he acquired a taste and information that would be of service to his countrymen when he returned. A lady he met in the Lichfield coach, for example, was alarmed when she learned he was an American and in despair at the rudeness he would presumably inflict upon her. But so gracious and helpful did her New England traveling companion prove that the lady would ever after think well of New England. As a token of her appreciation of the fact, she offered Barnard a recipe for the best bacon in England. With the same pleasure with which he recorded Colman's approval of his sermon, Barnard happily wrote that he brought the recipe home, scattered it about the countryside, "and from thence came all the right good bacon made in New England." [3]

Back in Boston in 1710, Barnard found his English experience had increased his attraction for his colonial countrymen. "It gave me some diversion to hear," he wrote, "(as I passed along the streets,) people in their shops saying to one another, 'How much better he preaches now than before he went to England;' though I often preached the sermons I had made before." [4] But while the new esteem brought him supply posts, it did not bring him a Boston pulpit and finally, in 1714, he accepted a call to Marblehead, where he served for the remainder of his long life.

If he could not be called to a civilized town, Barnard at least regarded his principal duty as seeing that the town to which he was called became civilized. When in 1766 he thought back on his fifty-two years of leadership in Marblehead, he remembered the economic and social changes that he believed he was instrumental in bringing about rather than his church activities. The minister, in his view, was principally a civilizer: a people brought to a better standard of life were a people more fit for religion. He derived great satisfaction from such facts as that there was now a regiment of seven smartly trained companies in his area, whereas when he had arrived there were but two ill-trained military groups, and that Marblehead now had thirty to forty ships engaged in foreign trade though when he had arrived there was none. "When I came," he wrote, "there was not so much as one proper carpenter, nor mason, nor tailor, nor butcher in the town, nor any thing of a market worth naming; but they had their houses built by country workmen, and their clothes made out of town, and supplied themselves with beef and pork from Boston, which drained the town of its money. But now we abound in artificers, and some of the best, and our markets large, even to a full supply. And what above all I would remark, there was not so much as one foreign trading vessel belonging to the town, nor for several years after I came to it; though no town had really greater advantage in their hands. The people contented themselves to be the slaves that digged in the mines, and left the merchants of Boston, Salem, and Europe to carry away the gains; by which means the town was always in dismally poor circumstances, involved in debt to the merchants more than they were worth; nor could I find twenty families in it that, upon the best examination, could stand upon their own legs; and they were generally as rude, swearing, drunken, and fighting a crew, as they were poor. Whereas, not only are the public ways vastly mended, but the manners of the people greatly cultivated; and we have many gentlemanlike and polite families, and the very fishermen scorn the rudeness of the former generation." [5]

Trade was what assured the upward sloping of the pyramid of provincial life. In spite of the war, which aggravated New England's perennial money shortage it prospered in continuance of patterns set earlier. John Higginson, minister of Salem, was by his very location an expert on trade and revealed his knowledge when he wrote his son Nathaniel, residing in India as a factor for the East Indian Company, to return to his native town and set up as a merchant there. The system he described was a familiar one: "Considering that money is of late grown so exceeding scarce amongst us, that the making of returns for England, by the way of Barbados, Leeward Islands, Bilboa, Oporto, Cadiz, and Isle of Wight would be more easy and safe than direct for England; and it's probable more advantageous; because, money being scarce, and returns direct, difficult whereas a man may sell more goods, and better get in his debts more speedily and certainly, for barter of goods for those markets, than direct." [6] So many were the trading ships of New England, and so frequently did they sail, he assured Nathaniel, that the merchant need not hire a ship for his express purposes but could readily find one going in his direction with cargo space available.

In proportion to the height of gentility the culture achieved was the breadth of its commercial base, and that base in the eighteenth century required commodities in greater demand than were those native to the colony. Accordingly, New England entrepreneurs developed the distilling of rum into the greatest single industry in their province and made that rum and African slaves a good part of the base on which they built. The slaves were, in the main, designed for other markets than New England but were some part of the foundation of the new provincialism for all that. By 1723 rum had surpassed all other goods as a medium of exchange on the Guinea slave coast, and in 1763 the Boston merchants estimated that Massachusetts produced yearly 15,000 hogsheads of rum, 100 gallons to the hogshead, distributed as follows: "9000 hogsheads for home consumption and the whale, cod, and mackrel fisheries; 3000 for the Southern Colonies; 1700 for Africa; and 1300 for Nova Scotia and Newfoundland." [7] Rum clearly had become a medium of exchange beyond the slave market.

Some slaves inevitably found their way to servitude in New England, and the number of slaves in Boston alone rose to 2000 by

1720, one-sixth of the town's total population, in Carl Bridenbaugh's estimate. That same Boston was the second largest printing and bookselling center in the British Empire.[8]

Puritan moral writings are lacking in extended considerations of the slave trade. The most notable reactions to it are the few that are opposed, but the silence with which these appear to have been received argues that they were regarded as so weightless as to demand no answer. If urbanity could be the possession of the godly as well as the worldly, as Colman argued, and if nature was to be the instrument of the rational as well as the justified man, then Negroes could, without great reservation, be assumed under a divine plan in which they fulfilled a role akin to that of the lower creatures. John Eliot, the venerable apostle to the Indians, shortly before his death had expressed concern for the well-being of the Negroes in Massachusetts. "He had long lamented it," Cotton Mather reports, "with a bleeding and a burning passion, that the English used their Negroes but as their horses or their oxen, and that so little care was taken about their immortal souls; he looked upon it as a prodigy that any wearing the name of Christians, should so much have the hearts of devils in them, as to prevent and hinder the instruction of the poor blackamores, and confine the souls of their miserable slaves to a destroying ignorance, merely for fear of thereby losing the benefit of their vassalage." [9]

Although the potential is there, Eliot is not centrally concerned with upsetting the institution of slavery but rather wants to improve the spiritual condition of the slave. He died in 1690 before he could formulate a plan for such improvement, but there is little doubt that it would have been ineffectual. The economic value of the slave was to be the determining factor, as Cotton Mather regretfully sensed, not his spiritual potential. Eliot's Indian plans had come to wreck on the rocks of Indian impediment to colonial growth; with the end of the fur trade Indians no longer served in the economy, but merely made difficult the cultivation of further lands. In view of the stark meaning of slavery, those held in such bondage were not potential brethren in church fellowship either. Sarah Kemble Knight reveals the swift certainty with which economic fact became social habit when, in 1704, she recorded her reaction, that of a Boston gentlewoman, to the way in which the coarser inhabitants of New England's frontier socialized with their slaves. They suffer, she says, "too great familiarity from them, permitting them to sit at table and eat with them (as they say to save time), and into the dish goes the black hoof as freely as the white hand." [10] She reveals that this frontier democracy comes about from economic necessity—the conservation of the housewife's labor and the maximization of the workers' time in the field—but mistrusts its social consequences.

Samuel Sewall, who retained an interest in propagating the Gospel to the Indians after this effort had lost any realistic appeal for most of his peers, concerned himself also with the evils of slavery. His most telling arguments, however, were addressed to that institution in Massachusetts, not to the trade, and were developed in the context of the social and economic well-being of his community. He had little effect immediately, but his arguments remain the best explanation of why slavery was not to have so long a continuance in New England as in colonies based on a plantation economy and why New England could also continue to serve those economies as slave-supplier. "It would conduce more to the welfare of the province to have white servants for a term of years," argued Sewall, "than to have slaves for life. Few can endure to hear of a Negro's being made free; and indeed they can seldom use their freedom well; yet their continual aspiring after their forbidden liberty, renders them unwilling servants. And there is such a disparity in their conditions, color & hair, that they can never embody with us, and grow up into orderly families, to the peopling of the land, but still remain in our body politic as a kind of *extravasat* blood. As many Negro men as there are among us, so many empty places there are in our train bands, and the places taken up of men that might make husbands for our daughters." [11] The art of political persuasion through appeal to social expedience was thus being developed in Boston six years before its greatest practitioner, Benjamin Franklin, was born there. The slaves, as Sewall saw, were finally to uphold the pyramid of society as the profitable commodities of New England trade rather than as a significant part of the New England labor force.

At the bottom of New England's internal social structure were the settlers who had pushed into the woods to clear land and wrest a crop from it without carrying with them the institutions of town, church, and school that had marked an earlier period of development. Their center, insofar as they had one, was the merchant's store where they came to renew their contact with the more finished settlements by staring at the goods displayed. Madam Knight observed their reverential awe in the presence of the merchant, and she mixed satirization of their rustic clownishness with distress at their debasement. Calling those she saw Bumpkin Simpers and Joan Tawdry, the gentlewoman who had composed poems to the moon as "Fair Cynthia" in closed iambic couplets opened her ears to the diverging diction that now characterized a separate class. "It's confounded gay, I vow," says Bumpkin, looking at the ribbon for sale at the merchant's, and Joan replies, "Law you, it's right gent, do you take it, 'tis dreadful pretty." [12] They are constantly indebted to the merchant, Madam Knight reports, and since they lack ready money and must usually pay in provisions promised, they pay double. Her scorn of the country clown with his jaws incessantly working on his cud of tobacco and his speech interspered with the spitting of the juice is tempered by her sense of native worth. "We may observe here the great necessity and benefit both of education and conversation," she says, "for those people have as large a portion of mother wit, and sometimes as larger, than those who have been brought up in cities; but, for want of improvements, render themselves almost ridiculous. . . . I should be glad if they would leave such follies, and am sure all that love clean houses (at least) would be glad on't too." [13]

The leaving of such follies was attached in great part in that society to the ability of the church to assume authority among the folk and to educate them to civility by organizing them into a congregation. Ministerial association, as it succeeded in the Connecticut woods that Madam Knight visited, accomplished this. The shifting Puritan emphasis from piety to morality took place because the minister's task was now to bring order to the lives of Bumpkin Simpers and Joan Tawdry and weld them to the larger society in more resonant ways than their consumption of town-made goods. The minister was as much the carrier of a social standard in the new villages formed on the New England frontier as he was the preacher of the word. His task was made trying by his constant struggle to retain outward trace of his gentility so that he could perform his task with authority. It was difficult to wrest from a country congregation a salary that would support him in some small style. Especially in the hard times brought on by the French and Indian Wars rural congregations were grudging.

"Very few besides the Boston minister . . . able to support themselves with what they receive from their people," complained Ebenezer Parkman from his rural manse. He felt that his ineffectiveness was the result of his undersupport, that his people were reaping sparsely from him because they had sowed sparsely. "He that would be just will attribute hereto and not to the want of either sufficient parts or eager inclination," he wrote, "if there are not so great men among us as were famous in New England in the days of fathers." So much for the standard of the original settlers, which, Parkman reveals in 1726, was becoming a measure of the diminishing stature of the clergy rather than a loss of strength in the believers, as the power of the purse was exerted by the pews. Parkman went on: "Most ministers do groan under their pressures and it is an addition to the weight that sinks them that the generality of people are of the sort and spirit that it scarce ever can prove to the advantage of men to complain, but it is best to suffer patiently, to obtain relief. They desire to be left to their own generosity, the extent of which is enough demonstrated. This reflection is the more melancholy when it is evident such evil conceits are daily propated to the dishonour of God with the disparagement of his ministry. For trifling as the following observation is, it is true: That their inward respect is much proportion'd to our external appearance; when therefore it becomes mean thro their neglect it will be in danger of becoming worse thro their contempt." [14]

As he noted that the still fashionable lamentation at declines and languishings was becoming a hollow theme, so Parkman, hard pressed by his constant squabbles about salary and the lack of respect this denoted in itself and promoted by reducing his capacity to make a decent appearance, also took sharp note in his diary of the hollowness of the special holy days of fast or thanksgiving that the Boston ministers managed to persuade the General Court to promulgate upon the countryside on every minor occasion. "They are such grab'd pieces of solemn mockery that I cannot but think God is greatly provok'd by them," he wrote in 1728. "They are loathsome to Him and He is weary to bear them. I cannot but conclude that one of the greatest reasons of the Lord's controversy with this land is taken from hence." [15] Here, indeed, was a new turn to an old matter. Fast days called to appeal to God had the reverse effect upon Him because they had become so frequent as to be but slightly observed. Such was the view from the rural parsonage.

That parsonage's bookshelves now contained "romances and tales; poems and plays." [16] In moods of despondency Parkman reproached himself for reading them, charging his indulgence to the sin of vanity. But in a ministry increasingly devoted to the improvement of the village's manners and morals rather than of its piety, Parkman could well have argued that such books were of professional use. "Example," he noted of himself, "seems to have a far greater influence upon me than precept, since it so gratifies my under powers, my imagination and curiosity; and thereby captivates my affections. It's sad that my understanding and judgment are no more employ'd upon the purity and perfection of the divine laws, and the infinite justice, supremacy and goodness of my God that injoins their observance. But I am glad I can any way be wrought upon and brought to my duty." [17] The times were ripening toward the moment of the Great Awakening, when a culture that was moved by example more than by precept could attach its under powers to religion without apology.

At the apex of the social pyramid the Boston ministry, freed relatively from any obligation to civilize its parishioners, improved its leisure to supply the want of a class devoted to the provision of a high culture. The spectrum of churches in Boston, circa 1735, all calling themselves Congregational, allowed for such ministers at one extreme as Mather Byles at Hollis Street, who imitated Pope in secular verse, sent him letters of devout adoration, and engaged in wars of wit in the periodical press with others, such as the distiller Joseph Green. Byles wanted to see Boston reflect the light of London. His hymn to God's wonder as manifested in the sea contained such verses as

> Round thee the scaly nation roves,
>   Thy op'ning hands their Joys bestow,
> Thro' all the blushing coral Groves,
>   These silent gay Retreats below.[18]

Distiller Green offered a parallel hymn parodying Byles's style thus:

> Fish of all kinds inhabit here,
>   And throng the dark abode.
> Here haddock, hake, and flounders are,
>   And eels and perch and cod.[19]

At the center of the spectrum Benjamin Colman bent all efforts to weld the sensibility to religion and the society to religious duty. "No man is made only for himself and his own private affairs, but to serve profit and benefit others," [20] he preached in apparent echo of John Donne. And his language was designed to exemplify as well as illustrate the theme of benign cosmopolitanism that he urged upon his listeners: "A man's private and domestic affairs are too *petite* to engross his noble soul; they are too small and narrow a compass for him to confine himself within. He is endowed for much greater things, and he much debases himself if he do not think so." [21] Colman and his parishioners had a moral obligation to extend their influence and their charity to the farthest ends of their society.

At the other end of the spectrum were those who, in the tradition of the Mathers, stopped short of mere secular literature or a direct development of the sensibility, but poured their stored energy into advancing the growth of science in New England. They too had an anxious eye on English approval. In his advanced age Cotton Mather championed smallpox inoculation against a town mob that was still sufficiently primitive in belief to regard such as tampering with God's will, and during the epidemic of 1721 characterized Boston as "an hell upon earth, a city full of lies, and murders, and blasphemies, as far as wishes and speeches can render it so." [22]

Culture by 1720 had become thoroughly provincial. It was from a provincial vantage point that the New Englanders of the early decades of the eighteenth century attempted to lift their society from the disregard of the life of the mind into which it had fallen in the years after King Philip's War and the end of the old charter. Those events had brought in their train a deterioration of institutions and a widespread demoralization. The dominant culture of seventeenth-century New England had been, in a limited fashion, a people's culture. It was based on widespread literacy, a respect for learning, and a mandated insistence upon community. Those of its own works that it cherished most highly were the productions of the learned—sermons, theological treatises, and excursions into ecclesiastical polemics—but these were not produced on a societal level separate from the people. They were produced by men who were regarded as the spokesmen of the people because they were the most able for the task, but who were not apart from them in assumptions or in aims. What their spokesmen produced, the people consumed with interest and with pleasure, and if this was not a folk culture because of its strong exclusion of a broad segment of the population, it nevertheless attempted, however mistakenly, to coerce the excluded into a joint participation in the appreciation of such products. It consistently held forth to them the ideal of inclusion if they yielded to such coercion.

The coherence of this culture was tried in the latter decades of the century, and the institutions of learning were enfeebled. When, in the new century, a concern for arts and letters reasserted itself, now seeking the forms of an age of sensibility and increasing technology, that concern, nevertheless, was clearly connected with the earlier insistence on a community of the literate. But the intellectual rebuilding took place in a dependent mercantile province rather than in an autonomous rural colony; in a province now conscious of social class and divided by economic specialization. The rebuilding, therefore, took the form of an alliance between wealth and those, such as the urban ministry, whom the wealthy endowed with leisure for study and creation. As a consequence a high culture began to detach itself, one that would, it was presumed, ultimately affect the general tone of life through superior example, but one which was intended for immediate effect only in a community of social and intellectual peers. American intellectuals in the provincial atmosphere were far more concerned with their peers in England than with their inferiors in New England. So began the tangled history of the American literary man's struggle for recognition in an indifferent imperial capital. This issue burns through the piqued vanity of Cotton Mather, for example, when in 1715 he complains about the difficulty in getting his *Biblia Americana* published. His clerical brethren in London, he says, "seem to be of the opinion that a poor *American* must never be allowed capable of doing any thing worth any one's regarding; or to have ever look'd on a book. And the truth is, we are under such disadvantages, that if we do any thing to purpose, it might carry in it a tacit rebuke to the sloth of people more advantageously circumstanced." [23] At that point Mather's sights were raised from an American audience to the limited British one of the leaders of the dissenting movement. But within five years he was attracted to the pattern of patronage that supported the literary endeavors of the leading English writers. "If the gentlemen whose wise expenses run in this channel," he reflected, "should sometimes have made unto them an handsome dedication of their books, which are by their goodness brought into operation in the world, it is but a very little of the acknowledgment that is due unto them, thus to erect statues for them." [24]

So the spiral twisted. From being intensely theological and theoretical, yet an expression of the people, learning had fallen into contempt as an interference with more vital new economic and political developments in the culture. It was reduced to scolding as the institutions that nourished the life of the mind decayed. It rose again when it was patronized by the merchants and adjusted itself to their concern for general benificence and their desire to refine their sensibilities so as to put the seal on their arrival into the gentry. In its revitalized form it was to be extended to the people rather than take its rise from their common concerns. It is no more curious than true that the dry reasonings of John Cotton's *Keys of the Kingdom of Heaven* had more of the common humanity of his culture in it than did the emotive strains of Mather Byles's "Hymn Written during a Voyage."

Ebenezer Parkman, uneasy in his preference for example over precept and embarrassed by his tendency to respond more fully to an appeal to his human feelings than to one made to his sense of divine justice, represents that class of intellectuals who were no longer in a position to contribute to the life of the mind, but who were still committed to transmitting its civilizing benefits. The people who attended the ministrations of such as he were also sensible of the gap that had opened in their lives between belief and feeling. The uses to which Colman put sensibility were too rarefied for them, and the authority presumed by the provincial leaders of the intellectual life was too opposite to their daily reality. But in their acceptance of a church made up of those who were not scandalous in behavior, as opposed to one consisting of devout believers; in their Sunday concern for morality rather than a weekly concern for piety, they had transformed their church into a formal organization rather than a vital fellowship. Creeds were statements of doctrine rather than statements of belief, and religious experience itself was standardized.[25] In such an institution, uninformed by zeal, the ministry were employees who, like all hired hands, were to be kept on as short wages as possible. The restoration of their authority could come in richer churches, as Colman had shown, by their assumption of superior grace. In the country churches, however, such assumption was countered by the people's adherence to the fundamental equality of believers. Authority was granted only to those ministers who set a superior moral example.

The church had become a specialized institution within society rather than a voluntary fellowship of believers who considered themselves the determiners of their society's future. The pattern deeply displeased thousands who were conscious that a force had gone out of their lives and that there was nothing to compensate them for its loss. No institution had supplied the place of the earlier church in giving daily reality a high purpose that converted physical trials into psychological triumphs and reduced the many indignities of daily life to trivialities that could and would be dominated by those illuminated with grace. Economic specialization had defined new communities in centers such as Boston, but in the rural areas the lost community of the church of professed saints was not replaced, and the isolation of the individual farmer and villager from his fellows was aggravated by his increasing separation, within the wider provincial society, from classes that were now emerging as economically and socially superior. The deadening condition was not one that could be broken when threat and experience of war were constantly felt; but at the close of the longest interlude in French and Indian hostilities revivalism finally erupted. Beginning around 1734 in individual congregations such as that of Jonathan Edwards in Northampton, it spread to a great and general conflagration that affected all the American colonies in the years from 1740 to 1742 and left its mark on American religion in the following decades. The Great Awakening again affirmed the absolute dividing power of grace and drew thousands to fellowship with their brother saints in a shared sense of overwhelming purpose that obliterated the earlier meaninglessness of their condition. Emotional release in religion became central to the new life awakened by the movement, rather than being peripheral, irrelevant, or opposed to religion. The politer, such as Colman, who had preached the development of a sensible religion, courageously supported its popular and more boisterous manifestations against colleagues committed to a view of Christian civility that abhorred the emotional outbreaks as contemptible signs of psychic aberration. At the center of revivalism stood Jonathan Edwards, whose deepest commitment was to the release of grace in common life and whose difficult task, brilliantly executed on an intellectual level, was to justify revivalism without condoning the anti-intellectual excesses that inevitably accompanied it; to bind emotionalism to religion as an essential part of it without accepting mere enthusiasm as a sign of the Spirit's presence.

In his detailed study of the Great Awakening, Edwin Scott Gaustad concludes that the central controversy it aroused was between those who would assert directly the supreme importance of the righteousness of God attained by faith in Jesus Christ and those who would substitute for this man's moral attainments. He writes: "This clear confrontation accounts to a major degree for the persistent appeal of the Great Awakening. For nowhere else in the western world did the double reaction against the devotional decline and theological pedantry of the seventeenth century focus on a single movement. In New England both pietism and the Enlightenment found their provocation in the revival's course and wake." [26] The movement that he thus identifies was American and, more specifically, of New England. But it became widespread and powerful because it was the culture's final assertion of its distinctive religious nature in terms of a universal divine plan rather than in the vocabulary of nationalism.

The torch was set to the tinder by the English evangelist George Whitfield, who first toured the colonies in 1740. The characteristic fashion in which the flames were fed and spread throughout the two years of the movement was through the ministry of itinerant preachers who traveled from town to town to awaken the dead and revivify the living. The many settled ministers who were part of the movement found they too were more effective preaching as visitors to other churches than they were in their own congregations. Jonathan Edwards' most memorable sermon in the period was preached to the congregation of Enfield, Connecticut, rather than to his own church. This method of propagation is clear indication that the reassertion of the dividing force of the spirit and the overwhelming comforts of fellowship to be derived from grace appealed to men as the means of membership in a community larger than their church, their town, or their province. Through participation in the Awakening men were asserting their membership in a universal community. The spiritual comforts they derived from their experience of the work of grace within them were amplified and, ultimately, took their dominant appeal from the fact that provincial social lines were destroyed in the emergence of the wider community promoted by visitors from England, another region, or the next town.

This phenomenon of universalism, in turn, indicates the severe limits of the economic and political potential of the movement. Although its central strength was drawn from plain folk who keenly felt their exclusion from a meaningful human community, the movement could appeal to members of all classes because its immediate thrust was without consequence in the established systems of property and political power. The revolution of religious emotions was, by its very universal assumptions, directed away from social concerns, and its most dramatic personal effects were moral.

When "he that was formerly a drunkard lives a sober life: when a vain, light and wanton person becomes grave, and sedate: when the blasphemer becomes a praiser of God. When laughter is turned into mourning; and carnal joy into heaviness; and that professedly on account of their souls' condition," said Samuel Finley; "when the ignorant are filled with knowledge in divine things, & the tongue that was dumb in the things of God, speaks the language of Canaan: when the erroneous are become orthodox in fundamental points: when such as never minded any religion do make religion their only business: when busy Marthas & covetous worldlings do neglect their worldly concerns to seek after God's ordinances. Now, these things, and such like, are discernible to those who are graceless, and according to their own rules they ought to judge the devil is cast out." [27] Such a casting out threatened no immediate institution and could well be acceded to by the high who were so disposed as well as the lowly. The Great Awakening was an American phenomenon, but its strength was derived from its ability to lift Americans out of their sense of inconsequential provinciality by belittling the importance for their true selves of the economic and political institutions that had come to control their lives. It imparted a feeling of personal adequacy that did not impair the status of those institutions.

Charles Chauncy of the First Church of Boston, the greatest of the spokesmen against the Awakening, did not hesitate to go to the time-honored source of alarm against religious enthusiasm, and to affirm in a sermon in 1742 that the movement "has made strong attempts to destroy all property, to make all things common"; and then to bring in the most striking features of such traditional frightenings, "wives as well as goods." [28] But he was arguing against use from abuse and scoring a lunatic few. As the movement began to wane, then, it is true that the more vehement itinerants, their power draining as the people cooled and the established ministers such as Edwards dissociated themselves from excess, did sound the economic note. But they did so also in a fashion as time-honored as Chauncy's alarmism, by turning on the dissociated ministers as hirelings when they addressed a debtor-class auditory. "Now observe that a little money can turn the concern of the hirelings from one flock to another as quickly as the prospect of increasing the goods presents," said Ebenezer Frothingham in the decline of the movement. "And many times some of these false teachers are so crafty, that they will get their salary stated upon silver, as so much per ounce, so that if Providence send famine and scarcity, or our common currency run never so low they will take care of one, and the poor entangled flock may shift as they can." [29] The heinousness of his opponents stands revealed in Frothingham's rhetoric because they seek a form of remuneration immune from economic depression and thus set themselves apart from the people, vulnerable to economic fluctuations, and from God, whose judgment causes the fluctuations.

The scattered references to politics and property such as those of Chauncy and Frothingham illustrate by contrast that the Great Awakening was centrally concerned with restructuring the perception of daily reality and that its most telling results were in the revitalized moral outlook of those who continued to accept the daily facts, but now felt a new confidence in dealing with them. The ultimate material promise held out by open lands to the west and further material resources to be derived from the French possessions once the foes had been driven from them; the ultimate social promise held out by the ability of the wealthy to become gentry: these confined the revitalization within spiritual channels. The Puritan movement as a whole had had but one brief flirtation with economic revolution, that represented by the Levellers and Diggers in the late 1640s. This was not reflected in New England, with its very different conditions, and by 1649 the intensity of religious fervor on which these groups had built was confined to religious denominationalism—Quakers, Fifth Monarchists, Ranters—who drew away the Levellers' manpower. The characteristic economic manifestation of Puritanism and of the more radical offshoots that grew on its trunk was its suitability to the opportunities of a post-medieval world in which credit was the basis of trade, fellowship the basis of growth, and unremitting labor the basis of personal advancement. The Great Awakening reaffirmed these values.

Significant among the attitudes revived in the Great Awakening was the ahistorical view peculiar to American Puritanism. The history of the chosen people was, most meaningfully, a history of the works of God on earth, ever spreading and yet, in any society in which saint had separated from sinner, ever complete. This view had suffered a decline in the general decline of religion, and New England history had turned from its eternal connections to a concern with the declension from primitive purity. But even in this turn it retained its central ahistoricity and traced that decline in biography —exemplary lives that served as models of the eternal condition— rather than in causal analysis of events. With the Great Awakening the predilection for eternal history returned. Just as the people were attracted to membership in a community that knew no national bounds, so they again were attracted to a depiction of their present as it located them relative to God's eternal disposition rather than to the conditions that had preceded them.

In 1739 Jonathan Edwards began his *History of the Work of Redemption* in a series of sermons, and he carried on his writing of that frequently interrupted history until his death in 1758. It was published posthumously. "I would observe," he wrote, "that the increase of gospel light, and carrying on the work of redemption, as it respects the elect church in general, from the first erecting of the church to the end of the world, is very much after the same manner as the carrying on of the same work and the same light in a particular soul, from the time of its conversion, till it is perfected and crowned in glory." [30] Here at the fore again was a view of human history completed in any given life even as it continued through the ages. He kept his parallel as controlling format in tracing "the great affair in general" from the days of the Bible to his present, and when he came to write of the successes of the Gospel after the Reformation he concerned himself with the conversion of the Indians as an important feature of its irresistible spread, but made no mention of the migration of the Puritans and their establishment in New England. He was concerned with attaching his readers not to an American reality, but to a vital eternal reality. The meaning of history was to be felt by them in their psychic makeup rather than in their connection with social institutions.

Charles Chauncy in opposition to the Great Awakening asserted a more continuous view of human history. "The work of the SPIRIT is different now from what it was in the first days of Christianity," he explained. "Men were then favored with the extraordinary presence of the Spirit. He came upon them in miraculous gifts and powers; as a spirit of prophecy, of knowledge, of revelation, of tongues, of miracles, but the Spirit is not now to be expected in these ways." Rather, now the Spirit operates in a more mundane fashion, turning men from sin to God, "and in fine, by carrying on the good work He has begun in them; assisting them in duty, strengthening them against temptation, and in a word preserving them blameless thro' faith unto salvation." [31] Although he is addressing himself to the process of salvation in the individual rather than to history, Chauncy is affirming a continuity of personal growth and development different from the revolution of faith advocated by the awakeners, and he reflects a wider view of history as a connected causal framework rather than a divine plan irresistibly working its way in its own time, but using the lives of men as instant examples of the slower cosmic process.

In America the characteristic pattern of rebellion against the stultifications of daily life was to be that of Edwards rather than of Chauncy, which is to say, it was to be that of an assertion of the quickened psyche for which the things of the world were made fresh and pliant, rather than a rearrangement of the things of this world.

The larger social promise of affluence and status was sufficiently convincing and sufficiently experienced to guide the highest moments of intellectual and emotional protest into the channels of spiritual renewal. In declaring that the day of miracles had passed, for example, Charles Chauncy was advancing the cause of rational religion that resulted in the Unitarian Church, from which Ralph Waldo Emerson a century later resigned his pastorate in order to lead a revolution of the spirit against the materialism of his society. Emerson's goal was to quicken his society's psychic awareness of its condition so that the world would become again as miraculous as it had ever been, and life as stirring, rather than to protest against the deadening material conditions themselves. The age of miracles never died, said Emerson, and Christ "spoke of miracles; for he felt that man's life was a miracle, and all that man doth, and he knew that this daily miracle shines as the character ascends. But the word Miracle, as pronounced by Christian churches, gives a false impression; it is Monster. It is not one with the blowing clover and the falling rain." [32] Thus does Emerson modernize the Puritan view, revivified before him by Edwards, and fit it to romanticism as Edwards did to sentiment. Man's psychic life, properly perceived, contains all history, says Emerson. So he would only reluctantly enter into political issues, these being trivial in comparison with the great issue of human existence, and so he could with good reason say that, although the Democrats had better political principles, he would vote for the Whigs because they had better men. The ascent of character was crucial.

The great fiction of the flowering of American literature was that of Hawthorne and Melville, and the defining tone was imparted by Hawthorne when he perceived that in America manners were drab and reality dull, but that the psyche contained the stuff of literature. He pioneered in the psychological novel as a literary form that derived its resonance from its containment of the cosmic drama, and Melville advanced the view. In their works there is no middle distance, as it were. Filling the foreground is the psyche, and filling the background are the workings of a divine plan, be it malignant or benificent, while between the two the institutions of the human community are dwarfed. Conscience in Hawthorne, as Austin Warren observes,[33] turns into the consciousness that becomes central for Henry James, in continuance of a tradition that sees American history as complete in the American psyche. And the overwhelming thrust of American critics' evaluation of their literary tradition continues into the latter decades of the twentieth century to be a recognition of characteristic psychic or mythic structures that are presented as having created art, rather than being a delineation of that art as it emerges from the social reality of the men who created it. James Joyce's monumental representation of the levels of consciousness found a responsive readership in America before it exerted its influence on other English-speaking cultures, and "Freudian" is a household word in Kansas City although not in Vienna.

Jonathan Edwards and Benjamin Franklin were exact contemporaries, and, as a result of Van Wyck Brooks's essay of 1915 "Highbrow and Lowbrow," are commonly viewed as the great originals of these two traditions of mind in America. Intellect in Edwards, Brooks wrote, "isolated and not responsible to other faculties, went on its way unchecked; and he was able to spin his inept sublimities by subtracting from his mind every trace of experience, every touch of human nature as it really was among his innocent countryfolk." Franklin, Brooks went on to say, was quite the opposite, "for the opposite of unmitigated theory is unmitigated practicality. Who can deny that in *Poor Richard* the 'Lowbrow' point of view for the first time took definitive shape, stayed itself with axioms, and found a sanction in the idea of 'policy'?" [34]

More than half a century after he offered it, Brooks's view of American intellectual history may require qualification, but his basic perception is still striking. Born within three years of each other in Puritan New England, Franklin and Edwards clearly retained habits of mind characteristic of their culture. They possessed remarkable self-discipline and exercised it according to a system originally developed to gain Protestants independence from hierarchy by training them to search their own souls. The early Puritans had insisted that since a man's possession of grace was crucial, all else in his life was to be subordinated to the question of whether or not he was pious, possessed that grace. The man who was pious would, as an inevitable result of his piety, be moral. But, they maintained, there were more seemly behavers, moral men, than there were pious men, so that although piety inevitably had its outward sign, morality, morality was not a sure sign of piety. In response some argued that the inward state was secondary; a tree, they said, is known by its fruits. But the Puritans answered that it was more important that the tree know itself by its roots.

The relationship between piety and morality had shifted in the wake of the old charter's death and the advent of mercantile dominance. A man's outward behavior came in New England to have a communal importance at least as great as his inward spiritual condition, and to encourage, as Cotton Mather deploringly wrote in 1721, "the religion of pews which with a proud, vain formal people seems now to be the chief religion." [35] Morality, in being increasingly accepted as the equivalent of piety, was converting the provincial from Puritan to Yankee.

Both Franklin and Edwards had radical effects upon this drift. The latter, having experienced grace and being consumed with a living sense of the beauty of the whole creation once the majesty of God was received as a sixth sense that quickened the other five, sought to restore his countrymen to a sense of the absolute priority of grace and the experiential joy it would confer. To accomplish this he realized that he should not continue the lifeless round of thundering imprecations at decline while invoking the memory of the fathers. Rather, he met the liberal drift to sensibility in its own terms, mastering his Locke and his Newton beyond the ability of the rational theologians whom he opposed, and turning their systems to the service of predestinarianism with a brilliance of intellectual execution that has scarcely been equaled in the subsequent history of American philosophy. As a result, he did revitalize a considerable segment of the American church.

Benjamin Franklin, amused by the slowness of the drift toward unimpeded practicality, sought to accelerate his countrymen in their realization that the public world was the world that mattered. In that world it was silly hair-splitting to ask what a man really was, apart from what he really did. If there was a discrepancy between the appearance of one who behaved well and his real character, then his continuing exercise of that behavior would erase it. There was little of importance to humanity that could be separated from human conduct.

The Puritan stream had divided and flowed primarily in one or another of the channels made distinct by Franklin and Edwards. But the distinction is not quite that which appeared to Brooks. Edwards, to be sure, in the full amplification of his intellectual powers may appear glacial, but, in point of fact, the logical writings that supply the evidence for such an assertion were, in great part, intended to restore feeling to religion. Piety had evaporated, Edwards perceived, when religion lost its experiential base and falsely became rational. His was a desire, heated white-hot, to restore to religion its emotional base. In demonstrating that one who was truly engaged with God was one who might be affected bodily and enter into transports, depressions, tremors, and enthusiasms, Edwards offered case histories as proof. His logical construction upon the *a priori* truths of Calvinism was balanced by his *a posteriori* validations drawn from documented experiences. The *Treatise on Religious Affections* is careful to show that physical and emotional experiences are not inevitable signs of the gracious person, but it insists that a religion of pure intellect that is above such passion is a dead religion. *A Divine and Supernatural Light* attempts an explanation of the inexpressible feeling that accompanies the receipt of grace, the sense of loveliness of God's holiness. It is, Edwards says, as difficult to do as to explain the taste of honey to one who has no taste at all. His autobiographical writings are documents of the undergoing that is for him at the heart of life, though again, he is aware, his words are faint substitutes for the feelings that lie there.

It is also inaccurate to see Franklin as the great progenitor of the crafty money-catcher. At most, one might say this of the Poor Richard who wrote *The Way of Wealth*, but Poor Richard is far from the whole of Benjamin Franklin. He is the best authorial voice for an address on economy aimed at the husbandmen of America, just as other subjects aimed at other audiences demanded, in Franklin's effective scheme, other voices. Because of his acute ability to stay personally detached from the subjects he handles through the construction of a personating voice, Franklin far more aptly attaches himself to social reality and works upon it more tellingly than does Edwards. But he is no more deeply concerned with experience itself, unless by such is meant the experience of living in society. Edwards' half of the divided stream, however, speaks of the experience of the self.

Edwards was very respectful of those under powers Ebenezer Parkman was ashamed to indulge. He insisted that preaching made its total impression at the time of delivery rather than after, when the doctrine preached was remembered. His literary emphasis was on the provision of a direct emotional experience, and, he observed, "though an after remembrance of what was heard in a sermon is oftentimes very profitable; yet, for the most part that remembrance is from an impression the words made on the heart in the time of it." [36] He recognized that so powerful was the imagination that it not only presented a source of strength but, in its limitless capacity for creation, could through imitating the effects of grace delude one. His doctrine of the imagination, therefore, sought continually to make it subservient to religion and to prevent it from asserting an idolatrous identity of its own. He cautioned: "Almighty power is no more requisite to represent the shape of man to the imagination, than the shape of anything else . . . that sort of power which can represent black or darkness to the imagination can also represent white and shining brightness." [37] Imagination, therefore, had to be held in fine control by the inspired speaker of the word, whose office it was to play with the dangerous fire in order to awaken men to a sense of their condition.

Young Benjamin Franklin was delighted with the first books he read that offered a relief from the extended expositions of the Puritan library by mixing in dialogue and drama, and he himself experimented with poetry. From his earliest *Dogood Papers* to his last bagatelles, his writings convey a sense of play, a delight in what the artful combination of words can achieve. But this play is always contained by his fundamental belief that the ultimate goal of writing is moralistic and that artistry is ultimately justified in that it packages advice attractively and influences action. Reason, not emotion, must be the literary governor.

Neither Edwards nor Franklin, then, encouraged a confidence in imaginative literature. The former, fully aware of the power of the imagination, distrusted its idolatrous potential. The latter, regarding it as a subordinate ally, dismissed its value except as a means of gracing utility and affording passing refreshment. Both shared an ambivalence toward the imaginative work, and this ambivalence was the farthest gesture Puritanism could make away from its earlier rigid distrust. The culture that followed was to inherit this ambivalence, which placed extraordinary demands on the stamina of American writers, leading them characteristically to add to the usual burdens of literary creation a perpetual self-justification of their vocation based on a deep distrust of it that they themselves shared.

The Great Awakening was the final widespread assertion of Puritan culture as potentially universal, one that pretended to be above material conditions and therefore applicable to all mankind. The chosen people who had developed their perception of their election as a special tribe in analogy to the biblical Israelites had permitted the analogy to metamorphose into a notion that their peculiarity was national, tied to political forms, rather than universal, tied to religious belief. Baffled by the death of the charter and the triumph of provincialism, they had been unable to realize this aspect of the analogy. The Great Awakening revitalized them for a significant historical moment by reminding them that the chosen people were separated spiritually not nationally, and that their special nature was tied to the Gospel not the government. Edwards was a remarkable preacher of the New Testament and a consistent interpreter of the Old Testament as Christian history.

In the wake of the enthusiasm, however, provincial problems reasserted themselves and political and material security came again to the fore as the French were finally defeated. The culture was never again to employ its sense of election in universal religious terms. Instead, the ideal that New England, and eventually America, had been selected for the fulfillment of a crucial cosmic purpose became secularized into a justification of the economic and political practices of the population—free trade and democracy—and attached to national goals. Benjamin Franklin advanced this cause. In its more modern international manifestations this aspect of the culture supports the society's duty to spread the wonders of democracy to the four corners of the earth with the same fervor that the first Puritans spread the clear sunshine of the Gospel, and with the same combination of ruthless righteousness and generous willingness to share the benefits of its civilization with those who are willing to accept its assumptions of superiority.

The persons who opposed the culture from within inherited the alienated position at which Jonathan Edwards arrived when, dismissed from his congregation in the hangover that followed the Awakening, he lived out the remainder of his life as a teacher in a frontier Indian mission. They spoke of reform of the self as the chief national priority, rather than reform of institutions. The American intellectual and the American artist most characteristically came to center their criticism of their country on the American psyche. Their arguments with their countrymen were conducted within the culture's vocabulary as they spoke for the potential of the psychic flux that was arrested by society's forms rather than in terms of new forms for old. In a society in which their efficient fellows, confident in their right to do so, were converting competence to affluence, they could afford a concern with personal renewal rather than social reconstruction.

Although the stream had divided, as Edwards and Franklin illustrate, both currents flowed from the same source, and each continued its dependence on the other. Puritanism as culture outlived provincialism as it outlived colonial autonomy. A culture of expansion, distrustful of volume as mere resistance, Puritanism asserts a remarkable capacity to reduce the abstract meanings of volume to the precisions of the word and to reduce the physical existence of the dimension of space—be it represented by an alien psyche, a wilderness, or outer space itself—to the two-dimensional plane of its technology. Created in response to the expansion of population, trade, and self-mastery in the post-medieval world, it suited the new world superlatively and will retain its suitability, it is to be presumed, until such time as expansion itself no longer suffices and stasis must be contemplated.

Notes

In citations from prose texts contemporary to the period of this study, the spelling has been modernized but the original punctuation has been retained, since to modernize it is to risk alteration of meaning. The abbreviation *CMHS* is used throughout the notes to signify *Collections of the Massachusetts Historical Society*.

CHAPTER ONE: *Man's Judgment of Himself*

1. William Haller, *Foxe's Book of Martyrs and the Elect Nation* (London, 1963), p. 110. This book is a principal source for the characterization of the content of Foxe's work that appears in this chapter.
2. Philip Hughes, *The Reformation in England* (London, 1950, 1953, 1954), 3 vols., is a principal source for facts in this chapter.
3. Haller, *Foxe's Book*, p. 187.
4. William Laud, *A Speech Delivered in the Star Chamber on Wednesday the XIVth of Iune at the Censure of Iohn Bastwick, Henry Burton, & William Prinn* (London, 1637), p. 47.
5. David Mathew, *The Age of Charles I* (London, 1951), p. 104.
6. Laud, *Speech*, p. 18.
7. Ernst Troeltsch, *The Social Teaching of the Christian Churches*, trans. Olive Wyon (London, 1931), I, 338.
8. On this topic see Charles H. and Katherine George, *The Protestant Mind of the English Reformation, 1570–1640* (Princeton, 1961), p. 106; and R. A. Knox, *Enthusiasm* (Oxford, 1950), p. 3.
9. Harry A. Wolfson, *Religious Philosophy* (Cambridge, Mass., 1961), p. 175.
10. John Neville Figgis, *The Divine Right of Kings* (Cambridge, 1922), 2nd ed., p. 105.
11. George P. Gooch, *English Democratic Ideas in the Seventeenth Century* (Cambridge, 1927), p. 7.
12. Eli F. Heckscher, *Mercantilism*, trans. Mendel Shapiro (London, 1934), I, 232; and Eleanor Trotter, *Seventeenth Century Life in the Country Parish* (Cambridge, 1919), *passim*.
13. John Smith, *A Description of New-England* (1616), in *Tracts & Other Papers*, ed. Peter Force (New York, 1947), II, 118–19.

14. William Ames, *Conscience with the Power and Cases Thereof* (London, 1643), I, 2. This was first published in 1632, but in 1643 was "translated out of Latin into English, for more public benefit."

15. U. Milo Kaufmann, *The Pilgrim's Progress and Tradition in Puritan Meditation* (New Haven, 1966), p. 23.

16. Ames, *Conscience*, V, 213.

17. Ibid., IV, 54.

18. Ibid.

19. Michael Walzer, *The Revolution of the Saints* (Cambridge, Mass., 1965) p. 110.

20. Ames, *Conscience*, V, 203.

21. Francis Bacon, *The Works*, ed. Basil Montagu (London, 1825), I, 23.

22. Christopher Hill, *Puritanism and Revolution* (London, 1958), p. 384.

23. William Bradford, *History of Plimouth Plantation* (Boston, 1899), pp. 26–27.

24. Samuel Clarke, *A Collection of the Lives of the Eminent Divines* (London, 1662), p. 11.

25. John Rogers, *A Godly & Fruitful Exposition upon All the First Epistle of Peter* (London, 1650), p. 291.

26. Christopher Hill, *Society and Puritanism in Pre-Revolutionary England* (London, 1964), p. 152.

27. Rogers, *A Godly*, pp. 24–25.

28. Daniel Neal, *The History of the Puritans* (London, 1723–1738), I, 579.

29. Ibid., I, 596–97.

30. Ibid., II, 123.

31. Ames, *Conscience*, V, 215.

32. Ibid., V, 219.

33. John Geree, *The Character of an Old English Puritaine, or Non-Conformist* (London, 1646), p. 4.

34. Ibid., p. 2.

35. Rogers, *A Godly*, p. 103.

36. Ibid., p. 316.

37. Ibid.

38. Ibid., p. 391.

39. Ibid., p. 411.

40. Ibid., p. 412.

41. Ibid., p. 456.

42. Thomas Shepard, "Certain Select Cases Resolved," in *The Works*, ed. John A. Albro (Hildersheim, 1971), I, 307–308.

43. John Rogers, *The Doctrine of Faith* (London, 1627), p. 472.

44. [John Ley], *A Discourse concerning Puritans* (London, 1641), p. 53.

45. [William Bradshaw], *English Puritanisme* (London, 1641), p. 16.

46. Neal, *History*, III, 196.

47. Richard Hooker, *Of the Laws of Ecclesiastical Polity* (Oxford, 1793), I, 294.

48. See Robert Middlekauff, *The Mathers* (New York, 1971), p. 32, for the lack of a sense of errand on the part of the first Puritans to migrate to America.

CHAPTER TWO: *Home Is Nowhere*

1. Rogers, *Doctrine*, pp. 507–508.
2. Ibid., pp. 432–33.
3. G. R. Elton, *Reformation Europe 1517–1559* (New York, 1966), p. 236. See also Walzer, op. cit.
4. Patrick Collinson, *The Elizabethan Puritan Movement* (London, 1967), p. 380.
5. Ibid., p. 175.
6. Perry Miller, *The New England Mind, the Seventeenth Century* (Cambridge, Mass., 1954), p. 441.
7. Hughes, *Reformation*, III, 212.
8. Rogers, *Doctrine*, p. 435.
9. *The Cambridge History of the British Empire* (Cambridge, 1929), I, 72.
10. Elton, *Reformation*, pp. 321 ff.
11. Marcus Wilson Jernegan, *Laboring and Dependent Classes in Colonial America, 1607–1783* (Chicago, 1931), p. 47.
12. Cotton Mather, *Magnalia Christi Americana* (Hartford, 1853), I, 263.
13. Rogers, *A Godly*, p. 7.
14. Mather, *Magnalia*, I, 69.
15. George F. Willison, *Saints and Strangers* (London, 1966), p. 53.
16. E. A. J. Johnson, *American Economic Thought in the Seventeenth Century* (London, 1932), pp. 227–28.
17. Bradford, *History*, p. 163.
18. Ibid., p. 164.
19. Ibid.
20. For physical details of the voyage, see John Josselyn, *An Account of Two Voyages to New-England* in *CMHS* (Cambridge, Mass., 1833), 3rd Series, Vol. III. His first voyage was in 1638.
21. Robert Cushman, "Reasons and Considerations Touching the Lawfulness of Removing out of England into the Parts of America" (1622), in *The Story of the Pilgrim Fathers 1606–1623 as Told by Themselves, Their Friends, and Their Enemies*, ed. Edward Arber (London, 1897), p. 497.
22. Mather, *Magnalia*, I, 43.
23. Thomas Morton, *New English Canaan* (London, 1632).
24. John Hull, *The Diaries* in *Transactions and Collections of the American Antiquarian Society* (Boston, 1857), III, 168.
25. Cushman, "Reasons," p. 499.
26. Ibid., p. 503.
27. Ibid., pp. 504–505.
28. Ames, *Conscience*, V, 193.
29. Edmund S. Morgan, *The Puritan Family* (Boston, 1944), p. 38.
30. Roger Williams, *Letters, 1632–1682*, ed. John Russell Bartlett, *Publications of the Narragansett Club* (Providence, 1874), 1st Series, IV, 89.
31. Mather, *Magnalia*, II, 400.

32. Smith, *Description*, p. 21.

33. Edward Winslow, "Good News from New England," (1624), in Arber, *Story of Pilgrim Fathers*, p. 597.

34. Ben Jonson, George Chapman, and John Marston, *Eastward Hoe*, III, iii, 29 –38.

35. Winslow, "Good News," p. 598.

36. Ibid.

37. Bradford, *History*, p. 175.

38. Francis Higginson, *New-Englands Plantation*, CMHS (Boston, 1806), 1st Series, I, 118.

39. Ibid., p. 121.

40. Ibid., p. 124.

41. Ibid., p. 122.

42. Winslow, "Good News," p. 596.

CHAPTER THREE: *The Smith's Dog*

1. Jernegan, *Laboring Classes*, p. 65.

2. Bradford, *History*, pp. 261 ff. and 315–16.

3. Larzer Ziff, *The Career of John Cotton* (Princeton, 1962), pp. 59–64.

4. John Cotton, "God's Promise to His Plantation," *Old South Leaflets*, No. 53.

5. John Cotton, *A Sermon Preached by the Reverend Mr. John Cotton Deliver'd at Salem, 1636* (Boston, 1713).

6. For a brief history of Massachusetts ecclesiastical history, see Larzer Ziff, "Introduction," *John Cotton on the Churches of New England* (Cambridge, Mass., 1968).

7. *Records of the Governor and Company of Massachusetts Bay*, ed. Nathaniel B. Shurtleff (Boston, 1853), I, 87.

8. John Winthrop, *Journal, 1630–1649*, ed. James Kendall Hosmer (New York, 1908), I, 135–36.

9. Norman Pettit, *The Heart Prepared: Grace and Conversion in Spiritual Life* (New Haven, 1966), p. 44.

10. Rogers, *Doctrine*, Sigs. A6–A6v.

11. Ibid., p. 63.

12. Ibid., p. 66.

13. Ibid., p. 68.

14. Ibid., p. 98.

15. Shepard, *Works*, I, clxxxvii.

16. Rogers, *Doctrine*, p. 269.

17. Shepard, *The Sincere Convert, Works*, I, 8.

18. Benjamin Franklin, *The Autobiography* (New York, 1952), p. 65.

19. Rogers, *A Godly*, p. 9.

20. Ibid., pp. 594–95.

21. Leonard Bacon, *Thirteen Historical Discourses on the Completion of Two Hundred Years from the Beginning of the First Church in New Haven* (New Haven, 1839), p. 22.

22. Peter Bulkeley, *The Gospel-Covenant* (London, 1651), p. 51.

23. Ibid., p. iv.

24. Samuel Whiting, "Concerning the Life of the Famous Mr. Cotton, Teacher to the Church at Boston in New-England," in *Chronicles of the First Planters of the Colony of Massachusetts Bay*, ed. Alexander Young (Boston, 1846), p. 427.

25. John Cotton, *Christ the Fountaine of Life* (London, 1651), p. 27.

26. For example, Shepard, *The Sound Believer, Works*, I, 162.

27. Cotton, *Christ the Fountaine*, p. 22.

28. John Cotton, *A Treatise of the Covenant of Grace* (London, 1659), pp. 199–200.

29. Ibid., pp. 97–98.

30. Winthrop, *Journal*, I, 162.

31. "The Examination of Mrs. Ann Hutchinson at the Court in Newtown, November, 1637," Thomas Hutchinson, *The History of the Colony and Province of Massachusetts-Bay* (Cambridge, Mass., 1936), II, 383–84.

32. John Winthrop, *A Short Story of the Rise, Reign, and Ruine of the Antinomians, Familists, and Libertines*, in *The Antinomian Controversy*, ed. David D. Hall (Middletown, Conn., 1968), p. 274.

33. Thomas Shepard, "Memoir of His own Life," *Chronicles*, ed. Young, p. 550.

34. *Records of Massachusetts*, I, 196.

35. John Winthrop, "A Defence of an Order of Court Made in the Year 1637," *Publications of the Prince Society* (Boston, 1865), I, 82.

36. Henry Vane, "A Brief Answer to a Certain Declaration Made to the Intent and Equitye of the Order of the Court," ibid., p. 92.

37. Mather, *Magnalia*, II, 515.

38. Thomas Shepard, *The Parable of the Ten Virgins, Works*, II, 260.

39. Ibid.

40. See the Appendices in Emery Battis, *Saints and Sectaries* (Chapel Hill, N.C., 1962).

41. Heckscher, *Mercantilism*, II, 286.

42. See the analysis of the market offered by Isaac Rasiere, secretary of the Dutch trading company, in the Massachusetts Historical Society edition of Bradford's *History* (Boston, 1912), II, 43n. See also William B. Weeden, *Economic and Social History of New-England, 1620–1789* (Boston, 1891), 2 vols.

43. "Leift. Lion Gardener His Relation of the Pequot Warres," *CMHS* (Cambridge, Mass., 1833), 3rd Series, III, 144.

44. Winthrop, *Short Story*, pp. 253–54.

45. "Winthrop Papers," *CMHS* (Boston, 1871), 5th Series, I, 232.

CHAPTER FOUR: *A Good Fence*

1. Troeltsch, *Social Teaching*, II, 599.

2. The fullest example is Edward Johnson, *Wonder-Working Providence, 1628–1651*, ed. J. Franklin Jameson (New York, 1910).

3. See Gooch, *English Democratic Ideas*.

4. See Geoffrey T. Nuttall, *Visible Saints* (Oxford, 1957).

5. "Winthrop Papers," *CMHS* (Boston, 1865), 4th Series, VII, 277.

6. Richard S. Dunn, *Puritans and Yankees* (Princeton, 1962), p. 37.

7. *New Englands First Fruits, CMHS* (Boston, 1806), 1st Series, I, 248.

8. *Cambridge History*, I, 181.

9. Bernard Bailyn, *The New England Merchants in the Seventeenth Century* (Cambridge, Mass., 1955), p. 43.

10. Ibid., p. 75.

11. Lorenzo Johnston Greene, *The Negro in Colonial New England, 1620–1776* (New York, 1942).

12. "Winthrop Papers," 5th Series, I, 301–302.

13. Bacon, *Thirteen Discourses*, p. 31.

14. "Winthrop Papers," 4th Series, VII, 28.

15. Lemuel Shattuck, *A History of the Town of Concord* (Concord, 1835), p. 17.

16. Shepard, *Ten Virgins, Works*, II, 260.

17. "Winthrop Papers," 4th Series, VII, 215.

18. Darret B. Rutman, *Winthrop's Boston, Portrait of a Puritan Town, 1630–1649* (Chapel Hill, N.C., 1965), p. 87.

19. Shepard, *Ten Virgins, Works*, II, 103.

20. Shepard, *Subjection to Christ in All His Ordinances and Appointments the Best Means to Preserve Our Liberty, Works*, III, 341.

21. Ibid., p. 344.

22. Ibid., p. 350.

23. Heckscher, *Mercantilism*, II, 165.

24. Shepard, *Subjection, Works*, III, 350.

25. Johnson, *Wonder-Working*, p. 83.

26. Rutman, *Winthrop's Boston*, p. 146.

27. Thomas Lechford, *Plain Dealing, CMHS* (Cambridge, 1833), III, 109.

28. Thomas Franklin Waters, *Ipswich in the Massachusetts Bay Colony* (Ipswich, 1905), I, 89.

29. Rutman, *Winthrop's Boston*, p. 163.

30. *Cambridge History*, I, 180.

31. "Gardener His Relation," p. 146.

32. John Underhill, *Newes from America, CMHS* (Boston, 1837), 3rd Series, VI, 23.

33. Ibid., p. 26.

34. Ibid., p. 27.

35. "Gardener His Relation," p. 154.

36. Winthrop, *Journal*, II, 136.

37. For the record of continuing church relations with this group, see Larzer Ziff, "The Social Bond of Church Covenant," *American Quarterly* (Winter 1958), Vol. X, No.4, pp. 454–62.

38. The fullest details of Gorton's life are to be found in John M. Mackie, "Life of Samuel Gorton," *Library of American Biography*, ed. Jared Sparks (Boston, 1845), Vol. XV.

39. Edward Winslow, *Hypocrisie Unmasked* (Providence, 1916), p. 7.

40. Samuel Gorton, *Simplicities Defence against Seven-Headed Policy*, in *Tracts and Other Papers*, ed. Peter Force (Washington, 1846), IV, 29–30.

41. Samuel Gorton, "Letter to Nathaniel Morton, Warwick, June 30th, 1669," ibid., p. 14.

42. Gorton, *Simplicities*, p. 31.

43. Ibid., p. 26.

44. Ibid., p. 41.

45. Ibid., pp. 50–51.

46. For the fullest analysis of the matter, see George Lyman Kittredge, "Dr. Robert Child the Remonstrant," *Publications of the Colonial Society of Massachusetts* (Boston, 1920), Vol. IX.

47. John Childe, *New Englands Jonas Cast up at London*, in *Tracts*, ed. Force, IV, 10.

48. Edward Winslow, *New Englands Salamander Discovered* (London, 1647).

CHAPTER FIVE: *Winter's Discourse*

1. This is the central concept of John Garrett, *Roger Williams, Witness beyond Christendom* (New York, 1970).

2. Roger Williams, *Complete Writings* (New York, 1963), V, 294.

3. See *John Cotton on the Churches*.

4. Williams, *Writings*, III, 42.

5. Ibid., VI, 219–20.

6. Ibid., I, 381.

7. Neal, *History*, IV, 272.

8. Ibid., III, 270.

9. Clarke, *Collection*, p. 260.

10. Ibid., p. 251.

11. Williams, *Writings*, VII, 169.

12. Ibid., VI, 262.

13. Roger Williams, "A Letter to Major Mason," *CMHS* (Boston, 1806), 1st Series, I, 283.

14. Ibid., p. 280.

15. "Copy of a Letter from Governor Prince to Roger Williams," ibid., p. 204.

16. See Knox, *Enthusiasm*, pp. 132–33.

17. Shepard, *Works*, II, 170.

18. Ibid., II, 551.

19. Ibid., II, 504.

20. Ibid., III, 382.

21. George E. Ellis, *The Puritan Age and Rule in the Colony of the Massachusetts-Bay, 1629–1685* (Boston, 1891), p. 264.

22. Ibid., p. 222.

23. Mather, *Magnalia*, II, 65.

24. Shepard, "Memoir," pp. 556–58.

25. Henry Martyn Dexter, *The Congregationalism of the Last Three Hundred Years as Seen in Its Literature* (London, n.d.), p. 446.

26. "The Diary of Michael Wigglesworth," ed. Edmund Morgan, *Publications of the Colonial Society of Massachusetts* (December 1946), XXXV, 328.

27. *The Diary of Cotton Mather* (New York, 1911), I, 475.

28. *A Iust and Necessary Apologie of Certain Christians, No Lesse Contumeiously then Commonly Called Brownists or Barrowists* (London, 1644), p. 21.

29. Mather, *Magnalia*, I, 301.

30. Ibid., pp. 301–302.

31. The most useful edition is *The Works of Anne Bradstreet*, ed. John H. Ellis (1867) and reissued (Gloucester, Mass., 1962). The phrase is from stanza 33 of *Contemplations*.

32. "In Memory of My Dear Grand-Child Elizabeth Bradstreet, Who Deceased August, 1665. Being a Year and Half Old," ibid.

33. Johnson, *Wonder-Working*, pp. 208–209.

34. Ibid., p. 207.

CHAPTER SIX: *White Coat, Blue Coat*

1. Leonard Verduin, *The Reformers and Their Stepchildren* (Exeter, 1966), p. 107.

2. For example [Daniel Cawdrey], *Vindiciae Clavium* (London, 1645).

3. *John Cotton on the Churches*, p. 75.

4. Ibid., p. 84.

5. John Robinson, *A Treatise of the Lawfulness of Hearing of the Ministers in the Church of England* (1634), p. 9.

6. Rutman, *Winthrop's Boston*, p. 148.

7. Shattuck, *Concord*, p. 156.

8. Mather, *Magnalia*, I, 400.

9. Shattuck, *Concord*, p. 160.

10. Ibid., p. 156.

11. John Clark, *Ill Newes from New-England* (London, 1652), p. 7.

12. Ibid., p. 19.

13. Ibid., p. 22.

14. Williams, *Letters*, p. 227.

15. Verduin, *Reformers*, p. 211.

16. John Cotton, *The Grounds and Ends of the Baptisme of the Children of the Faithful* (London, 1647), p. 4.

17. Ibid., p. 167.

18. Ibid., p. 159.

19. Rufus M. Jones, *The Quakers in the American Colonies* (London, 1911), p. xx.

20. William C. Brathwaite, *The Beginnings of Quakerism* (London, 1923), p. 51.

21. Ibid., p. 152.

22. Frederick B. Tolles, *Quakers and the Atlantic Culture* (New York, 1960), p. 58.

23. Mather, *Magnalia*, I, 492.

24. Tolles, *Quakers*, p. 63.

25. Kai T. Erikson, *Wayward Puritans* (New York, 1966), pp. 188–89.

26. Samuel Clarke, *The Marrow of Ecclesiastical History* (London, 1654), p. 801.

27. "Mather Papers," *CMHS* (Boston, 1868), 4th Series, VIII, 4–5.

28. William L. Sachse, "The Migration of New Englanders to England, 1640–1660," *The American Historical Review* (January 1948), LIII, 251–78. See also Sachse, *The Colonial American in Britain* (Madison, Wis., 1956).

29. Thomas Hutchinson, *History*, I, 82.

30. Increase Mather, "Autobiography," ed. M. G. Hall, *Proceedings of the American Antiquarian Society* (Worcester, Mass., 1961), Vol. 71, Part 2, p. 286.

31. Weeden, *Economic History*, I, 289.

32. Robert Barclay, *An Apology for the True Christian Divinity* (London, 1825), p. 529. First Latin edition 1676; first English edition 1678.

33. William Potter, *The Key to Wealth* (London, 1650), p. 1.

34. John Cotton, *The Way of Life* (London, 1641), p. 270.

35. *The Apologia of Robert Keayne*, ed. Bernard Bailyn (New York, 1965), p. 82.

36. Weeden, *Economic History*, I, 249.

37. *The Literature of America: Colonial Period*, ed. Larzer Ziff (New York, 1970), pp. 207–208.

38. *The Glorious Revolution in America*, eds. Michael G. Hall, Lawrence H. Leder, and Michael G. Kammen (Chapel Hill, N.C., 1964), p. 14.

39. Joseph Dorfman, *The Economic Mind in American Civilization* (London, 1947), I, 53.

40. Josselyn, *Account*, p. 331.

41. Ibid., p. 352.

CHAPTER SEVEN: *Saint Pompion*

1. See Gerald R. Cragg, *Puritanism in the Period of the Great Persecution, 1660–1688* (Cambridge, 1957).

2. "Mather Papers," p. 262.

3. *The Peacable Design: Being a Modest Account of the Non-Conformists Meetings* (London, 1675), p. 32.

4. Ibid., pp. 35–36.

5. Ibid., p. 54.

6. Edward Holyoke, *The Doctrine of Life, or of Mans Redemption* (London, 1658), p. 316.

7. Ibid., p. 317.

8. Ibid., p. 318.

9. Ibid.

10. Ibid., p. 320.

11. Ibid., p. 321.

12. Thomas Walley, *Balm in Gilead to Heal Sions Wounds* (Cambridge, Mass., 1669), p. 9.

13. Benjamin Tompson, *His Poems*, ed. Howard Judson Hall (Cambridge, Mass., 1924), p. 49.

14. Ibid.

15. Ibid., p. 50.

16. Ibid., p. 49.

17. Ibid., p. 51.

18. Holyoke, *Doctrine*, p. 318.

19. Ibid.

20. Thomas Goddard Wright, *Literary Culture in New England, 1620–1730* (New Haven, 1920), p. 92.

21. Roger Williams, *A Key into the Language of the Indians of New England,* CMHS (Boston, 1806), 1st Series, III, 237–38.

22. *The Day of Doom,* ed. Kenneth B. Murdock (New York, 1929), p. iii.

23. Neal, *History,* IV, 423.

24. William Prynne, *Histrio-mastix* (London, 1633), p. 965.

25. Ibid., p. 966.

26. Ibid.

27. "Mather Papers," p. 565.

28. Ibid., pp. 566–67.

29. Mather, *Magnalia,* I, 558.

30. Ibid., p. 573.

31. Williams, *Key,* p. 214.

32. Ibid., p. 228.

33. Williams, *Letters,* p. 270.

34. Shepard, *Works,* III, 478.

35. Ibid.

36. John Eliot, *The Christian Commonwealth,* CMHS (Boston, 1846), 3rd Series, IX, 128.

37. Ibid., p. 133.

38. William Kellaway, *The New England Company, 1649–1776* (London, 1961), p. 116.

39. "Winthrop Papers," 5th Series, I, 106.

40. Ibid., pp. 106–107.

41. Daniel Gookin, *Historical Collections of the Indians,* CMHS (Boston, 1806), 1st Series, I, 183.

42. "Winthrop Papers," 5th Series, I, 109.

43. Mary Rowlandson, *The Narrative of the Captivity and Restoration of Mrs. Mary Rowlandson* (Lancaster, Mass., 1903), facsimile of 1682 edition, p. 50.

44. Benjamin Church, *The History of King Philip's War* (Boston, 1825), p. 101.

45. Ibid., pp. 114–15.

46. Ibid., pp. 117–18.

47. Peter Folger, *A Looking Glass for the Times* (Boston? 1725), p. 6.

48. Ibid., p. 8.

CHAPTER EIGHT: *Courtly Pomp and Decay*

1. See John Davenport, *Letters,* ed. Isabel M. Calder (New Haven, 1937).

2. See Hamilton Andrews Hill, *History of the Old South Church* (Boston, 1890), 2 vols.

3. Ibid., I, 54.

4. Ibid., I, 190.

5. John Gorham Palfrey, *History of New England* (Boston, 1865), III, 84.

6. Ibid., p. 85.

7. Ibid., p. 84n.

8. The sermon is reprinted in its entirety with valuable notes in *The Wall and the Garden, Selected Massachusetts Election Sermons, 1670–1775,* ed. A. W. Plumstead (Minneapolis, 1968).

9. Ibid., p. 69.

10. Ibid., p. 72.
11. Ibid.
12. Ibid.
13. Dunn, *Puritans and Yankees*, p. 173.
14. Carl Bridenbaugh, *Cities in the Wilderness* (New York, 1955), p. 108.
15. "Mather Papers," p. 598.
16. Ibid., p. 582.
17. *A Case of Great and Present Use. Whether We May Lawfully Hear the Now Conforming Ministers Who Are Re-ordained and Have Renounced the Covenant, and Some of Them Supposed to Be Scandalous in Their Lives?* (London, 1677), p. 2.
18. Ibid.
19. Morgan, *Puritan Family*, p. 88.
20. Weeden, *Economic History*, I, 275.
21. Ibid., p. 270.
22. For an example of settlement in the day, see Herbert Collins Parson, *A Puritan Outpost* (New York, 1937).
23. "Mather Papers," p. 305.
24. Ibid., p. 624.
25. William Hubbard, *A General History of New England, from the Discovery to MDCLXXX, CMHS* (Boston, 1815), 2nd Series, V–VI, 621.
26. Williston Walker, *The Creeds and Platforms of Congregationalism* (New York, 1893), p. 416.
27. Ibid., pp. 427–28.
28. Ibid., p. 429.
29. Ibid., p. 430.
30. Ibid., p. 431.
31. Ibid., p. 280n.
32. Ibid., p. 437.
33. John Flavel, *Works* (London, 1820), V, 5.
34. Ibid., p. 7.
35. Rogers, *A Godly*, p. 72.
36. Ibid., p. 97.
37. Flavel, *Works*, V, 15.
38. Perry Miller, *The New England Mind, from Colony to Province* (Cambridge, Mass., 1953), p. 52.

CHAPTER NINE: *Jack and Tom*

1. Palfrey, *History*, II, 588.
2. "The Andros Tracts," *Publications of the Prince Society* (Boston, 1868–74), VI, 153.
3. "Hutchinson Papers," *CMHS* (Boston, 1825), 3rd Series, I, 109–10.
4. Ibid., p. 109.
5. Henry Norwood, "A Voyage to Virginia," in *A Collection of Voyages and Travels*, ed. A. Churchill (London, 1746), VI, 168–69.
6. Ibid., p. 169.

7. Bridenbaugh, *Cities*, p. 97n.
8. John Dunton, *The Life and Errors* (London, 1818), I, 94.
9. Ibid., I, 112.
10. Ibid., p. 94.
11. Ibid., p. 101.
12. Ibid., p. 124.
13. Ibid., p. 79.
14. Ibid., p. 104.
15. Hall et al. *Glorious Revolution*, p. 24.
16. Palfrey, *History*, III, 56n.
17. "Mather Papers," p. 284.
18. Ibid.
19. Increase Mather, *Remarkable Providences* (London, 1890), p. [xxvii].
20. Ibid., pp. [xxvi–xxvii].
21. Miller, *New England Mind, Colony to Province*, p. 146.
22. *Narratives of the Witchcraft Cases, 1648–1706*, ed. George Lincoln Burr (New York, 1914), p. 99.
23. Ibid., p. 96.
24. Palfrey, *History*, III, 547.
25. Burr, *Narratives*, p. 114.
26. Peter Gay, *A Loss of Mastery* (Berkeley, Calif., 1966).
27. "Mather Papers," p. 514.
28. Dunton, *Life*, I, 94.
29. Benjamin Franklin, *Autobiography and Selected Writings* (New York, 1964), p. 287.
30. Ibid.
31. See Michael G. Hall, *Edward Randolph and the American Colonies* (Chapel Hill, N.C., 1960).
32 Palfrey, *History*, III, 384–85.
33. Ibid., p. 384.
34. "Andros Tracts," V, 47.
35. Ibid., p. 35.
36. Ibid., p. 89.
37. Ibid., p. 50.
38. Ibid., VI, 254.
39. Ibid.
40. Ibid., p. 255.
41. See David W. Petegorsky, *Left-Wing Democracy in the English Civil War* (Cambridge, 1940).
42. Waters, *Ipswich*, I, 260.

CHAPTER TEN: *This Monday*

1. I. Mather, "Autobiography," p. 320.
2. See Hall et al., *Glorious Revolution*.
3. *Cambridge History*, I, 262.

4. See Dunn, *Puritans and Yankees.*
5. See Richard L. Bushman, *From Puritan to Yankee* (Cambridge, Mass., 1967).
6. Bailyn, *New England Merchants,* p. 194.
7. Samuel Richardson, *Pamela* (New York, 1958), p. 132.
8. Dunn, *Puritans and Yankees,* p. 284.
9. "Andros Tracts," V, 200.
10. Ibid., p. 201.
11. Ibid.
12. Ibid., p. 208.
13. Ibid., VI, 251.
14. For details of Phips's life, see Viola F. Barnes, "The Rise of William Phips," *New England Quarterly* (July 1928), Vol. I, No. 3., and "Phippius Maximus," ibid. (October 1928), Vol. I, No. 4; and Alice Lounsberry, *Sir William Phips* (New York, 1941).
15. Barnes, *NEQ,* I, No. 3, p. 284.
16. Lounsberry, *Phips,* p. 214.
17. *Proceedings of the Massachusetts Historical Society* (Boston, 1902), XV, 290.
18. Ibid., p. 317.
19. Gooch, *Democratic Ideas,* p. 298.
20. Mather, *Magnalia,* I, 215.
21. Jernegan, *Laboring Classes,* p. 202.
22. Weeden, *Economic History,* I, 364.
23. See Greene, *The Negro in Colonial New England.*
24. The literature on the New England witchcraft craze is considerable. George L. Burr indicates the most significant works to 1914 in his Preface to the *Narratives.* Since that date the list has continued to grow, the most popular extended account being Marion L. Starkey, *The Devil in Massachusetts* (New York, 1950), and the most recent Chadwick Hansen, *Witchcraft at Salem* (New York, 1969). The interpretation here differs from both.
25. Burr, *Narratives,* p. 156.
26. Samuel Sewall, *Diary, 1674–1729, CMHS* (Boston, 1878–82), 5th Series, Vols. V–VII; V, 110.
27. Burr, *Narratives,* p. 179.
28. Ibid.
29. Ibid., p. 211.
30. H. R. Trevor-Roper, *The European Witch-Craze of the 16th and 17th Centuries* (Harmondsworth, England, 1969), p. 120. This is a revision of essays that first appeared in 1967 as part of *Religion, the Reformation and Social Change.*
31. Allan I. Ludwig, *Graven Images* (Middletown, Conn., 1966), p. 107.
32. Ibid., p. 271.

CHAPTER ELEVEN: *Loose Stones*

1. Sewall, *Diary,* V, 115.
2. See T. B. Strandness, *Samuel Sewall* (East Lansing, Mich., 1967), and Ola Winslow, *Samuel Sewall of Boston* (New York, 1964).
3. Sewall, *Diary,* V, 114.

4. Ibid., p. 271.

5. Ibid., p. 443.

6. Samuel Sewall, *Phaenomena* (Boston, 1697), p. 59.

7. See Norman S. Grabo, *Edward Taylor* (New Haven, Conn., 1961).

8. See Perry Miller, "Introduction," to John Wise, *A Vindication of the Government of New-England Churches* (Gainesville, Fla., 1958): facsimile of the 1717 edition.

9. *The Poems of Edward Taylor*, ed. Donald E. Stanford (New Haven, Conn., 1960), p. 384.

10. Sewall, *Diary*, VII, 385.

11. "Mather Papers," p. 258.

12. Ibid., pp. 314–15.

13. Dunton, *Life*, I, 94.

14. John Barnard, *Autobiography*, CMHS (Boston, 1836), 3rd Series, V, 182–83.

15. Ibid., p. 186.

16. Mather, *Magnalia*, II, 649.

17. Ibid., p. 538.

18. Joshua Scottow, *A Narrative of the Planting of the Massachusetts Colony*, CMHS (Boston, 1858), 4th Series, IV, 322.

19. Sewall, *Diary*, VII, 131.

20. Ibid., V, 493.

21. I. Mather, "Autobiography," p. 352.

22. "Mather Papers," p. 35.

23. George Allan Cook, *John Wise, Early American Democrat* (New York, 1952), p. 88.

24. See Samuel Kirkland Lothrop, *A History of the Church in Brattle Street, Boston* (Boston, 1851).

25. Mather, *Magnalia*, II, 259.

26. Increase Mather, *The Order of the Gospel* (Boston, 1700), p. 47.

27. Ibid., p. 81.

28. Ibid., p. 68.

29. Ibid., p. 141. Mather is here citing the Savoy Confession.

30. Lothrop, *Brattle Street*, p. 40n.

31. Ibid., p. 41n.

32. Ebenezer Turell, *The Life . . . of . . . Benjamin Colman* (Boston, 1749), pp. 26–27.

33. Ibid., p. 32.

34. *Boswell's Life of Johnson*, ed. George B. Hill and L. F. Powell (Oxford, 1934), I, 312.

35. Elizabeth Rowe, *The Miscellaneous Works* (London, 1739), I, 112.

36. Mark Twain, *Huckleberry Finn* (New York, 1948), p. 103.

37. Rowe, *Works*, I, xxxvi.

38. Ibid., pp. xi–xii.

39. *Boswell's Life of Johnson*, I, 312.

40. Isaac Watts, *A Guide to Prayer, Works* (London, 1813), V, 125.

41. Ibid., p. 86.

42. Ibid., p. 128.

43. Turell, *Life of Colman*, p. 169.

44. Ibid., p. 172.

45. Benjamin Colman, *Practical Discourses on the Parable of the Ten Virgins* (Boston, 1747), p. 2.
46. Mather, *Diary*, I, 239.
47. Turell, *Life of Colman*, p. 187.
48. Ibid., p. 99.
49. Dexter, *Congregationalism*, p. 489.
50. Mather, *Diary*, II, 327.
51. John Wise, *The Churches Quarrel Espoused* (Gainesville, Fla., 1966), p. 13: facsimile of 1713 edition.
52. Ibid., p. 14.
53. Ibid.
54. Wise, *Vindication*, pp. 37–38.
55. Thomas Paine, *Common Sense and Other Political Writings* (New York, 1963), p. 4.
56. Ibid., p. 25.

CHAPTER TWELVE: *An Abundance of Artificers*

1. Barnard, *Autobiography*, p. 189.
2. Dunn, *Puritans and Yankees*, p. 344.
3. Barnard, *Autobiography*, p. 204.
4. Ibid., p. 214.
5. Ibid., pp. 239–40.
6. "Higginson Letter," *CMHS* (Boston, 1838), 3rd Series, VII, 220.
7. Charles M. Andrews, *Colonial Folkways* (New Haven, Conn., 1919), p. 106n.
8. Bridenbaugh, *Cities*, p. 134.
9. Mather, *Magnalia*, I, 576.
10. Sarah Kemble Knight, *The Journals of Madam Knight and Rev. Mr. Buckingham* (New York, 1825), p. 258.
11. Samuel Sewall, *The Selling of Joseph*, *CMHS* (Boston, 1878), 5th Series, VI, 17n–18n.
12. Knight, *Journals*, p. 259.
13. Ibid., p. 260.
14. Ebenezer Parkman, "Diary," ed. Francis G. Wallet, *Proceedings of the American Antiquarian Society* (Worcester, Mass., 1961), Vol. 71, 144.
15. Ibid., p. 216.
16. Ibid., p. 369.
17. Ibid., p. 174.
18. Mather Byles, *Poems on Several Occasions* (New York, 1940), p. 432.
19. *A Library of American Literature*, ed. Edmund Clarence Stedman and Ellen Mackay Hutchinson (New York, 1894), II, 434.
20. Benjamin Colman, *The Religious Regards We Owe to Our Country* (Boston, 1718), p. 15.
21. Ibid., p. 16.
22. Mather, *Diary*, II, 639.
23. Ibid., p. 331.

24. "Mather Papers," pp. 440–41.

25. For the prevalence of this pattern of establishment, rigidification, and reform, see Anton F. Boisen, *Religion in Crisis and Custom* (New York, 1945), p. 89.

26. Edwin Scott Gaustad, *The Great Awakening in New England* (New York, 1957), p. 138.

27. *The Great Awakening*, ed. Alan Heimert and Perry Miller (Indianapolis, 1967), pp. 153–54.

28. Ibid., p. 243.

29. Ibid., p. 449.

30. Jonathan Edwards, *A History of the Work of Redemption, Works* (New York, 1843), I, 315.

31. Heimert and Miller, *Great Awakening*, pp. 244–45.

32. Ralph Waldo Emerson, "The Divinity School Address," *Selections*, ed. Stephen E. Whicher (Boston, 1957), p. 105.

33. Austin Warren, *The New England Conscience* (Ann Arbor, Mich., 1966), p. 190.

34. Van Wyck Brooks, *America's Coming of Age* (New York, 1958), p. 7.

35. Mather, *Diary*, II, 615.

36. Jonathan Edwards, *Thoughts on the Revival of Religion in New England, Works*, III, 342.

37. Jonathan Edwards, *A Treatise concerning Religious Affections, Works*, III, 178.

Index